岭南名著丛书

林雄 顾作义 主编

西学东渐记

导读本

（清）容闳 著

王杰 整理导读

SPM 南方传媒　广东人民出版社
·广州·

图书在版编目（CIP）数据

西学东渐记：导读本 / （清）容闳著；王杰整理导读. —广州：
广东人民出版社，2024.5
（岭南名著丛书 / 林雄，顾作义主编）
ISBN 978-7-218-16346-8

Ⅰ.①西… Ⅱ.①容… ②王… Ⅲ.①容闳（1828—1912）—回
忆录 Ⅳ.①K827=6

中国版本图书馆CIP数据核字（2022）第248102号

XIXUE DONGJIAN JI（DAODUBEN）
西 学 东 渐 记 （导读本）
（清）容 闳 著 王 杰 整理导读

出 版 人：肖风华

策划编辑：王俊辉
责任编辑：罗 丹
责任技编：吴彦斌　马 健

出版发行：广东人民出版社
地　　址：广州市越秀区大沙头四马路10号（邮政编码：510199）
电　　话：（020）85716809（总编室）
传　　真：（020）83289585
网　　址：http://www.gdpph.com
印　　刷：广州市豪威彩色印务有限公司
开　　本：889毫米×1194毫米　1/32
印　　张：10.625　　字　　数：248千
版　　次：2024年5月第1版
印　　次：2024年5月第1次印刷
定　　价：58.00元

如发现印装质量问题，影响阅读，请与出版社（020-85716849）联系调换。
售书热线：（020）87716172

《西学东渐记》导读

　　容闳是近代以降中国与美国文化交流初期的产儿。他的横空出世，是中西文化碰撞的造化；他传奇的人生，谱写了中美文化交流先驱者的开篇。

　　170多年前，容闳与黄胜、黄宽跟随马礼逊学校（Morrison School）校长鲍留云（Samuel Robins Brown，1810—1880，亦译布朗、勃朗）远赴美国留学，毕业于耶鲁，成为第一位获得美国大学文凭的中国人，1854年学成归国。他历17年之功，走上倡议和筹划政府组织幼童留学美国的艰辛旅程，促成那个时代幼童留美的惊天大业，被后人誉为"留学生之父"；他以促进中美文化交流为使命，以使者的身份于潜移默化之中，开创了中国文化走向美国、走向世界的先河，无愧为中美文化交流的先驱。2013年10月21日，国家主席习近平出席欧美同学会成立100周年庆祝大会并发表重要讲话，在讲话中指出"百余年的留学史是'索我理想之中华'的奋斗史"。而这奋斗史源于香山，始于容闳。作为跨越中西、享誉中美的文化符号，容闳是中国不朽的文化名片。

　　容闳毕生唯一的传世之作《西学东渐记》，从问世伊始，风行于世，至今尤炙。其版本之多，发行量之大，可谓洛阳纸贵，经久不衰。

　　《西学东渐记》以自传的体裁，叙述了容闳在中国与美国的生活与经历，展示了中美早期文化交流典型个案的原真态貌，吐露了中美早期文化人交集的心路轨迹，透析了中西文化的内蕴与异同，揭示了西学东渐与东学西渐的内幕与前景，催促着两国先驱志士睁眼看彼此，进而推动着中西方文化交流的拓展与深化。换句话说是，一个人，一本书，揭示了尘封中国人走向世界历史的开篇；一本书，一个人，拉开了中华民族与文明世界互动的序幕。

生平与功业

容闳，族名光照，字达萌，号纯甫，英文名 Yung Wing；道光八年（1828）11 月 17 日出生于广东省广州府香山县恭常都沙尾村（后改名南屏，今珠海市南屏镇），该地濒临南海，直线距离澳门 4 公里。十五年（1835），七岁的容闳读不起私塾，被父亲送到澳门免费入读附设于郭实猎所办女校的马礼逊学校习西学；十九年（1839）辍学；次年回校复学；二十二年（1842）随该校迁至香港就学；二十七年（1847）随校长鲍留云赴美留学，入读康州孟松学院（Monson Academy）；三十年（1850）考入耶鲁学院（Yale college，后更名耶鲁大学）文学院；咸丰二年（1852）入籍美国 ①；四年（1854）学成回中国，先后在广州、香港、上海等地谋职；十年（1860）赴南京访问太平天国；同治元年（1862）赴安庆拜访曾国藩；次年，被曾氏派往美国采买机器；五年（1866）返国；次年由曾国藩保奏"以同知留于苏州，遇缺即补"；九年（1870）作为译员随丁日昌赴天津协办"教案"；次年，任'出洋肄业局'帮办，在上海从总办陈兰彬筹备幼童

———————
① 其时，清朝还没有国籍概念，美国允许双重国籍。

留美事务；十一年（1872）率先赴美为幼童安排食宿和就学事务；十二年（1873）携在美采买的军械回国；次年赴秘鲁调查华工受虐状况；光绪元年（1875）与美国本土女子祁洛（Mary Louisa Kellogg）在哈特福德结婚[①]，受任出使美国、日斯巴尼亚（西班牙）、秘鲁三国副大臣；次年长子容觐彤（Morrison Brown Yung）出生，本人获耶鲁荣誉法学博士学位，成为首位获西方荣誉博士的中国人；四年（1878）随陈兰彬前往华盛顿白宫递交国书履任；翌年次子容觐槐（Bartlett Golden Yung）出生；七年（1881），三年公使任满；次年回国述职；九年（1883）回美定居；十二年（1886）妻子祁洛去世；二十一年（1895）由两江总督张之洞派往英国借款，旋回国任江南交涉委员；次年递交创办银行和修筑铁路条陈；二十六（1900）应康有为之邀赴新加坡考察，又赴上海参加"中国国会"，当选议长，旋因自立军失败，逃往日本，与孙中山相识相交；二十八年（1902）赴美定居；三十一年（1905）陪同康有为、荷马李（Homer Lea）等前往白宫拜会美国总统西奥多·罗斯福（Theodore Roosevelt）；宣统元年（1909）回忆录 *My Life in China and America* 在美国纽约出版；次年运筹孙中山与荷马李、美国银行家布斯（Charles Beach Boothe）、艾伦（Walter W. Allen）等人谋划"中国红龙计划"；三年（1911）与谢瓒泰频繁通信关注国内武昌起义事；民国元年（1912）4 月 21 日在哈特福德家中辞世，与妻子合葬于美国康涅狄格州哈特福德西带山墓地（Cedar Hill Cemetery）[②]。

容闳从美国耶鲁毕业后，毅然回国，满怀爱国救国报国的热情，为晚清时期正在掀动的洋务事业及民主进步运动披肝沥胆。

---

① 关于容闳婚姻，下文将有展开。

② 西带山墓地（Cedar Hill Cemetery），又译作雪松山墓地。此处为容闳家族的墓地，后来的孙子孙女都长眠于此。

其功业可谓筚路蓝缕：

第一，奉命赴美国，采购机器，有力促成中国第一家民族工业企业——上海机器局（江南制造总局）的诞生；

第二，历经17年，游说朝廷官派留学生，促成清政府于1872年开创幼童留美事业，分四批赴美留学的120名幼童，后来成为铁路、电报、西医、海军、矿业等新兴行业的领军人物，其中，詹天佑、唐国安、唐绍仪、梁敦彦、梁诚等卓然成家。

第三，衔命赴秘鲁查访华工受虐状况，整理实情禀报朝廷，助朝廷适时善后，保护南美华人权益；

第四，出使美国、日斯巴尼亚（即西班牙）、秘鲁三国副公使。驻扎华盛顿，协助公使陈兰彬，保护旅美华工华商，维护中国合法权益；

第五，为耶鲁图书馆捐赠中国典籍，支持卫三畏在耶鲁开设汉学讲席，推动美国汉学发展，传扬中国文化；

第六，中日甲午战争期间，受委前往英国借款，支持政府与日本海战，决不妥协退让；

第七，先后向朝廷递交禁止鸦片、创办"中央银行"及修筑津镇铁路等方案，呼吁致力中国近代化建设；

第八，支持康有为倡导的维新改革，转而支持孙中山的民主革命运动，践行为中国的独立民主富强助力。

容闳的一生，经历鸦片战争到辛亥革命，他是中国近代近八十年历史的见证者、参与者和推动者，在近代中国的若干重大事件中均扮演过重要角色。他致力于"西学东渐"与"中学西渐"的探索，先后将西方的军械、学术、教育、铁路、纺织、银行等新兴行业引入中国，努力改变中国落后挨打的命运，从而谱写了于中西交流中勇立潮流的一生。与晚清时期立于时代潮头的其他志士仁人相较，容闳更多表现在"践于行"。他的大智慧、大勇气、大才干，都是在敢为人先精神的驱动下，于专制高压、封建守旧的社会环境中拼搏而成就的。他因践于行而寡于述，没有留下多少文献史料，《西学东渐记》算是他难得的传世精品著述了。

著作与译作

容闳撰述的自传，原名 *My Life in China and America*，中文直译为《我在中国和美国的生活》，于清宣统元年在美国纽约出版发行。1915 年由徐凤石、恽铁樵译成中文，提炼其一生功业之真谛，题名《西学东渐记》[①]，先在是年的《小说月报》第 6 卷第 1—8 号连载，轰动一时，同年在上海商务印书馆出版。本书选用"徐凤石、恽铁樵译本"，即是综合考虑其译作最早、文字最优，流传最广，影响最大而择优录选。从此，成为国人了解中美文化交流的经典著作，并多方印行，热销不减（此后还有 1991 年"王蓁译本"——《我在美国和在中国的生活追忆》[②]、2003 年"石霓译本"——《容闳自传——我在中国和美国的生活》[③]和 2018 年"王志通和左滕慧子译本"——《耶鲁中国人——容闳自传》[④]，以及 1969 年百濑弘的日文译本[⑤]）。在这个意义上说，"西学东渐"成了中国向西方学习的代名词，容闳即成为西学东渐的代言人。

---

① 容纯甫：《西学东渐记》，徐凤石、恽铁樵译，商务印书馆，1915。

② 容闳：《我在美国和在中国的生活追忆》，王蓁译，中华书局，1991。容闳：《西学东渐记》，王蓁译，中国人民大学出版社，2011。

③ 容闳：《容闳自传——我在中国和美国的生活》，石霓译注，百家出版社，2003。

④ 容闳：《耶鲁中国人——容闳自传》，王志通、左滕慧子译注，江苏凤凰文艺出版社，2018。

⑤ 容闳：《西学东渐记——容闳自传》，百濑弘译，阪野正高解说，平凡社，1969。

本书风行中国百年，尤以作者容闳本人的事功引人注目。"自序"开篇，激情洋溢，叩人肺腑：容闳的爱国精神和对同胞的热爱都不曾衰减；正好相反，这些都由于同情心而更加强了。因此，接下去的几章专门用来阐述容闳苦心孤诣地完成派遣留学生的计划：这是容闳对中国的永恒热爱的表现，也是他认为改革和复兴中国的最为切实可行的办法。

《西学东渐记》全书凡22章，记叙了作者赴美留学，学成归国，向太平天国提出政治建议，协助曾国藩、李鸿章办江南制造局，实施教育救国计划，组织中国幼童留学生出洋，保护美洲华侨，参加维新变法运动，因清政府通缉而避难美国的经历等。其涉及人物之多、事件之广，时间跨度超越半个世纪，近乎一部中国近代史。全书以回忆录的笔调，逐年追忆，间以评述、议论，抒发己意，旨在说明和呼吁中国如欲富强，"则非行一完全之新政策，决不能恢复其原有之荣誉"。其初衷不改，天地可鉴。

需要指出的是，该书是容闳暮年八十岁前后撰述的著作，未免存在一些记忆与事实的误差。本次整理出版，对其中某些与史实不符的记载，即在当页的注释中加以说明。

从温情与敬意的角度审视，容闳是人不是神，同样有喜怒哀乐、七情六欲，他有个性，有己见，他对曾国藩和美国的师长表示推崇与敬意，对李鸿章、陈兰彬、吴嘉善、盛宣怀、翁同龢等上司或同僚的记述时露情绪化，其评论文字难免有失偏颇，需要理解。他毕竟是由西学哺育出来的中国人，中西文化的差异无时不在他的思想与行为中显现出相互的矛盾与碰撞，对此我们不能苛求。

举个例子：关于容闳本人的婚姻，他在自传中就有意隐去一位"中国夫人"的事实，仅谈及一位美国的妻子祁洛。其实，他在与美国夫人结婚前，曾于1869年"9月15日，经朋友徐润等人的介绍，容闳与一位苏州郑氏姑娘在上海结婚，住上海天同路唐家弄43弄6号。郑氏女没有子女，《容氏谱牒》记载为'副郑氏'，后离异"[①]。《容氏谱牒》中记载郑氏"生道光戊申年十一月二十七日（1848年12月22日）……郑寄葬上海"[②]。这一"隐去"，似不难理解——或许是因为容闳身为基督教徒，需恪守一夫一妻约章，而不能像其他有条件的中国人一样妻妾成群，以免招致非议。这可以理解为中西方文化理念在容闳身上的反映。

引人注目的是，容闳在自传的扉页，将其身份标明为"耶鲁大学文学士，法学博士，出洋肄业局监督，中国驻美副公使，江苏候补道"。其中"法学博士"应是"名誉法学博士"，省去了"名誉"二字；"出洋肄业局监督"应是"出洋肄业局帮办"（副手），一直未"转正"为"监督"；"江苏候补道"仅是一个虚衔，无实权者也。如何考量容闳自己选用的"名片"，当待读者见仁见智了。谨此敬请读者审慎分辨。

本书采用徐、恽译本，并附有《西学东渐记》英文原版（*My Life in China and America*），以方便熟悉英文的读者阅读。

评价与导读

读史可以鉴知，感知有利阅读。也就是说，了解对历史人物的基本评价，具体说来，了解对容闳历史事功的评价，有利于加深对容闳著作的理解，既可增加"历史感"的体验，又可

[①] 陈汉才：《容闳评传》，广东高等教育出版社，2008，第346页。

[②] 《容氏谱牒》卷十五。转引自容应英：《容若兰是容闳的儿子吗？》，《近代史研究》2003年第4期，第283页。按，郑氏何因离异，几时分手，因资料缺乏，亦无从得知。

升华对时代人物的认知。从宏观角度审视，就是要把握容闳对民族、国家的建树及其历史影响。

1840年以降，时代场景举目疮痍。由于西方列强入侵和清朝封建统治腐败，中国逐步沦为半殖民地、半封建社会，国家蒙辱、人民蒙难、文明蒙尘，中华民族遭受了前所未有的劫难。为了拯救民族危亡，中国人民奋起反抗，仁人志士奔走呐喊，进行了艰苦卓绝的斗争。

容闳就是这些先驱志士中的一员。他生于忧患，长于忧患，国家有难，激发了他不甘于忧患，奋发于忧患，从而报国于忧患的决心。容闳不愧为可歌可泣的先驱者，他对中华民族建立的功业，永垂青史。

一、爱国者与报国士

容闳是一位伟大的爱国主义者，又是一位筚路蓝缕的报国者。爱国与报国一直流淌在他的血液里，形铸于他的日常生活中。

他的爱国主义激情首先体现在对西方知识的渴求。1850年圣诞节，他在致卫三畏的信中写道："我入学前花在语言学习上的时间是一年半。当我问及他人所花的时间时，我惊奇地发现，绝大多数同班同学都花了至少3年时间，有些人更花了6年时间。因此学术水平差异显现出来，相互之间在不同的基础上竞争。"[1]这足以说明他在美国学习之刻苦与用功。此外，他还要承受桑梓乃至至亲的误解。有如其对卫三畏所坦言："如您所熟知，中国人偏见甚深，颠倒本末，无法像您或其他开明人士那样理解求学之旨趣、优势和价值。无知和迷信蒙蔽了他们大

---

① 吴义雄、恽文捷编译：《美国所藏容闳文献初编》，社会科学文献出版社，2015，第16页。

脑的多数机能，因而不能欣赏真正有价值的事物。"① 完全可以想见，晚近时期的中国人，对近代西方文明和西学教育还缺乏应有的了解，乡人自然难以明白他为何在外国留学的时间如此之长。事实上，经过十余年的西学教育，容闳已深切领悟到美国新式教育的先鞭之着，倘能将之移植祖国，这种优质教育必将产生巨大的功效。所以，对于容闳来说，必须坚定信心，踔厉前行，要比其他同学更自律更自觉更著成效，以便未来报效祖国。

容闳大学毕业，美国友人劝他留在美国，享受优渥的生活与工作待遇，但他毅然决然回国，立志反哺贫穷落后的故园，为振兴华夏之邦建功立业。

自 1854 年告别耶鲁求学生涯，容闳怀抱"以西方之学术灌输于中国，使中国日趋于文明富强之境"的远大理想与信念，回到了阔别七年的祖国。他于晚年回忆道："大学最后一年结束之前，我已在心中规划出自己将要付诸行动的事业。我决心要做的事就是：中国的年轻一代应当享受与我同样的教育条件；这样，通过西方教育，中国将得以复兴，日趋文明富强②。"这是容闳发自内心的期冀，以西学改造中国，实现中国复兴富强，并渴盼祖国能造就一大批深谙西方政治学说、掌握先进科学技术、通晓世界近代文明的青年一辈肩负改造中国的大任。正是因为容闳矢志不移的奔走呼号，最终得以遂愿——他所倡导的海外留学运动修成正果。容闳对此欣慰不已："我的志向就是去

---

① 吴义雄、恽文捷编译：《美国所藏容闳文献初编》，社会科学文献出版社,2015,第 14 页。

② 徐凤石、恽铁樵所译《西学东渐记》将此句译为"以西方之学术灌输于中国，使中国日趋于文明富强之境"，堪称经典，为学界所广泛引用。

实现这一目标。朝着这一目标，我倾尽了所有心力与精力。"①这一功业光耀千秋，载入了华夏史册。

在往后58年间，于探寻报国的人生道路上，容闳参与了太平天国运动、洋务运动、戊戌变法、辛亥革命等国家自强、民族自救运动。具体而言，曾经造访太平天国，提出七项改革主张；投身曾国藩、李鸿章主导的洋务运动，促成詹天佑、唐绍仪、唐国安等120名幼童留学美国，协力推动近代中国的转型，被誉为"中国留学生之父"；晚年参与康有为、梁启超发起的戊戌变法；曾助力孙中山领导的辛亥革命；1912年4月，于生命垂危之际，鼓励两个耶鲁大学毕业的儿子弃所固之业，回国支持新生国家的建设。他84岁的爱国人生，是近代中国历史的真实写照。

报效祖国的信念，是容闳的本愿，也是经过审慎思考的抉择。他如是将心仪表白："我远渡重洋，求学深造，凭借勤奋刻苦和自我克制，最终在竞争中得到梦寐以求的收获。尽管收获所得并不如期待的那么完美圆满，但我完全达到了大学教育的常规标准，获得了人文教育的理念。因此，我能够称自己是一个受过教育的人，而且有必要问一下自己：'我将用自己所学去做些什么呢？'"②不难理解，正是强烈渴望中国富强的使命感，驱使容闳不留美国，而是回国献身。容闳的挚友杜渣（Joseph Hopkins Twichell）牧师曾经这般追忆：容闳届临毕业，《圣经》的一条经文仿如上帝的声音一直萦绕在他的心头、盘旋于耳边："如果一个人不能供养他自己，尤其是不能供养他自己的家人，

① Yung Wing, *My Life in China and America*（New york: Henry Holt and Company, 1909），p.15.

② 同上。

那么他就已经背弃了信仰，于是比一个不信仰者更坏。"① 这 "对容闳来说，'他自己'（his own）和'他自己的家人'（his own house），这些字眼意味着孕育他的祖国。这条经文赢得了胜利。可以说，他所获得的利益是从整整一个国家的人民中挑选出来的，他的正义之感和感恩之心都不允许他只为自己的利益着想。所以，虽然他不知道自己将会遭遇什么，但是依然决定返回中国；于是他就去做那些他已经做过的事情。"② 有美国友人赞誉容闳：他从头到脚，每个纤维神经都爱国；梁启超称许说：他舍忧国之外，无他思想无他事业；在孙中山的书信中也有这样的褒词：他虽久别乡井，却祖国萦怀。有学人如是强调，容闳决意归国，"他把西方基督（宗）教的使命感与奉献精神，与中国传统文化的以天下为己任与回报祖国整合起来；又把西方近代化以个性解放为基础的 ambition（雄心），与中国古代经典所提倡的大丈夫气概贯通起来。因此，他留学美国的起因与归宿都是以近代西学改造中国，而不是纯粹归化于西方"③。举凡，应该是较为客观和精准的诠释。

二、留学生与中学使

30 年前，学人对容闳的研究，都将其主要贡献定位于西学东渐，即一直将容闳视为近代中国西学东渐的鲜明标识。直到

---

① 出自《圣经·新约》"提摩太前书" 5：8，英译为："If any provide not for his own, and specially for those of his own house, he hath denied the faith, and is worse than an infidel."《圣经》（和合本）汉译为："人若不看顾亲属，就是背了真道，比不信的人还不好。不看顾自己家里的人，更是如此。"

② "An address by the Rev. Joseph H. Twichell, delivered before the Kent Club of the Yale Law School, April 10,1878." in Yung Wing, *My Life in China and America* (New york: Henry Holt and Company, 1909), p.89.

③ 章开沅：《先驱者的足迹——耶鲁馆藏容闳文献述评》，载氏著：《传播与植根——基督教与中西文化交流论集》，广东人民出版社，2005，第 121 页。

1989 年章开沅先生在耶鲁大学图书馆发现了容闳的大量档案资料之后，容闳的东学（中学）西传，才开始为学人注目，即容氏在西方构建中国形象之开创性的建树，渐次引起学界的足够重视。东西文化的互动——辩证性和准确性地概括了容闳"西学东渐"与"东学西传"毕生的主要功绩。

据史料展示，容闳于 1847—1854 年在美留学期间，不仅倾心致力于西学东渐，成为近代西学东渐的先驱者，而且利用可凭借之渠道展开东学西传，始而成为晚清东学西传的开拓者。一方面，他主动通过不同途径、各种方式将中华优秀文化传播到西方；另一方面，在当时罕有中国人踪影的美国，展现了中华文化的鲜活符号。可以说，他是筚路蓝缕身体力行地为中华文化代言。①

留美期间，容闳不仅对《四书》和若干中国史书、诗歌有所了解，而且善用这些典籍中的名言佳句为 1854 年届众多美国级友作毕业赠别。1872 年后，他肩任中国出洋肄业局帮办，辅助出洋肄业局总办陈兰彬等人在哈特福德工作八年之久，既督促留美幼童学习中文经典，还向耶鲁赠送《纲鉴易知录》《三字经》《千字文》《四书》《五经》《山海经》《康熙字典》《三国演义》《李太白诗集》等中国典籍，前后计捐赠 40 种 1237 卷。应该指出，中西文化交流本来是双向互补，即令是先进文明与落后文明之间也存在着互动链条，何况中国传统文化还具有几千年悠久的历史和极为灿烂的内蕴。西方人为东方文化的固有魅力所吸引，故国文化的基因必然要在与美国同学、友人长期相处中有所展现，这就是容闳致力于东（中）学西传的潜在因由。就传统文化的素养与实力而言，容闳诚然不及王韬、薛福成、郭嵩焘以及同僚陈兰

---

① 参见陈才俊：《容闳赴美留学与东学西传》，《唐廷枢研究》第 1 期（2019 年 12 月），第 128—148 页。

彬等学者，但他对西学和西方社会的熟谙，却使他在东学西传工作中具有自己的明显优势。诚然，因受物质条件、生活阅历、认知水平、影响范围等因素制约，容闳所践行的东学西传尚属处在初级的、较低层次的范畴，然而，无论在个人形象上还是在实际运筹上，他都彰显了中国文化在美国传播的早期开拓者的风貌，其先声性与开创性的贡献是不可磨灭的。尽管容闳留美期间躬身践行东学西传所产生的效果至今见仁见智，但起码可以肯定，通过他，华夏文化给新英格兰地区一部分美国人留下了良好的印象，并使他们增加认识和了解中华民族、中国文化的兴趣。西方人本来就为东方文化的固有魅力所吸引，加之容闳故国文化的基因也在其与美国师友长期相处中有所展现，于是乎，美国人早期关于中国的形象就慢慢构筑起来了。

容闳自幼接触西方教会，年轻时皈依耶稣基督，在海外接受完备的西式教育，并渐趋形成适应于西方文明的价值观与世界观，因此有人误将其视为业已归化美国的"香蕉人"。他的中国文化底蕴乃是幼年于乡间传统习俗耳濡目染的积淀，稍长，即在留学之前，又在澳门、香港等近邻地方学习生活了一段时间，得益于本土文化的沐浴，中华传统文化的基因就铭刻于其幼稚的心田，由是，其本位文化仍然是东方文化，中华文化早已根植其心。其实，无论在中国还是在美国，容闳始终深怀浓郁故国情结，秉持传统中华美德，其跃然书信中的忠孝、思乡之衷情，便是中华文化底蕴的深沉体现。古往今来，人类的文化交流是双向互动的，即使难免有主动与被动之分，有先进与落后之别。总体而言，东西方文化交流一直是彼此互动的，很难说有什么绝对的主动与绝对的被动，更何况中华传统文化还具有极其悠久的历史和极为丰富的内涵。晚清以降，虽然由于西方的强盛与东方的衰落，西学长期以强劲的态势东渐，但是源远流长的中华文化也并没有完全中断自己的西传。容闳赴美留学期间积极致力的东学西传即是明证。

1881 年，英国人 H. N. 肖尔（H. N. Shore）曾经通过对容闳的评价来认识中国："一个能够产生这样人物的国家，就能够成就伟大的事业。这个国家的前途不会是卑贱的……可以在真正完全摆脱迷信的重担和对过去的崇拜时，迅速给自己以新生，把自己建成一个真正伟大的国家。"①历史亦证明，西方人正是通过对中国人的认识和交流，进而认识和了解中华民族和中国文化，从而诱发进一步认识和理解博大精深中国文化的强烈愿望，促使中西文化的广泛交流。

2014 年 9 月 24 日，习近平在纪念孔子诞辰 2565 周年国际学术研讨会暨国际儒学联合会第五届会员大会开幕会上的讲话中说："正确进行文明学习借鉴。文明因交流而多彩，文明因互鉴而丰富。任何一种文明，不管它产生于哪个国家、哪个民族的社会土壤之中，都是流动的、开放的。这是文明传播和发展的一条重要规律。在长期演化过程中，中华文明从与其他文明的交流中获得了丰富营养，也为人类文明进步作出了重要贡献。丝绸之路的开辟，遣隋遣唐使大批来华，法显、玄奘西行取经，郑和七下远洋，等等，都是中外文明交流互鉴的生动事例。儒学本是中国的学问，但也早已走向世界，成为人类文明的一部分。'独学而无友，则孤陋而寡闻。'对人类社会创造的各种文明，无论是古代的中华文明、希腊文明、罗马文明、埃及文明、两河文明、印度文明等，还是现在的亚洲文明、非洲文明、欧洲文明、美洲文明、大洋洲文明等，我们都应该采取学习借鉴

---

① 转引自钟叔河：《容闳与西学东渐》，载氏著：《走向世界 —— 近代知识分子考察西方的历史》，中华书局，1985，第 138—139 页。

的态度，都应该积极吸纳其中的有益成分，使人类创造的一切
文明中的优秀文化基因与当代文化相适应、与现代社会相协调，
把跨越时空、超越国度、富有永恒魅力、具有当代价值的优秀
文化精神弘扬起来。"[1]这一表述，为文化承传指明了方向，意义
非同寻常。

容闳作为中国文化的符号和代表，则自然而然地向美国人
展示、传播中国文化。这种展示、传播是无形的、潜移默化的。
从这个意义来说，容闳不仅是近代中国西学东渐的先驱者，而
且是晚清早期东学西传的开拓者，更是中西文化交流的积极推
动者和巨大的贡献者。

三、基督徒与改革者

西学出身的容闳，从孩童伊始接受西方教育，在孟松学校
皈依耶稣基督，成为一名美国公理教会（American Congregational
Church）基督徒。大学时期形成了适应于西方近代文明的世界
观，回国投身维新与革命活动。同是基督徒入世的香山同乡孙
中山，亦在西式教育中完成大学学业，1884 年 5 月 4 日，在香
港由美国公理教会喜嘉理（Charles Robert Hagar）牧师施洗成为
基督徒。[2]两人均切身体认到美国基督宗教文明与中国封建专制
顽蔽之差异，触发改革祖国之宏志。[3]两人以西方文明的世界观
来审视中国，矢志为中国的进步事业贡献毕生，鞠躬尽瘁。显
然，他们与中国其他本土的先驱志士不一样，后者大多是长期
接受传统教育，旋走出国门看世界，获取新知以后返国推动各

---

① 《习近平：在纪念孔子诞辰 2565 周年国际学术研讨会上的讲话》，2014
年 9 月 24 日，新华网，http://xinhuanet.com/politics/2014–09/24/c_11126/2018_2.htm。

② 参见黄宇和：《中山先生与英国》，台湾学生书局，2005，第 56 页。

③ 参见梁寿华：《革命先驱——基督徒与晚清中国革命的起源》，宣道出
版社 ,2007，第 298 页。

项新政改革。

不同的文化背景塑造不同的世界观，不少学人称道容闳的可贵在于"与时俱进"，意即他的革新主张与实践经历器物（办工厂）、精神（创新学）、制度（从变法到革命）三个层面。这种看法是把容闳等同于其他中国现代化的先驱者，不尽符合容闳的心路历程。因为，容闳在美国所接受的多年文化熏陶，特别是耶鲁的系统教育，使他早已具有民主、自由与共和国思想。所以，他在1854年毕业的临别赠言，才会出现"希望获悉你的故土从专制统治下和愚昧锁链中解放出来""愿你回归天朝帝国之时，将发现它已成为神圣的共和国，而你将参与获致推翻压迫的胜利"等诚挚的话语。1860年他从上海前往南京，对太平天国进行相当认真的实地考察，给洪仁玕的七条建议，已经包括政治、军事、经济、教育各方面的革新。其后在《西学东渐记》第十章（"太平军中之访察"）和十一章（"对于太平军战争之观感"）中，他也毫不讳言自己对于革命的同情和推翻清朝政府并建业新国家的向往。[①]

可以说，信仰成为他们共同的革命救国动力，革命救国行动又反过来映显出其共同的信仰价值追求。[②]

容闳走上革命救国之途，乃缘于其族弟（亦称堂弟）容星桥[③]的牵线。戊戌政变之后，容闳"以素表同情于维新党，寓所

---

① 章开沅：《对于容闳的新认识》，《华中师范大学学报（哲学社会科学）》第38卷第3期，1999年5月。

② 陈才俊：《容闳与孙中山：两位基督徒"总统"的革命缘愫》《"辛亥革命与澳门"学术研讨论会论文集》，澳门理工学院，2012。

③ 中国大陆、台湾地区及日本诸多学者曾误认容闳与容星桥为叔侄，或是因为1900年容星桥在自立军起义计划失败后逃亡日本时，对他人介绍自己乃容闳之侄，并被其时之日本特高警察记录在案所致。此后学者多据此说，以讹传讹。至于容星桥为何自称容闳之侄，则可能是因为二人年龄相差37岁，看上去更像叔侄。

又有会议场之目，故亦犯隐匿党人之嫌，不得不迁徙以逃生"①，遂匿避于上海租界，旋于 1899 年迁居香港。此时他对清政府的幻想渐趋破灭，通过时任香港兴中会总部《中国日报》事务的容星桥，与兴中会的核心人物、基督徒爱国华侨谢缵泰联络。

谢缵泰记述，1900 年 3 月底，他在香港托马斯酒店（Thomas Hotel）会见容闳，与"容闳讨论了政治局势"。4 月 2 日，两人"密谈很久"；容闳同意"在能干的基督徒领导下而联合与合作"。翌日，他"为容闳和杨衢云安排了一个秘密会议，讨论赶快联合与合作的问题"②。自此，"革命事业获得容闳之赞许"③。双方取得了互信。4 月 18 日，杨衢云拜访谢缵泰。谢氏为防止拟"联合与合作"的各党派领导间的自私竞争和妒忌，"强烈建议推选容闳博士为维新联合党派的主席"④。

1900 年 7 月 26 日，唐才常在上海愚园（亦称张园）召开"中国国会"（即"自立会"），准备发动自立军起义。"公推容闳为会长，严复为副会长，唐为总干事"⑤。容闳与会并以英文起草大会宣言，"向大家宣讲宗旨，声如洪钟，在会人意气奋发，鼓掌雷动"⑥。此见容闳声望如领袖群伦。

此间（是年 6—7 月），孙中山等兴中会志士试图与时任两

---

① 容闳：《西学东渐记》，徐凤石、恽铁憔译，岳麓书社，2008，第 122 页。

② 参见谢缵泰：《中华民国革命秘史》，江煦棠、马颂明译，载中国人民政治协商会议广东省委员会文史资料研究委员会编：《孙中山与辛亥革命史料专辑》，广东人民出版社，1981，第 308 页。

③ 罗家伦主编：《国父年谱》（上册），中国国民党中央委员会党史史料编纂委员会，1969，第 117 页。

④ 谢缵泰：《中华民国革命秘史》，江煦棠、马颂明译，载中国人民政治协商会议广东省委员会文史资料研究委员会编：《孙中山与辛亥革命史料专辑》，广东人民出版社，1981，第 309 页。

⑤ 参见冯自由：《革命逸史》（第一册），台湾商务印书馆，1969，第 80 页。

⑥ 孙宝瑄：《日益斋日记》，资料丛刊《戊戌变法》（一），第 540 页。

广总督李鸿章"合作"，谋划两广独立。孙中山致函李之幕僚刘学询，谈及独立后的政府外交工作，谓可让何启与容闳"各当一面"①。8月22日，孙中山于横滨谈话指出："在中国的政治改革派的力量中，尽管分成多派，但我相信今天由于历史的进展和一些感情因素，照理不致争执不休，而可设法将各派很好地联成一体。作为众望所归的领袖，当推容闳。"②这说明孙中山与容闳的神交程度。

往后，容闳和孙中山以及革命派的关系渐形密切。孙中山对容闳这位热心改革中国的前贤敬慕不已，并加紧互动。1900年10月下旬，孙中山在其计划的新政府案中推举容闳为外国派遣特使。③1901年，容闳曾对革命党人刘禹生提及孙中山称许"其人宽广诚明有大志，予勖以华盛顿、弗兰克林之心志。他日见面，汝当助其成功"④。两人由是建立了相知之谊。

1900年9月至1902年5月，容闳基本居于香港，与革命党人过从甚密。此间，谢缵泰、李纪堂等部分兴中会基督徒和另一位基督徒、太平天国遗臣洪全福，谋划于1903年除夕在广州起事，预立国号"大明顺天国"，"提议推举容闳博士为临时政府大总统，众无异义"⑤。"此实为容氏于革命党人具有极大

———————

① 冯自由：《革命逸史》（第四集），中华书局，1981，第99页。

② 日本外务省外交史料馆：《各国内政关系杂纂：支那之部》，明治三十三年八月二十二日神奈川县知县发，秘甲第334号。转引自《孙中山全集》第一卷，中华书局，1981，第198—199页。

③ 孙中山：《致刘学询函》，载《孙中山全集》（第一卷），中华书局，1981，第202页。

④ 刘禹生：《纪先师容纯父先生》，载刘禹生：《世载堂杂忆》，中华书局，1960，第115页。

⑤ 冯自由：《革命逸史》（第四集），中华书局，1981，第71—72页。

信用所致。"① 容闳对起事"极表同情"②，对谢缵泰的谋略、李纪堂的疏财和洪全福的勇武，极为赞许，并亲赴美国争取国际声援。大明顺天国革命未果，容闳仍积极活跃于美国，寻求救国图强国之策。他于 1907 年 9 月 10 日，"提出了促使中国革命成功的计划"③；又分别于 1908 年 7 月 14 日和 1910 年 4 月 13 日致函谢缵泰，"谴责康有为及其保皇会"，"强烈抨击康有为及其信徒"④。也就是在这个时候，容闳最终彻底与维新派决绝。

1908 年 11 月，光绪皇帝与慈禧太后相继离世，容闳致函荷马李，敦促他乘时发动武装反清，倘能取得中国一省，即任命其为总督。容闳还把中国各秘密会社的名单寄给荷马李，建议他邀请各会社领袖来美共商组织临时政府内阁及顾问委员会，其中就有孙中山。1909 年底，孙中山应容闳之邀抵达纽约，共同商讨武装起义的计划，容闳允诺承担筹款任务。他们制定了"中国红龙计划"（Red Dragon–China），内容包括：（1）暂停在中国南方准备未周的起义，以便集中人力财力发动更大规模的起义；（2）由孙中山任命布思为同盟会驻美全权财务代表，向纽约的大财团筹措巨款；在美国为同盟会训练军官；筹组临时政府。容闳估计实施这一计划约需 500 万美元、10 万支枪支、

---

① 李志刚：《容闳与近代中国》，正中书局，1981，第 165 页。

② 陈春生：《壬寅洪全福广州举义记》，资料丛刊《辛亥革命》（一），第 316 页。

③ 谢缵泰：《中华民国革命秘史》，江煦棠、马颂明译，载中国人民政治协商会议广东省委员会文史资料研究委员会编：《孙中山与辛亥革命史料专辑》，广东人民出版社，1981，第 319 页。

④ 谢缵泰：《中华民国革命秘史》，江煦棠、马颂明译，载中国人民政治协商会议广东省委员会文史资料研究委员会编：《孙中山与辛亥革命史料专辑》，广东人民出版社，1981，第 320 页。

1 亿发弹药。而荷马李则估计需要美金 5000 万元。[①]1910 年 2 月 16 日，容闳向孙中山提供了进行步骤：（1）自银行贷借 150 万至 200 万元作为活动基金；（2）成立一个临时政府，任用有能力的人来管理占领的城市；（3）任用一位有能力的人统率军队；（4）训练海军。[②]孙中山随即赴旧金山、洛杉矶等地，与荷马李、布思等人进行了多次策划。其间容闳不断函驰荷马李和布思，表示支持孙的立场，希望他们迅速筹款，以便大计付诸实施。容闳还向布思提出具体借款方案：向美国政府借款，总数为 1000 万美元，分 5 次付款，年利息为 15%，期限为 10 年。其后，孙、容与荷马李、布思往返通信讨论计划的实施。尽管贷款没有任何成果，容闳为民主革命呕心沥血的努力还是令人敬佩的。

1911 年武昌起义成功消息传出，中风卧床的容闳在大洋彼岸喜出望外。他接连致函谢缵泰等革命领导者，高度评价这场史无前例的民主革命是"了不起的大革命"，"它已经在短短的期间内，使满清政府不得不跪地求饶"，"想想你们的革命给你们和子孙后代开辟了一番多么壮丽的事业！"[③]容闳在信中委托谢缵泰向被推举为临时大总统的孙中山表示祝贺。他说："你得一直等到新生的中华民国的新总统孙逸仙博士就职：到那时，你就能够向我报导他的就职典礼，并给我寄一份完整的内阁名单。在南京参加就职典礼的时候，假如你见到他，千万替我向

---

① 参见吴相湘：《国父传记新资料》，《传记文学》第 11 卷第 5 期，第 22 页。

② 参见吴相湘：《国父传记新资料》，《传记文学》第 11 卷第 5 期，第 23 页。

③ 谢缵泰：《中华民国革命秘史》，江煦棠、马颂明译，载中国人民政治协商会议广东省委员会文史资料研究委员会编：《孙中山与辛亥革命史料专辑》，广东人民出版社，1981，第 324—325 页。

他致以衷心的祝贺。"还表示，"我的健康情况逐渐好转，或许会到中国来，参观参观这个新共和国。""我希望能活到看见我的朋友当选下届大总统，他已经为中国和中国人奋斗了二十二年之久。""我真希望在没死之前，能够和所有其他革命领导人亲自认识认识。"①一个已临垂暮之年的老人，尚如此关心国事，着实令人钦佩。

容闳以几十年之政治经验，不仅对前景并不乐观，而且预见到隐藏着的危机。他分析当时国内国外的政治形势，向革命党人提出了一些颇有见地的忠告：为新民国的建设着想，容闳认为应聘用一定数量的外国人为我所用。他指出："如果聘用外国人，宁可聘用美国人好得多。我们可以按照自己的意愿留用或解雇，并以此为条件与他们签订合同。这样一个重要问题，应当由代表在参议会（National Convention）上冷静讨论，并作出坚决的决定。"②

1912年元旦，孙中山在南京就任中华民国临时大总统，特地给容闳写了一封热情洋溢的信，并附上一张照片。信中对容闳"因谋复满清之专制，而建伟大之事业，以还吾人自由平等之幸福，致有此逃之异域"表示深切的慰问。企盼容闳早日回国参加新民国建设："况当此破坏后，民国建设，在在需才。素仰盛名，播震寰宇，加以才智学识，达练过人，用敢备极欢迎，恳请先生归国。而在此中华民国创立一完全之政府，以巩固我

---

① 谢缵泰：《中华民国革命秘史》，江煦棠、马颂明译，载中国人民政治协商会议广东省委员会文史资料研究委员会编：《孙中山与辛亥革命史料专辑》，广东人民出版社，1981，第326页。

② 参见谢缵泰：《中华民国革命秘史》，江煦棠、马颂明译，载中国人民政治协商会议广东省委员会文史资料研究委员会编：《孙中山与辛亥革命史料专辑》，广东人民出版社，1981，第324—326页，第323—326页。

幼稚之共和。倘俯允所请，则他日吾人得安享自由平等之幸福，悉自先生所赐矣。"① 容闳得悉孙中山书信，欣慰无似。遗憾的是，他已重病在身，无法实现归国的夙愿。于是，他说服同样毕业于耶鲁大学的两个儿子觐彤和觐槐回国，代其为新的共和国家服务。

晚清时期的中国基督徒接受基督宗教信仰和文明后，在中国传统以外多了一种价值的选择。他们虽然不一定反对传统，但往往视新接受的基督宗教价值比本国固有的传统更高。对这些基督徒来说，基督宗教所具有的价值，是中国传统和现实所无的。其中最为当时基督徒革命者推崇的就是人道主义（humanitarianism），这种人道主义往往成为其中一些基督徒参加革命的动力。② 这也许正是容闳与孙中山"殊途同归"走上革命救国之道的深层缘愫。

1912 年 4 月 21 日，容闳在美国康狄涅格州哈特福德市的寓所逝世，安葬于该市西带山公墓。谢缵泰称誉他"是个真正的爱国者，他深深热爱祖国，晚年切望回国，为祖国效劳"③。他虽然被安葬在曾经学习、工作、生活多年的哈特福德，而墓碑上所镌刻的那个"容"字图案，却象征着那颗永远期盼东归之心，铭刻着他对祖国土地和人民的终身眷恋。

王杰

---

① 中国社会科学院近代史研究所中华民国史研究室编：《孙中山全集》（第二卷），中华书局，1982，第 144 页。

② 参见梁寿华：《中国革命的先驱 —— 晚清基督徒革命者》，《中国神学研究院期刊》第 18 期（1995 年 1 月），第 28 页。

③ 谢缵泰：《中华民国革命秘史》，江煦棠、马颂明译，载中国人民政治协商会议广东省委员会文史资料研究委员会编：《孙中山与辛亥革命史料专辑》，广东人民出版社，1981，第 324—326 页，第 330 页。

目录

西学东渐记

自　序

　　本书前五章缕述我赴美国前的早期教育，以及到美国后的继续学习，先是在马萨诸塞州芒森城（旧译马沙朱色得士省孟松）的芒森学校，后来在耶鲁大学（旧译耶路大学）。

　　第六章从我出国八年后重返中国开始。一向被当作西方文明表征的西方教育，如果不能使一个东方人变化其内在的气质，使他在面对感情和举止截然不同的人时，觉得自己倒像来自另一个世界似的，那不就可怪了吗？我的情况正好如此。然而，我的爱国精神和对同胞的热爱都不曾衰减；正好相反，这些都由于同情心而更加强了。因此，接下去的几章专门用来阐述我苦心孤诣地完成派遣留学生的计划：这是我对中国的永恒热爱的表现，也是我认为改革和复兴中国的最为切实可行的办法。

　　随着中国留学事务所的突然撤销和已经成为中国现代教育先行者的一百二十名留学生的召回，我的教育事业也从而告终了。

　　1872 年那批留学生的仅存者中，有几人由于艰苦努力，勤奋不懈，终能跻身于中国重要的经世之才的前列。而且正是由于他们，原先的留学事务所也复活了，虽然形式上已有变更。因此，如今人们可以看到中国学生翩翩联袂，从遥远的海角天涯，来到欧美接受科学教育。

　　1909 年 11 月于康涅狄格州哈特福德阿特伍德街 16 号

第一章　幼稚时代

1828 年 11 月 17 日，予生于彼多罗岛（Pedro Island）[①]之南屏镇。镇距澳门西南可四英里。澳门，葡萄牙殖民地也。[②]岛与澳门间，有海峡广半英里许。予第三，有一兄一姊一弟。今兄弟若姊俱已谢世[③]，惟予仅存（按：先生于一九一二年逝世，著

---

① 彼多罗岛（Pedro Island）：即湾仔岛。

② 原文有误，应为租占地。香山县和粤海关在澳门有派驻机构，葡人须向广东地方政府交租金。

③ 据《容氏谱牒》记载，容闳家族情况如下：

祖父容活生，育五子：名建、名著、名彰（Yung Ming Cheong）、名嘉、名培。

父亲容丙炎（1795—1840）"名建，讳丙炎，号立亭，诰赠中宪大夫，晋赠资政大夫，生乾隆乙卯年（1795）十二月廿三日，卒道光庚子年（1840）八月廿二日，娶林氏，本村德熙公女，诰赠恭人，晋赠二品夫人，生嘉庆丙辰年（1796）八月十五日，卒咸丰庚申年（1860）十月廿七日，寿六十五岁，同葬山萝亭（坤申），生三子：达苗、达萌、达芽（出嗣），一女（适造贝林家）"。

母亲林莲娣（1796—1860），英文名 Lin Lien Tai，南屏林德熙之女。

叔父"名培，讳绍祥，号云亭，生嘉庆丁卯年（1807）四月廿一日，卒道光癸巳年（1833）十一月十二日，娶黄氏，公葬山萝亭，妣生卒葬俱失书。嗣子达芽，名建公三子"。

长兄光杰（1822—1892），字达苗，号穗邨，娶张氏、陈氏，生四子：鹤兰（尚勤，号廉臣，张氏所生）、征兰（尚谦，又名良南，号辉珊，陈出）、爵（张出）、攀（陈出），一女（张出）。次兄容乾（1825—1850），字达芽，出嗣名培公，娶黄氏，无子，育子容申。容申（1871—1914），族名若兰，号尚书，娶北山杨氏，生三子：泽华、家萧、能华，一女适本村张祥。姐容氏，嫁南屏对岸的造贝村林家。

次兄"达芽，讳乾，生道光乙酉年（1825）十月十八日，卒道光庚戌年（1850）八月十七日，娶黄氏，公葬山萝亭，妣生卒葬俱失书，育一子若兰。"

容闳（1828.11.17—1912.4.21），族名达萌，号纯甫，英文名 Yung Wing，先后娶苏州郑氏（1848—？）和美国祁洛氏（Mary Louise Kellogg，1851—1886），生二子咏兰、嘉兰。

3

书时为 1900 年 ① ）。

1834 年，伦敦妇女会议在远东提倡女学。英教士古特拉富② 之夫人（Mrs. Gutzlaff）遂于是时莅澳，初设一塾，专授女生。未几复设附塾，兼收男生。其司事某君，予同里而父执也，常为予父母道古夫人设塾授徒事。其后予得入塾肄业，此君与有力焉。惟是时中国为纯粹之旧世界，仕进显达，赖八股为敲门砖，予兄方在旧塾读书，而父母独命予入西塾，此则百思不得其故。意者通商而后，所谓洋务渐趋重要，吾父母欲先着人鞭，冀儿子能出人头地，得一翻译或洋务委员之优缺乎？至于予后来所成之事业，似为时世所趋，或非予父母所及料也。

1835 年，随父至澳门，入古夫人所设西塾，予见西国妇女始此 —— 时才七龄。当时情形深印脑中，今虽事隔数十年，犹能记忆。古夫人躯干修长，体态合度，貌秀而有威，眼碧色，深陷眶中，唇薄颐方，眉浓发厚，望而知为果毅明决之女丈夫。

---

① 译者有误，容氏著书时为 1909 年。

② 英教士古特拉富：即普鲁士籍新教传教士郭实猎（Karl Friedrich August Gützlaff，1803—1851），汉名郭士立、郭实腊、郭实猎，生于普鲁士东部波美拉尼亚斯德丁（今波兰什切青）。1821 年入柏林神学院，1823 年到鹿特丹入荷兰传道学院进修。1826 年毕业，入荷兰传道会为牧师，被派往南洋传教。1828 年到新加坡。1829 年脱离荷兰教会，在马六甲主持伦敦会，与该传道会首位女传教士玛丽·纽惠露（Maria Newell）结婚。1830 年携妻往暹罗。1831 年 2 月 16 日纽惠露难产，母女先后去世，于 6 月 3 日乘帆船前往中国北方考察，12 月到澳门行医传教。1832 年 2 月陪同英国东印度公司商船北上考察，至朝鲜、日本，9 月返澳门；10 月再次乘船北上，到牛庄（今营口）。1833 年夏回澳门，8 月在广州创办中国境内第一份中文报刊——《东西洋每月统记传》。1834 年与伦敦妇女教育会派往马六甲华英书院工作的温施娣（Mary Wanstall）结婚，6 月返回澳门定居。1935 年 9 月 30 日，与温施娣在澳门设立一所女子学校。1840 年鸦片战争爆发，任英军司令官的翻译和向导，以及英军占领下的定海知县、宁波知府；参与起草《南京条约》。1843 年任首任香港总督璞鼎查的中文秘书。1844 年在香港成立传教组织"福汉会"，创立中国传教会。1851 年 8 月 9 日在香港逝世。

时方盛夏，衣裳全白，飘飘若仙，两袖圆博如球，为当年时制。夫人御此服饰，乃益形其修伟。予睹状，殊惊愕，依吾父肘下，逡巡不前。虽夫人和颜悦色，终惴惴也。我生之初，足迹不出里巷，骤易处境，自非童稚所堪。迨后思家之念稍杀，外界接触渐习，乃觉古夫人者和蔼仁厚，视之若母矣。予于学生中齿最稚，乃益邀夫人怜悯，入塾后即命居女院中，不与男童杂处，盖特别优待也。

予儿时颇顽劣，第一年入塾时曾逃学，其事至今不忘。古夫人之居予于女院，本为优遇，予不知其用意。男生等皆居楼下层，能作户外运动。而予与诸女生，则禁锢于三层楼上，惟以露台为游戏场。以为有所厚薄，心不能甘。常课余潜至楼下，与男生嬉。又见彼等皆许自由出门，散步街市，而予等犹无此权利，心益不平。乃时时潜出至埠头，见小舟舣集，忽发异想，思假此逃出藩笼，以复我自由之旧。同院女生，年事皆长于予。中有数人，因禁闭过严，亦久蛰思启，故于予之计划，深表同情。既得同志六人，胆益壮。定计予先至埠头，雇定盖篷小船，乘间脱逃。翌晨早餐后，古夫人方就膳，予等七人遂于此时潜行出校，匆匆登舟，向对岸进发。对岸为彼多罗岛，予家在也。谓同伴六人先至予家小住，然后分别还乡。在予固自以为计出万全，不谓渡江未半，追者踵至。来船极速，转瞬且及。予乃惶急，促舟子努力前进，许渡登彼岸时酬以重金。但予舟只二橹，来舟则四橹。舟子知势力悬殊，见来舟手巾一挥，即戢耳听命，而予等七人束手受缚矣。放豚入笠，乃施惩戒。古夫人旋命予等排列成行，巡行全校。且于晚课后，课堂中设一长桌，命七人立其上一小时。予立中央，左右各三人，头戴顶尖纸帽，胸前悬一方牌大书"逃徒"，不啻越狱罪囚也。予受此惩创，羞愧无地。而古夫人意犹未足，故将果饼橙子等分给他生剥食，使予等馋涎欲流，绝不一顾。苦乐相形，难堪滋甚，古夫人洵恶作剧哉！

古夫人所设塾，本专教女生。其附设男塾，不过为玛礼孙学校（Morrison School）①之预备耳。玛礼孙学校发起于1835年，至1839年成立。未成立时，以生徒附属古夫人塾中，酌拨该校经费，以资补助。是予本玛礼孙校学生而寄生于此者。忆予初入塾时，塾中男生，合予共二人耳。后此塾逐渐扩张，规画益宏。夫人乃邀其侄女派克司女士（Miss Parkes）姊妹二人，来华襄助。派女士之兄海雷派克司（Mr. Harry Parkes），即1864年主张第二次之鸦片战争者，因其于此事著异常劳绩，故英皇锡以勋爵云。②予于此短期内，得亲炙于派克司女士二人，亦幸事也。

其后此塾因故停办，予等遂亦星散。古夫人携盲女三人赴美，此三女乃经予教以凸字读书之法，及予辍教时，彼等已自能诵习《圣经》及《天路历程》二书矣。派克司姊妹则一嫁陆克哈医士（Dr. William Lockhart），一嫁麦克来穿教士（Rev. MacClatchy），仍受伦敦传道会之委任，在中国服务甚久云。

予既还家，从事汉文。迨1840年夏秋之交，方鸦片战争剧烈时，适予父逝世，身后萧条，家无担石。予等兄弟姊妹四人，三人年齿稍长，能博微资。予兄业渔，予姊躬操井臼，予亦来往于本乡及邻镇之间贩卖糖果，兢兢业业，不敢视为儿戏。每日清晨三时即起，至晚上六时始归，日获银币二角五分，悉以奉母。所得无多，仅仅小补。家中揭挂，惟长兄是赖耳。予母

① 玛礼孙学校（Morrison School），今译马礼逊学校。

② 原文意为：海雷派克司实为第二次鸦片战争之发动者，因其于此事卓著劳绩，故于1864年得授勋爵。海雷派克司即巴夏礼（Harry Smith Parke，1828—1885），英国外交官，1863年任驻上海领事，1883—1885年任驻公使兼驻朝鲜公使，1885年逝于北京。

得予等臂助，尚能勉强度日。如是者五阅月，而严冬忽至，店铺咸停制糖果。予乃不得已而改业，随老农后，芸草阡陌间 ①。予姊恒与予偕。相传古有卢斯（Ruth）者，割禾无所获，遇波亚士（Boaz）② 时时周给之，予惜无此佳遇。幸予粗通西文，窘迫时竟赖以解厄。予之能读写英文，农人本不之知。予姊告之，乃忽动其好奇心，招予至前，曰："孺子，试作红毛人之语。"予初怩怩不能出口，后予姊从旁怂恿，谓："汝试为之。彼农或有以犒汝。"农人欣然曰："老夫生平从未闻洋话。孺子能言者，吾将以禾一巨捆酬汝劳，重至汝不能负也。"予闻此重赏，胆立壮，乃为之背诵二十六字母。农人闻所未闻，咸惊奇诧异。予为此第一次演说时，稻田中之泥水深且没胫。演说既毕，获奖禾数捆，予与予姊果不能负，乃速返家邀人同往荷归。予之拉杂英文，早年时即著此奇效，是则始愿所不及。时予年十二岁，即古时卢斯之获六斛，其成绩亦不予过矣。

刘禾时期甚短，无他事足述。其后有一比邻，向在天主教士某处，为印刷书报工人。适由澳门请假归，偶与予母言教士欲雇用童子折叠书页，仅识英字母及号码无误即得，程度不必过高。予母告以此事予能为之，乃请其介绍于教士。条约既定，别母赴澳门就新事，月获工资四元五角，以一元五角付膳宿费，余三元按月汇寄堂上。然予亦不遽因此致富。可四阅月，忽有梦想不到之人来函招予，而上帝又似命予速往勿失时机者。函盖来自霍白生医生（Dr. Hobson），医生亦传道者，其所主任之医院，距予执业之印刷所仅一英里。予在古夫人西塾时数见之，故稔识其人。此次见招，初不解其故，以为霍氏欲予从其学医

---

① 原文意为：随获者之后而拾其落穗。
② 波亚士（Boaz）：人名。

也。继乃知古夫人赴美时，其临别之末一语，即托予于霍白生，谓必访得予所在，俟玛礼孙学校开课时送予入校云。霍氏负此宿诺，无日或忘。盖觅予不得，已数月于兹。相见时霍氏谓予："玛礼孙学校已开课，汝亟归家请命，必先得若母允汝入塾，然后舍去汝业，来此伴余数月，使予得熟知汝之为人，乃可介绍汝于该校教习也。"时予母方深资予助，闻言意颇不乐；然卒亦从予请，命予往澳门辞别天主教教士。该教士虽沉静缄默，四月之中从未与予交一语，然亦未尝吹毛求疵，故予去时颇觉恋恋。予辞出后，迳往医院，从霍医生终日臼臼丁丁，制药膏丸散。霍氏巡行医院，抚视病人时，则捧盆随其后。如是者二阅月，霍君乃引予至玛礼孙学校，谒见校长勃朗先生（Rev. Brown）。

第二章　小学时代

玛礼孙学校于 1839 年 11 月 1 日开课，主持校务者为勃朗先生。先生美国人，1832 年由耶路大学（Yale University）毕业，旋复得名誉博士学位①。乃于是年（1839 年）2 月 19 日偕其夫人莅澳，以其生平经验从事教育，实为中国创办西塾之第一人。予入是校在 1841 年，先我一年而入者已有五人，黄君胜、李君刚、周君文、唐君杰与黄君宽也。校中教科，为初等之算术、地文及英文。英文教课列在上午，国文教课则在下午。予惟英文一科，与其余五人同时授课，读音颇正确，进步亦速。予等六人为开校之创始班，予年最幼。迨后 1846 年之 12 月，勃朗先生因病归国，六人中竟半数得附骥尾，亦难得之时会也。

玛礼孙学校何由而来乎，读者宜急欲知之矣。1834 年 8 月 1 日，玛礼孙博士（Dr. Robert Morrison）卒于中国，其翌年 1 月 26 日，乃有传单发布于寓澳之西人，提议

鲍留云（Samuel Robbins Brown，1810—1880）

---

①　原文为神学博士学位。

组织玛礼孙教育会，以纪念其一生事迹。并建议设学校，及设施他种方法，以促进中国之泰西教育。至玛礼孙博士之来中国，乃为英国传道会所委派。彼为中国之第一传道师。博士于 1807 年 1 月 31 日由伦敦启程，经大西洋而至纽约，改乘帆船名"屈利亥登"（Trident）者而至中国。原拟在澳门登陆，因为天主教士之嫉忌，不果，乃折至广州。后因中外适起交涉，中政府与西商感情颇恶，乃往麻拉甲（Malacca）暂时驻足，以植基础。于是从事著作，成第一部之华英字典①，分订三册；并以耶教《圣经》译成汉文，以供华人披阅。又有第一信徒名梁亚发者，助其宣讲，为传道界别开生面，成效卓著。此后寓华之教士，咸奉玛礼孙所著之字典及其所译之《圣经》，以为圭臬。玛礼孙博士既在中国成如许事业，其名永垂不朽，允宜建一大学以纪念之。乃所建者只区区一塾，规模褊小，且因经费仅仅恃侨寓西商，时虞匮乏。以玛氏之丰功伟烈，而纪念之成绩，乃不过如是，庸非一憾事哉！

　　1840 年鸦片战争起，其后结果，即以香港让于英人。玛礼

马礼逊学校首批学生唐廷桂
（1828—1897，原名植，字茂枝）

马礼逊学校第二批学生
唐廷枢（1832—1892，字建时）

---

① 原文为英华字典。

孙学校遂于1842年迁于香港某山之巅，高出海平线几六百英尺。山在维多利亚殖民地（Victoria Colony）之东端。登山眺望，自东至西，港口全境毕现。即此一处，已足见香港为中国南部形胜，无怪外人垂涎。且港口深阔，足为英国海军根据地。有此特点，故此岛终不我属，卒为英国有也。玛礼孙学校既设于山顶，其后此山遂亦以玛礼孙得名云。

1845年3月12日，威廉·麦克（William Macy）先生来港，为玛礼孙学校之助教。是校自澳门徙此以来，大加扩张，学生之数已达四十余人。新增三班，教授一人之力不能兼顾，故须延聘教习，相助为理。麦先生之来校，适当其会。勃朗先生则仍专心校务，毫无间断。直至次年秋间回美，乃以麦先生继之。盖其时麦先生已有一年之经验矣。

勃朗与麦克二君之品性大相悬殊。勃先生一望而知为自立之人，性情态度沉静自若，遇事调处秩序井然。其为人和蔼可亲，温然有礼；且常操乐观主义，不厌不倦，故与学生之感情甚佳。其讲授教课，殆别具天才，不须远证，而自能使学生明白了解。此虽由于赋性聪敏，要亦阅历所致。盖当其未来中国、未入耶路大学之前，固已具有教育上之经验矣。故对于各种学生，无论其为华人、为日人、或为美人，均能审其心理而管束之。知师莫若弟，以才具论，实为一良好校长。其后先生回国，任阿朋学校（Auburn Academy）之监院，后往日本亦从事教育，皆功效大著，足证是言之不谬也。至于助教麦克先生，亦为耶路大学之毕业生。第未来中国之先，未尝执教鞭，故经验绝少。而于中国将择何种事业，亦未有方针。然其天性敏捷，德行纯懿，思想卓荦，使君自不凡也。

1850年玛礼孙学校解散，麦克与其母返美，复入耶路大学圣教科学道，1854年复经美国公会派至中国传道。其时予已毕业于耶路大学，准备回国，乃与之偕归。自桑得阿克（Sandy Hook）启程以至香港，计历百五十四日之久，始达目的地。长途寂寂，无聊殊甚，当于第六章中详之。

1846 年冬，勃朗先生回国。去之前四月，先生以此意布告生徒，略谓己与家属均身体羸弱，拟暂时离华，庶几迁地为良。并谓对于本校，感情甚深，此次归国，极愿携三五旧徒，同赴新大陆，俾受完全之教育；诸生中如有愿意同行者，可即起立。全堂学生聆其言，爽然如有所失，默不发声。其后数日间，课余之暇，聚谈及此，每为之愀然不乐。其欣欣然有喜色者，惟愿与赴美之数人耳，即黄胜①、黄宽②与予是也。当勃先生布告游

---

① 黄胜（1827—1902），又名黄达权，字平甫，广东香山县人。道光二十一年（1841）入读马礼逊学校。次年随校迁往香港继续学业。二十七年（1847）与容闳、黄宽跟随校长鲍留云夫妇留学美国。次年回国，任职《德臣西报》及英华书院印刷所。咸丰三年（1853）任英华书院印刷所监督，参与创办《遐迩贯珍》，并协助理雅各翻译《四书》。八年（1858）参与创办《中外新报》，并成为首位香港华人陪审员。同治三年（1864）任上海同文馆英文教习。六年（1867）就职英华书院印刷所。八年（1869）参与创办香港东华医院，兼任总理。十年（1871）参与创办中华印务总局。次年参与创办《华字日报》。十二年（1873）携带第二批幼童赴美。次年参与创办《循环日报》。光绪二年（1876）与唐廷枢在香港选取福建船政学堂学生。次年任驻美使馆翻译。四年（1878）任驻旧金山翻译。八年（1882）任满返港。次年加入英籍，并委为非官守太平绅士，出任定例局议员（1883—1890）。十二年（1886）任香港东华医院主席。著有《西洋火器略说》，与王韬合译《火器略说》。

② 黄宽（1829—1878），名杰臣，号绰卿，广东香山人。道光二十一年（1841）入读马礼逊学校。二十二年（1842）随学校迁至香港继续就读。二十七年（1847）与容闳、黄胜随校长鲍留云夫妇前往美国入学求学。道光三十年（1850）赴英国苏格兰爱丁堡大学学习医科，肄业五年得医学博士学位。后继续留英研究病理学、解剖学二年。咸丰七年（1857）回香港开西医所，次年迁广州行医，后接办英国医生在金利埠创设的惠爱医馆，兼任博济医院医生。十年（1860）辞去惠爱医馆职务。同治元年（1862）被李鸿章聘为上海幕府任医官，未及半载即辞职，返广州自设诊所。二年（1863）被聘为海关医务处医官。五年（1866）博济医院附设之南华医学堂成立，担任解剖学、生理学及外科学教学任务。六年（1867）博济医院院长嘉约翰因病回国，代理院长职务。光绪元年（1875）兼任西南施医局主任。四年因病早逝。

美方针时，予首先起立，次黄胜，次黄宽。第予等虽有此意，然年幼无能自主。归白诸母，母意颇不乐。予再四请行，乃勉强曰："诺。"然已凄然泪下矣。予见状，意良不忍，竭力劝慰之曰："儿虽远去，尚有兄弟与姊三人，且长兄行将娶妇，得有兄嫂承欢膝下，不致寂寞。母其善自珍摄，弗念儿也！"母闻予言，为之首肯。由今思之，殆望予成器，勉强忍痛也。呜呼！

黄胜（1827—1902）

　　予等均贫苦，若自备资斧，则无米安能为炊。幸勃先生未宣言前，已与校董妥筹办法。故予等留美期内，不特经费有着，即父母等亦至少得二年之养赡。既惠我身，又及家族，仁人君子之用心，可谓至矣。资助予等之人，本定二年为期限，其中三人之名，予尚能记忆。一为蓄德鲁特君（Andrew Shortrede），苏格兰人，香港《中国日报》（*China Mail*）之主笔。其人素鳏居，慷慨明决，有当仁不让之风。一为美商李企君（Ritchie）。一为苏格兰人康白尔君（Campbell）。其余诸人，惜不相识，故无从记其名姓。此外又有阿立芬特公司（The Olyphant Brothers）者，为美国纽

容闳和唐廷枢合影

约巨商兄弟三人所设；有帆船一艘名"亨特利思"（Huntress），专来中国运载茶叶，予等即乘是船赴美。蒙公司主人美意，自

香港至纽约不取船资，亦盛德也。此数君者，解囊相助，俾予得受完全之教育，盖全为基督教慈善性质，并无他种目的。今则人事代谢，已为古人，即称道其名，亦已不及。然其后裔闻之，知黄宽、黄胜与予之教育，全为其先人所培植，亦一快心惬意事也。

第三章　初游美国

　　1847 年 1 月 4 日，予等由黄浦^①首途，船名"亨特利思"（Huntress），帆船也，属于阿立芬特兄弟公司^②，前章已言之。船主名格拉司彼（Captain Gillespie）。时值东北风大作，解缆扬帆，自黄浦抵圣希利那岛（St. Helena），波平船稳。过好望角时，小有风浪，自船后来，势乃至猛，恍若恶魔之逐人。入夜天则黑暗，浓云如幕，不漏星斗。于此茫茫黑夜中，仰望桅上电灯星星，摇荡空际，飘忽不定，有若墟墓间之磷火。此种愁惨景象，印入脑际，迄今犹历历在目。惟彼时予年尚幼，不自知其危险，故虽扁舟颠簸于惊涛骇浪中，不特无恐怖之念，且转以为乐；竟若此波涛汹涌，入予目中，皆成为不世之奇观者。迨舟既过好望角，驶入大西洋，较前转平静。至圣希利那岛稍停，装载粮食淡水。凡帆船之自东来者，中途乏饮食料，辄假此岛为暂时停泊之所。

　　自舟中遥望圣希利那岛，但见火成石焦黑如炭，草木不生，有若牛山濯濯。予等乘此停舟之际，由约姆司坦（Jamestown）登陆，游览风景。入其村，居民稀少，田间植物则甚多，浓绿芸芸，良堪娱目。居民中有我国同胞数人，乃前乘东印度公司船以来者，年事方盛，咸有眷属。此岛即拿破仑战败被幽之地，

---

　　①　黄浦：此为翻译之错，当作黄埔，乃属广州，而黄浦是上海之地。
　　②　阿立芬特兄弟公司：即前文之阿立芬特公司。

15

拿氏遂终老于此。其坟在岛之浪奥特（Longwood）地方，予等咸往登临，抚今吊古，怅触余怀。坟前有大柳树一，乃各折一枝，携归舟中，培养而灌溉之，以为异日之纪念。后抵美国，勃朗先生遂移此柳枝，植诸纽约省之阿朋学校中。勃朗即在此校任教授数年，后乃往游日本。迨1854年予至阿朋学校游览时，则见此枝已长成茂树，垂条万缕矣。

舟既过圣希利那岛，折向西北行，遇"海湾水溜"（Gulf Stream），水急风顺，舟去如矢，未几遂抵纽约。时在1847年4月12日，即予初履美土之第一日也。是行计居舟中凡九十八日，而此九十八日中，天气清朗，绝少阴霾，洵始愿所不及。1847年纽约之情形，绝非今日[①]。当时居民仅二十五万乃至三十万耳，今则已成极大之都会，危楼摩天，华屋林立，教堂塔尖高耸云表，人烟之稠密，商业之繁盛，与伦敦相颉颃矣。犹忆1845年予在玛礼孙学校肄业时，曾为一文，题曰《意想之纽约游》。当尔时搦管为文，讵料果身履其境者。由是观之，吾人之意想，固亦有时成为事实，初不必尽属虚幻。予之意想得成为事实者，尚有二事：一为予之教育计划，愿遣多数青年子弟游学美国；一则愿得美妇以为室。今此二事，亦皆如愿以偿。则予今日胸中，尚怀有种种梦想，又安知将来不一一见诸实行耶。

予之勾留纽约，为日无多。于此新世界中第一次所遇之良友，为巴脱拉脱夫妇二人（Mr. and Mrs. David E. Bartlett）。巴君时在纽约聋哑学校教授，后乃迁于哈特福德，仍为同类之事业。今巴君已于1879年逝世，其夫人居孀约三十年，于1907年春间亦溘然长逝矣。巴夫人之为人，品格高尚，有足令人敬爱。其宗教之信仰尤诚笃，本其慈善之怀，常热心于社会公益事业。影响所及，中国亦蒙其福。盖有中国学生数人，皆为巴夫人教

① 指1909年。

育而成有用之材。故巴夫人者，予美国良友之一也。

自纽约乘舟赴纽海纹，以机会之佳，得晤耶路大学校长谭君（President Day of Yale University），数年之后，竟得毕业此校，当时固非敢有此奢望也。予等离纽海纹后，经威哈斯角（Warehouse Point）而至东温若（East Windsor），迳造勃朗夫人家。勃夫人之父母尔时尚存，父名巴脱拉脱（Rev. Shubael Bartlett，与前节之巴君为另一人）①，为东温若教堂之牧师。予等入教堂瞻仰，即随众祈祷，人皆怪之。予座次牧师之左，由侧面可周瞩全堂，几无一人不注目予等者。盖此中有中国童子，事属创见，宜其然也。予知当日众人神志既专注予等，于牧师之宣讲，必听而不闻矣。

巴牧师乃一清教徒（Puritan，清教徒为耶稣教徒之一派，最先来美洲者），其人足为新英国省清教徒之模范（按新英国省［New England States］为美国东部之数省，纽约省亦在其内），宣讲时语声清朗，意态诚恳。闻其生平兢兢所事，绝不稍稍草率。凡初晤巴牧师者，每疑其人严刻寡恩，实则其心地甚仁厚也。惟以束身极谨，故面目异常严肃，从未闻其纵笑失声，尤无一谐谑语。每日起居有定时，坐卧有常处，晨兴后则将《圣经》及祈祷文置于一定之处，端正无少偏。举止动作，终年如一日。总其一生之行事，殆如时计针之移动，周而复始，不爽暴刻。故凡与巴牧师久处者，未见巴牧师之面，咸能言巴牧师方事之事，历历无少差也。

巴牧师之夫人，则与其夫旨趣大异：长日欢乐，时有笑容；遇人接物尤蔼吉，每一启口，辄善气迎人，可知其宅心之仁慈。凡牧师堂中恒多教友，酬酢颇繁。巴牧师有此贤内助，故教友咸乐巴君夫妇。牧师年俸不过四百美金，以此供衣食犹虞其不

---

① 前节之巴君即为此巴脱拉脱之子。

足，乃巴夫人且不时款享宾客。余不解其点金何术，而能措置裕如。后乃知巴牧师有田园数亩，岁入虽微，不无小补。又其幼子但以礼（Daniel）尤勤于所事，以所得资归奉父母。牧师得常以酒食交欢宾客，殆赖有此也。

后予在孟松中学及耶路大学肄业时，每值假期，辄过巴牧师家。

第四章　中学时代

　　予在东温若，小住勃朗家一星期，乃赴马沙朱色得士省
（Massachusetts），入孟松学校（Monson Academy）肄业。彼时美
国尚无高等中学，仅有预备学校，孟松即预备学校中之最著名
者。全国好学之士，莫不负笈远来肄业此校，为入大学之预备。
按孟松在新英国省中，所以名誉特著，以自创设以来，长得品
学纯粹之士，为之校长故。当予在孟松时，其校长名海门（Rev.
Charles Hammond），亦德高望重，品学兼优者。海君毕业于耶路
大学，夙好古文，兼嗜英国文艺，故胸怀超逸，气宇宽宏。当
时在新英国省，殆无人不知其为大教育家。且其为人富自立性，
生平主张俭德，提倡戒酒。总其言行，无可訾议，不愧为新英
国省师表。以校长道德文章之高尚，而学校名誉亦顿增。自海
门来长此校，日益发达，气象蓬勃，为前此未有云。而斯时中
国人入该校者，惟予等三人耳。海校长对于予等特加礼遇，当
非以中国人之罕观，遂以少为贵，而加以优礼；盖亦对于中国
素抱热诚，甚望予等学成归国，能有所设施耳。

　　在孟松学校之第一年，予等列英文班中，所习者为算术、
文法、生理、心理及哲学等课。其生理、心理两科，则为勃朗
女师（Miss Rebekah Brown）所授。美国学校通例，凡行毕业礼
时，其毕业生中之成绩最优者，则代表全体对教师来宾而致谢
词。勃朗女师尝为此致谢词之代表者，毕业于霍来克玉山女校
（Mt. Holyoke School）之第一人也，后与医学博士麦克林（Dr. A.

S. McClean）结婚，遂寓于斯丕林费尔（Springfield）。勃朗女师之为人，操行既端正，心术仁慈，尤勇于为善，热心于教育。夫妇二人，待予咸极诚挚。每值放假，必邀予过其家。及予入耶路大学肄业，处境甚窘，赖渠夫妇资助之力尤多。归国后，彼此犹音问不绝。及再至美国，复下榻其家。斯丕林费尔有此良友，令人每念不忘。1872年予携第一批留学生游美时，即赁屋邻麦博士，公暇期常得与吾友把晤也。

勃朗君（此指勃朗牧师）之至美也，以予等三人托付于其老母。母予余等殊周到，每餐必同食。惟勃君有妹已媾，挈子三人，寄居母家，遂无余室可容予等。乃别赁一屋，与勃朗对门而居。

方予游学美国时，生活程度不若今日之高。学生贫乏者，稍稍为人工作，即不难得学费。尚忆彼时膳宿、燃料、洗衣等费，每星期苟得一元二角五之美金，足以支付一切。惟居室之洒扫拂拭，及冬令炽炭于炉，劈柴、生火诸琐事，须自为之。然予甚乐为此，借以运动筋脉，流通血液，实健身良法也。予等寓处去校约半英里，每日往返三次，虽严寒雪深三尺，亦必徒步。如此长日运动，胃乃大健，食量兼人。

于今回忆勃朗母夫人之为人，实觉其可敬可爱，得未曾有。其道德品行，都不可及。凡知媪之历史者，当能证予此言不谬。计其一生艰苦备尝，不如意之事，十有八九，然卒能自拔于颠沛之中。尝自著一诗自况，立言幽闲沉静，怡然自足，如其为人。

校长海门君之志趣，既如前所述。其于古诗人中，尤好莎士比亚；于古之大演说家，则服膺威白斯特，于此可想见其所学。其教授法极佳，能令学生于古今文艺佳妙处，一一了解而无扞格。每日登堂授课，初不屑屑于文法之规则，独于词句之构造及精义所在，则批郤导窾，详释无遗。以彼文学大家，出其为文之长技，用于演讲，故出言咸确当而有精神。大教育家阿那博士（Dr. Arnold）之言曰：善于教育者，必能注意于学生之道德，以养成其优美之品格；否则仅仅以学问知识授于学生，自谓尽其能事，充乎其极，不过使学生成一能行之百科全书，或一具有灵性之鹦鹉耳，曷足贵哉！海君之为教授，盖能深合阿那博士所云教育之本旨者也。予在孟松学校时，曾诵习多数英国之文集，皆海君所亲授者。

在孟松之第一年，予未敢冀入大学。盖予等出发时，仅以二年为限，1849年即须回国也。三人中，以黄胜齿为最长。1848年秋，黄胜以病归国，仅予与黄宽二人。居恒晤谈，辄话及二年后之方针。予之本志，固深愿继续求学。惟1849年后，将恃何人资助予等学费，此问题之困难，殆不啻古所谓"戈登结"，几于无人能解者，则亦惟有商之于海门校长及勃朗君耳。幸得二君厚意，允为函询香港资助予等之人。迨得覆书，则谓二年后如予二人愿至英国苏格兰省爱丁堡大学习专门科者，则彼等仍可继续资助云云。予等蒙其慷慨解囊，历久不倦，诚为可感。嗣予等互商进止，黄宽决计二年后至苏格兰补此学额。予则甚欲入耶路大学，故愿仍留美。议既定，于是黄宽学费，已可无恐。予于1849年后，借何资以求学，此问题固仍悬而未决也。亦惟有泰然处之，任予运命之自然，不复为无益之虑。

此事既决，予于1849年暑假

黄宽（1829—1878）留学英国时留影

后，遂不更治英国文学，而习正科初等之书。翌年之夏，二人同时毕业。黄宽旋即妥备行装，迳赴苏格兰入爱丁堡大学。予则仍留美国，后亦卒得入耶路大学。予与黄宽二人，自1840年①同读书于澳门玛礼孙学校，嗣后朝夕切磋共笔砚者垂十年，至是始分袂焉。

黄宽后在爱丁堡大学习医，历七年之苦学，卒以第三人毕业，为中国学生界增一荣誉，于1857年归国悬壶，营业颇发达。以黄宽之才之学，遂成为好望角以东最负盛名之良外科。继复寓粤，事业益盛，声誉益隆。旅粤西人欢迎黄宽，较之欢迎欧美医士有加，积资亦富，于1879年逝世。中西人士临吊者无不悼惜，盖其品行纯笃，富有热忱，故遗爱在人，不仅医术工也。

---

① 应为1841年，见第二章。

第五章　大学时代

　　予未入耶路大学时，经济问题既未解决，果何恃以求学乎？虽美国通例，学生之贫乏者，不难工作以得学费。然此亦言之非艰行之惟艰，身履其境，实有种种困难，而舍此更无良策。计予友在美国人中可恃以谋缓急者，惟勃朗及海门二君。勃朗即携予赴美者，海门则予在孟松学校时，尝受其教育者也。予既无术自解此厄，乃乞二人援手。彼等谓予："孟松学校定制，固有学额资送大学，盖为勤学寒士而设。汝诚有意于此，不妨姑试之。第此权操诸校董，且愿受其资助者，须先具志愿书，毕业后愿充教士以传道，乃克享此利益。"予闻言爽然自失，不待思索，已知无补额希望，故亦决意不向该校请求。数日后，诸校董忽召予往面议资遣入学事。是殆勃朗与海门二君，未悟予意，已预为予先容矣。校董之言正与勃朗、海门同，谓毕业后归国传道则可，第具一志愿书存查耳。

　　此在校董一方面，固对予极抱热诚。而予之对于此等条件，则不能轻诺。予虽贫，自由所固有。他日竟学，无论何业，将择其最有益于中国者为之。纵政府不录用，不必遂大

容闳 1854 年毕业照

有为，要亦不难造一新时势，以竟吾素志。若限于一业，则范围甚狭，有用之身，必致无用。且传道固佳，未必即为造福中国独一无二之事业。以吾国幅员若是其辽阔，人苟具真正之宗教精神，何往而不利。然中国国民信仰果何如者？在信力薄弱之人，其然诺将如春冰之遇旭日，不久消灭，谁能禁之？况志愿书一经签字，即动受拘束，将来虽有良好机会，可为中国谋福利者，亦必形格势禁，坐视失之乎？余既有此意，以为始基宜慎，则对于校董诸人之盛意，宁抱歉衷，不得不婉辞谢之。嗣海门悉予意，深表同情。盖人类有应尽之天职，决不能以食贫故，遽变宗旨也。

人生际会，往往非所逆料。当予却孟松校董资助时，为1850 年之夏，勃朗方至南部探视其姊，顺道访乔治亚省萨伐那妇女会（The Ladies Association in Savannah, Ga.）之会员。谈次偶及予事，遂将得好消息以归。尤幸者，勃朗之归，适逢其会。设更晚者，则予或更作他图，不知成如何结果矣。渠对于予之意见，亦深以为然，因语余萨伐那妇女会会员，已允资助。此岂前此梦想所及者？遂束装东行，赴纽海文，迳趋耶路大学投考，居然不在孙山之外。盖予于入大学之预备，仅治拉丁文十五月，希拉文十二月，算术十阅月。于此短促之岁月中，复因孟松左近地方新造铁路，筑路之际学校不得不暂时停辍，而予之学业遂亦因以间断。同学之友，学程皆优于余。竟得入彀，事后追思，不知其所以然。余之入耶路大学，虽尚无不及格之学科，然在教室受课，辄觉预备工夫实为未足，以故备形困难。盖一方面须筹画经费，使无缺乏之虞；一方面又须致力所业，以冀不落人后也。尚忆在第一年级时，读书恒至夜半，日间亦无余暇为游戏运动。坐是体魄日就羸弱，曾因精力不支，请假赴东温若休息一星期，乃能继续求学焉。

至第二年级，有一事尤足困予，则微积学是也。予素视算术为畏途，于微积分尤甚。所习学科中，惟此一门，总觉有所捍格。虽日日习之，亦无丝毫裨益，每试常不及格。以如是成绩，颇惧受降级之惩戒，或被斥退。后竟得越过此难关，则赖有英文为助。美国大学制，每级分数班，每班有主任教员，专司此班中学生功课之分数。学生欲自知其分数多寡者，可问主任教员。予班之主任教员，曰白洛及（Blodget），乃教拉丁文①者。予在二年级时，自惭分数过少，至不敢向教员探询，私意或且降级。幸英文论说颇优，第二第三两学期连获首奖，故平均分数，犹得以有余补不足。自经两次获奖，校中师生异常器重，即校外人亦以青眼相向。然余未敢略存自满心，以予四学年中平均分数之少，扪心惭汗。若因人之誉己而趾高气扬，抑自欺之甚矣。

第二学年之末及第三学年，学费渐充裕。以校中有二三年级学生约二十人，结为一会，共屋而居，另倩一人为之司饮膳。予竭力经营，获充是职。晨则为之购办蔬肴，饭则为之供应左右。后此二年中予之膳费，盖皆取给于此。虽所获无多，不无小补。萨伐那妇女会既助予以常年经费，阿立芬公司②亦有特捐相助。此外予更得一职：为兄弟会管理书籍。兄弟会者，校中两辩驳会之一也。会有一小藏书楼，予以会员之资格，得与是选，博微资焉。

第四学年，兄弟会中仍举予为司书人，每岁酬予美金三十元。予既得此数项进款，客囊乃觉稍裕，不复以举债为生。若例以小村落中之牧师，每年薪俸所入，亦不过二三百金。彼且

---

①　原文为希腊文。

②　原文误，应为阿立芬特公司。

1854 年容闳毕业纪念册封面

以赡养八口之家而无缺乏，则予以个人而有此，又有妇女会赠予以袜履等物，更不必自耗囊金。于此犹云不足，则亦过矣。

予于 1854 年毕业。同班中毕业者，共九十八人。以中国人而毕业于美国第一等之大学校，实自予始。以故美国人对予感情至佳。时校中中国学生，绝无仅有，易于令人注目。又因予尝任兄弟会藏书楼中司书之职二年，故相识之人尤多。同校前后三级中之学生，稔予者几过半。故余熟悉美国情形，而于学界中交游尤广。予在校时，名誉颇佳。于今思之，亦无甚关系。浮云过眼，不过博得一时虚荣耳。

予当修业期内，中国之腐败情形，时触予怀，迨末年而尤甚。每一念及，辄为之怏怏不乐，转愿不受此良教育之为愈。盖既受教育，则予心中之理想既高，而道德之范围亦广，遂觉此身负荷极重，若在毫无知识时代，转不之觉也。更念中国国民，身受无限痛苦，无限压制。此痛苦与压制，在彼未受教育之人，亦转毫无感觉，初不知其为痛苦与压制也。故予尝谓知识益高者，痛苦亦多，而快乐益少。反之，愈无知识，则痛苦愈少，而快乐乃愈多。快乐与知识，殆天然成一反比例乎！

虽然，持此观念以论人生之苦乐，则其所见亦甚卑，惟怯懦者为之耳。此其人必不足以成伟大之事业，而趋于高尚之境域也。在予个人而论，尤不应存此悲观。何也？予既远涉重洋，身受文明之教育，且以辛勤刻苦，幸遂予求学之志，虽未能事事如愿以偿，然律以普通教育之资格，予固大可自命为已受教育之人矣。既自命为已受教育之人，则当旦夕图维，以冀生平所学，得以见诸实用。此种观念，予无时不耿耿于心。盖当第四学年中尚未毕业时，已预计将来应行之事，规画大略于胸中矣。予意以为予之一身，既受此文明之教育，则当使后予之人，亦享此同等之利益。以西方之学术，灌输于中国，使中国日趋于文明富强之境。予后来之事业，盖皆以此为标准，专心致志以为之。溯自1854年予毕业之时，以至1872年中国有第一批留学生之派遣，则此志愿之成熟时也。

第六章　学成归国

自予毕业耶路大学，屈指去国之日，忽忽十年[①]。予之初志，所望甚奢，本欲延长留学年限，冀可学成专科。盖当予在耶路大学时，校中方创一雪费尔专门学院（Sheffield Scientific School），院长为诺德君（Prof. Norton）。予修业时，曾入此院附习测量科，拟为将来学习工程之预备。设予果能学成专科以归国者，自信予所企望之事业，将益易于着手也。惜以贫乏，不能自筹资斧。助予之友，又不愿予久居美国。彼盖目予为中国有用之人材，虑予久居不归，乐不思蜀也。于是捐弃学习专科之奢愿，而留学时期，于以告终。美人中劝予归国最力者，其一为白礼特（Perit），其人执业于美国某东方公司中；其二为阿立芬特兄弟公司之主人翁。所谓阿立芬特公司，即八年前曾以帆船载予来美而不取值者。此数人之见解皆甚高尚，其所以怂恿予归中国，非有私意存于其间；盖欲予归国后热心传道，使中国信仰上帝，人人为耶稣教徒耳。

有麦克教士者，于1845年至香港代勃朗为玛礼孙学校教员，于前第二章中已言及之。迨后玛礼孙学校解散，麦克乃重归美国，复入耶路为学生。兹复经美国教会派往中国传道，遂于1854年11月13日，与予同乘纽约某公司帆船名"欧里加"（Eureka）者，自纽约首途。时值冬令，为过好望角最恶劣之时

---

① 应为八年。

会。盖隆冬之际，东北风极大，凡帆船向东方行，必遇逆风，无可倖免，而欧里加船此时正依此航路以进行也。此船本为运货以赴香港者，舟中乘客，除予及麦克外，实无第三人。起程之日，适彤云密布，严寒袭人。舟又停泊于东河（East River）中流，不能傍岸，予等乃觅小舟以渡。当登舟时，回顾岸旁，不见有一人挥巾空际，送予远行者。及舟既起碇，岸上亦无高呼欢送之声，此境此情，甚萧条也。

　　船初行，先以他船拖至桑得阿克（Sandy Hook），迨出口后乃解缆自飏。正值逆风迎面而来，势殊猛烈。风篷不能扯满，则张半帆，旁行斜上，曲折以进。船中载货极少，即欲觅一压舱之重物，亦不可得。以故冲击风浪中，颠簸愈甚。沧海一粟，如明星倒影水中，荡漾不定。此航路之恶，为夙昔所著称，固非自今日始也。由桑得阿克以至香港，几无平稳之一日。计水程凡一万三千海里，船行历一百五十四日乃达目的。予生平航海不为不多，然寂寞无聊，则未有如此行之甚者。

　　船主名辉布（Whipple），籍隶费拉特尔费亚（Philadelphia）城。为人粗犷无文，以口吃故，举止尤燥急。每日于船中所为，令人可笑之事极多，而于晨间则尤甚。彼每晨必登甲板，自船首至船尾，来回急走，以测候天空气象。有时忽骤止其步，驻足痴立，对逆风吹来之方向，仰首瞩天，筋涨面赤，眼珠几欲突出。暴怒之极，则伸两手尽力自搔其发，一若与此烦恼丝有无穷夙憾，必欲根根拔而去之者。如是往来跳跃，啮齿有声。或以足与甲板斗其坚，力跄不已。口中作种种亵语，对天漫骂，谓天公之作此逆风，盖有意与之为难，阻其进行也。顾船主虽毒骂，而口吃乃期期不可辨，其状可笑亦复可怜。予初见其狂暴如疯，颇生怜悯之念。迨后见其无日不如是，乃觉其人可鄙，殊不足怜惜。彼每次向天示威之后，必至力尽筋疲，乃于甲板上独据胡床，枯坐历数小时。舟中虽无人愿与之接谈，而彼固怡然自得，恒力搓其两手，自语自笑，状若无辜之疯人。长途中凡其举动，非疯非俱。船中水手，司空见惯，不以为奇。虽外貌不敢显轻侮之色，而心中固无不匿笑其为人也。

舟行之际，一切调度，全由大副一人指挥。此大副之专制，不啻海中一暴君。幸水手皆为挪威及瑞典两国之人，故尚肯服从其命令。若在美国人遇此野蛮无人理之事，必不能堪，或且起暴动以为对待矣。盖此船主、大副之役使水手，有如牛马，日夜无少停。途中所得暂事休息者，惟船行至热带时，适风波平静之数日耳。予稽旅行之日记册，计自解缆后约行两星期，始至马加撒海峡（Macassar Strait）①，舟中人殆无一不生厌倦之心。过海峡后，船主乃扬言于众曰：“予此行所以不幸而遇逆风者，以舟中有约拿其人在也。”②语时故使予友麦克闻之，其意盖以约拿况麦克也。予友闻是言，绝不介意，惟对予目笑而存之。时予方与麦克谈论舟过海峡事，乃语麦克曰：“设以予司此船者，过此海峡不过十日足矣。”语时亦故高其声浪，使船主闻之。一则报复其语侵麦克，一则使彼自知其航术未精也。

当隆冬之际，设行舟不过好望角，而绕亨角（Cape Horn）以进，利便实甚。盖如是则可得顺风，不独缩短航海之期，且可省船主无数气力。但予以乘客资格，亦莫知其内容真相。该公司驶行此船，既无甚货物，又必逆东北风而行，岂其于经济上有特别之目的耶？若以予意，则必经亨角遵新航路以行，而予又可借此耳目一新矣。

---

① 原文意为：过马加撒海峡，计须抢风行驶约两星期之久。

② 相传约拿为古时先知，运最蹇。一日航海遇暴风，舟且覆，同舟者拈阄以求罪人，适得约拿，举而投诸海，风乃立止云。

船近香港时，有领港人至船上。船主见其为中国人，乃倩予为舌人，询其近处有无危险之暗礁及沙滩。予默念此暗礁与沙滩者，中国语不知当作何辞，久思不属，竟莫达其意。幸领港人适解英语，乃转告予以暗礁、沙滩之中国名词。噫，此领港人者，竟为予回国后之第一国语教授，不亦异乎！船主及麦克等见予状，咸笑不可仰。予自念以中国人而不能作中国语，亦无词以自解也。

　　登陆后予第一关怀之事，为往视予友蓄德鲁特。蓄德鲁特者，《中国日报》主笔。予在孟松学校时，彼曾以资助予一年有余，盖予之老友也。把晤后，彼即邀予过其家，小作勾留。旋赴澳门，省视吾母。予去家日久，慈母倚闾悬念，必至望眼欲穿矣。予见母之日，以一时无从易中国衣，乃仍西装以进。是时予已须矣，若循中国习惯，则少年未娶者，不应若是早须也。予见母无恙，胸中感谢之心，达于极点，转无一语能出诸口。质言之，予此时喜极欲涕，此种状况，实非语言笔墨所能形容于万一。

　　母见予立现一种慈爱之色，以手抚摩予身且遍，谓此十年[1]中思见儿而不可得也。予知母尚未悉予旅美之详情，乃依坐膝下，告之曰："母乎！儿方经一五六阅月可厌之长期旅行也。然今幸无恙，已得抵家省母矣。儿自离膝下，前后已有八年。此八年中，在在皆遇良友，能善视儿，故儿身常健无疾病。儿在校肄业，常思借此时学习，以为将来效力祖国之预备。守此宗旨，八年如一日。当未入大学之前，又曾先入一预备学校。于预备学校毕业后，乃入耶路大学。耶路大学在美国为最著名大学之一，校内所订课程，必四年乃能毕业，此儿所以久客异乡。

---

　　[1]　应该是八年。

今既毕业于该校，遂得一学士学位。美国之学士，盖与中国之秀才相仿。"语次随出一羊皮纸以示母，且告之曰，"此即毕业文凭也。凡得毕业于耶路大学者，即在美国人犹视为荣誉，况儿以中国人而得与其列耶？"

予母闻言，乃询予此文凭与学位，可博奖金几何？盖予母固未知其效用如何也。予乃告母曰："此非可以得奖金者。第有文凭，则较无文凭之人，谋事为易。至大学之给学位，亦非有金钱之效用。惟已造就一种品格高尚之人材，使其将来得有势力，以为他人之领袖耳。大学校所授之教育，实较金钱尤为宝贵。盖人必受教育，然后乃有知识，知识即势力也。势力之效用，较金钱为大。儿今既以第一中国留学生毕业于耶路大学，今后吾母即为数万万人中第一中国留学生毕业于美国第一等大学者之母。此乃稀贵之荣誉，为常人所难得。儿此后在世一日，必侍奉吾母，俾母得安享幸福，不使少有缺乏也。"

予之为此大言不惭，非敢自矜自满，不过欲博吾母欢心耳。母闻予言果甚乐，面有笑容。旋谓予曰："吾见儿已蓄须，上有一兄尚未蓄须，故吾意汝去须为佳。"予闻母言，即如命趋出，召匠立薙之。母见予状，乐乃益甚。察其意以为吾子虽受外国教育，固未失其中国固有之道德，仍能尽孝于亲也。予此时胸中爱母之忱，恨未能剖心相示。此后予每尽力所能及，以奉予母，颐养天年。迨1858年予母弃养，寿六十有四；计去予失怙时，凡二十四年。予母逝时，予适在上海，未能见一面，实为终天遗憾。

1855年予居粤中，与美教士富文（Vrooman）君同寓，地名"咸虾栏"，与行刑场颇近。场在城外西南隅，邻珠江之滨。予之寓此，除补习汉文而外，他无所事。以予久居美洲，于本国语言，几尽忘之，至是乃渐复其旧。不及六月，竟能重操粤语，惟唇舌间尚觉生硬耳。至予之汉文，乃于 1846 年游美之前所习者，为时不过四年。以习汉文，学期实为至短，根基之浅，自不待言。故今日之温习，颇极困难，进步极缓。夫文字之与语言，在英文中虽间有不同之点，究不若中国之悬殊特甚。以中国之文字而论，辉煌华丽，变化万端，虽应用普及全国，而文字之发音，则南北互异，东西悬殊。至于语言，则尤庞杂不可究诘。如福建、江苏、安徽等省，即一省之中，亦有无数不同之方言。每值甲乙两地人相遇，设各操其乡谈，则几如异国之人，彼此不能通解。此乃中国语言文字上特别困难之处，为各国所无者。

当予在粤时，粤中适有一暴动，秩序因之大乱。此际太平天国之军队，方横行内地，所向披靡，而粤乱亦适起于是时。顾粤人之暴动，初与太平军无涉。彼两广总督叶名琛者，于此暴动发生之始，出极残暴之手段以镇压之，意在摧残方苞之花，使无萌芽之患也。统计是夏所杀，凡七万五千余人。以予所知，其中强半，皆无辜冤死。予寓去刑场才半英里，一日予忽发奇想，思赴刑场一觇其异。至则但见场中流血成渠，道旁无首之尸纵横遍地。盖以杀戮过众，不及掩埋。且因骤觅一辽旷之地，为大圹以容此众尸，一时颇不易得，故索任其暴露于烈日下也。时方盛夏，寒暑表在九十度或九十度以上，致刑场四围二千码以内，空气恶劣如毒雾。此累累之陈尸，最新者暴露亦已二三日。地上之土，吸血既饱，皆作赭色。余血盈科而进，汇为污池。空气中毒菌之弥漫，殆不可以言语形容。据此景象，加以粤省人烟之稠密，在理当发生极大之瘟疫，乃竟得安然无恙，宁非怪事？后闻于城西远僻处觅得一极大沟渠，投尸其中，任其自然堆叠，以满为度，遂谓尽掩埋之能事矣。当时有往观者，谓此掩埋之法，简易实甚。掷尸沟中后，无需人力更施覆盖。以尸中血色之蛆，已足代赤土而有余，不令群尸露少隙也。此种情形，非独当时观者酸鼻，至今言之，犹令人欲作三日呕。人或告予，是被杀者有与暴动毫无关系，徒以一般虎狼胥役，敲诈不遂，遂任意诬陷置之死地云。似此不分良莠之屠戮，不独今世纪中无事可与比拟，即古昔尼罗（Nero）王之残暴，及法国革命时代之惨剧，杀人亦无如是之多。罪魁祸首，惟两广总督叶名琛一人，实尸其咎。

叶为汉阳人。汉阳于太平军起事时即被占据，遂遭兵火之劫。人谓叶在汉阳本有极富之财产，此役尽付焚如，故对于太平军恨之切齿。而太平军之首领，又多籍隶两广，于是叶乃迁怒于两广人民。1854年，既攫得两广总督之权位，遂假公济私，以报其夙怨，粤人乃无辜而受其殃矣。叶之戮人，不讯口供，捕得即杀，有如牛羊之入屠肆。此杀人之恶魔，天所不容，其罪恶满盈之一日，且不旋踵而至，彼固犹在梦中也。未几，叶因事与英政府酿成大交涉，为英兵所掳，幽之印度极边杳无居人之处。遂于此荒凉寂寞之区，苟延残喘，以度其含垢忍辱之余生，不特为全国同胞所唾骂，抑亦为全世界人所鄙弃也。

予自刑场归寓后，神志懊丧，胸中烦闷万状，食不下咽，寝不安枕。日间所见种种惨状，时时缠绕于予脑筋中。愤懑之极，乃深恶满人之无状，而许太平天国之举动为正当。予既表同情于太平军，乃几欲起而为之响应。及后深思静虑，乃觉此举卤莽，究非妥善之策；不若仍予旧有计划，先习国语与汉文，俟其娴熟，乃依一定之方针，循序而进，庶可达予夙昔之希望也。

第七章　入世谋生

前章言予习国文既极困难，未可遂云有得。而于中国语言，则渐复旧观，谈话无虞扦格。于时颇思于社会中得一职守，此非仅为家人衣食，欲有所藉手，达予维新中国之目的：谋食亦谋道也。

有美教士曰派克（Parker）者，彼邦医学博士，奉美教会之命来华传道，悬壶于粤有年。此时方为美政府之特别委员，暂代公使事。时吾华尚无各国全权公使；北京之应设公使与否，在磋商中，国际上尚未有互派公使之条约。派克博士之于外交，非有特别经验，其于律学亦非专门；徒以其旅华日久，习中国之语言风俗，故美政府以此任之。予有友曰歇区可克（Mr. M. N. Hitchcock），亦美人，与派克有旧，乃绍介予为派克处书记。予前在古夫人小学时，已耳派克博士名。渠亦毕业于耶路大学者，因与予有同校之谊，颇相得。其办事地点，在粤之省垣，惟夏季则至澳门避暑焉。予在派克处，事少薪薄，月十五金耳。予乐就之，意本不在金钱，欲借派克力识中国达官，庶几得行予志。顾派克虽摄公使，乃非近水楼台，与予之计划甚左。三月后遽自行辞职，赴香港习法律。

香港有老友蓄德鲁特君，遇予素厚，因主其家。无何，蓄荐予于香港高等审判厅为译员，月薪七十五金。处境略裕，乃稍稍放胆，潜心治法律。英国审判厅制度，律师资格凡两种：曰小律师（Solicitors），专司收集证据、抄阅公文及摘述案情始末，以备辩护之材料，而己不出庭；曰大律师（Barristers），则出庭司辩护者。予从予友蓄德鲁特之言，学习第一种律师事业。余之为此，可谓铸错。盖香港为英国之殖民地，予以中国人而律师于此，是以外人侵入英国法律团体，损彼利益，分我杯羹，必召英律师之恶感。以余之鲁钝，未计及此，一误也。又予所师事者，乃一寻常律师；此时有一总律师，思罗致予于门下，乃舍此就彼，二误也。一时失检，有此二误。他日之离香港，即种因于此矣。

因第一着之误，致香港律师合群力以拒予。一时新闻界，惟予友蓄德鲁特主笔之《中国日报》差无贬词，余皆连篇累牍，肆意攻击。若辈以为予于中西文字，皆所擅长，设于香港律师界得占一席，则将来凡涉于华人诉讼事件，必为予个人垄断，英律师且相将归国，故对于予之学法律，出全力以拒之。因第二着之误，又得罪于总律师。其人曰安师德（Anstey），曾欲就其权力所及，为予辟一实习律师之途。因上书英政府，请允中国人之在香港者，苟试验及格，有充律师之权利；并草拟章程，附于请愿书后。按法定手续，此举必须经英国议会之通过，乃成为殖民地之单行法，则其事之不易可知。旋竟邀英政府之允准，著为定律，是总律师之所以为予尽力者，不可为不至。顾予乃不就笼络，事后始知，予诚为负负。予既另事律师派森（Parson）为师，总律师则大恚，每相值于法庭翻译时，辄事事苛求予短，不复如前之谦和。于是予以一身，受双方冲击，觉在香港已无立足余地。抑不独予处境困难，予师派森亦复日坐针毡，身为众矢之的，而无可抵抗。彼乃不得不自谋，取消予学律之合同。予既受此排挤，自念恋恋于此殊非计，不如辞职，去而之他。予去未久，派森亦以他故弃其香港事业，买棹归英。

今回忆在港时短期历史，转觉学律未成，为予生幸事。

使当日果成一香港律师，则所成事业，必甚微末。且久居英国殖民地，身体为所拘束，不能至中国内地，与上流社会交游。纵使成一著名律师，博得多金，亦安所用之？余既去香港，于1856年8月，乘一运茶船北赴上海。船名"佛罗棱司"（Florence），乃自美国波司顿来者。船主名都玛勒司克（Dumaresque），此船为所自有。船之名，即船主女公子名也。忆1855年予自美归国时，所乘"欧里加"船之船主，以较今日之都船主，不可同日语。都之为人，仁厚而通达，彬彬有礼。彼闻予名后，即极表欢迎，立以由港至上海之船票赠予，不取值。此行程期仅七日，船未抵岸，而予与船主二人，已于此短期内成莫逆交矣。

予抵上海未久，于海关翻译处谋得一职，月薪七十五两，折合墨银可百元。因中国向无银元，墨西哥银币输入遂流行也。此职之薪金，固已较香港高等法庭译员为优，即所事亦不若彼

上海江海关

繁重可厌。惟予性好劳动，转嫌太简易耳。此时办公时刻外，颇多余晷，在寓读书。如是者三月，旋觉此事于予，亦不相宜。使予果愿独善其身，为一洁己奉公之人，则绝不应混迹于此。盖此间有一恶习，中国船上商人与海关中通事，咸通声气，狼狈为奸，以图中饱。予既知此，乃深恶其卑鄙，不屑与伍，以自污吾名誉，乃决意辞职，而苦无词。

某日予迳访总税务司，故问之曰："以予在海关中奉职，将来希望若何？亦能升至总税务司之地位乎？"彼告予曰："凡中国人为翻译者，无论何人，绝不能有此希望。"予闻言退出，立作一辞职书投之。书谓予与彼受同等教育，且予以中国人为中国国家服务，奈何独不能与彼英人享同等之权利，而终不可以为总税务司耶？予书入后，总税务司来（Mr. Lay）君，初不允予请，面加慰留，令勿去职；且误会予之此举为嫌俸薄，故以辞职相要挟，因许月增予俸至二百两。噫！彼固以为中国人殆无一不以金钱为生命者，宁知众人皆醉之中，犹有能以廉隅自守，视道德为重、金钱为轻者耶？且予之为此，别有高尚志趣，并不以得升总税务司为目的。予意凡欲见重于人者，必其人先能自重。今海关中通事及其余司一职者，几无一不受贿赂。以予独处此浊流中，决不能实行予志，此辞职之本意也。辞职书中，亦不明言及此。四阅月后，卒离去海关，而另觅光明磊落之事业。

同事诸友，见予弃此二百两厚俸，图不可必之事，莫不目予为痴，是燕雀不知鸿鹄也。予之操行差堪自信者，惟廉洁二字。无论何往，必保全名誉，永远不使玷污。予非不自知，归国以来，未及一年，已三迁其业。其长此见异思迁，则所希望之事业，或且如幻灯泡影，终无所成。又非不自觉予之希望过奢，志向过高，颇难见诸实行也。第念吾人竞存于世界，必有一定之希望，方能造成真实之事业。予之生于斯世，既非为哺啜而来；予之受此教育，尤非易易。则含辛茹苦所得者，又安能不望其实行于中国耶？一旦遇有机会，能多用我一分学问，即多获一分效果，此岂为一人利益计，抑欲谋全中国之幸福也！予于所事，屡次中辍，岂好为变迁哉？

第八章　经商之阅历

　　予离海关后，至某英商公司为书记。此公司专收中国丝茶者。予之入此，不过暂借枝栖。然虽相处仅数月，获益良多，于商家内幕及经商方法，已略知梗概，于他日事业，关系实多。该公司自余就事六阅月，而停止营业，予乃重为失业之人。此时如投身大海中，四顾茫茫，不知方针当何向。计予为书记，六阅月中，值意外之事二，是亦不可不纪。

　　某星期四之夕，予自苏州河边礼拜堂行祷礼归，经四川路。见有西人成群在前，人各手一中国纸灯，高举过顶，晃荡不定。行路则左倾右斜，作折线而前，且行且唱，亦有狂呼者，状似甚乐。道旁中国人见之，皆四窜奔走，若有虎狼追逐者。予行既近，与之相距约百码。此时颇有骑虎之势，即欲退避，亦已无及。予仆本执灯为予导，此时乃退匿予后。予告以无恐，迤逦前进，不数武，三四被酒西人已迎面至。一人夺予仆手中灯，一则举足思蹴予；顾被酒已甚，足方举，身已摇摇欲仆。予见其醉态蹒跚，亦不与较，惟避而过之。旋见在后有清醒者，乃目睹其伴侣之行为，不加劝止，且顾而乐之。予乃伫立与语，先告以予名，并询以适欲蹴予及夺仆灯者之名。彼等初不肯吐实，继予力言纵知其人，必不与之为难。彼乃告予其中一人名，及在某船中所操之业。嘻，异矣！彼所告之人名，盖即"欧里加"船中大副也。此船非他，即于1855年载予归国者，今此船又适为予所处之公司运货。予乃于翌晨作一函，致其船主，详告一切。船主阅函甚怒，掷示大副。大副读未竟，色立变，急奔登岸，向予谢罪。予仍遇以和蔼之色，婉言告之曰："君当知美人之在中国，固极受中国人之敬礼者。故凡美人之至中国，尤当自知其所处地位之尊贵，善自保惜，不宜有强暴行为以自丧其名誉，而伤中国人感情。予之作此函，非欲与君为难，第欲借此以尽予之忠告耳。"大副闻言，备道感愧。并邀予至其船中，杯酒言欢，订为朋友。予谢之，旋自去。此事遂和平了结。

二月后，又值一意外事。此事迥不如前，其结果乃令人不适，当予所处公司停止贸易，所有什物尽付拍卖。是日中外人士来者夥多，予亦厕人丛中骈肩立。适有一体量高六尺余，雄伟无伦之苏格兰人，立于予后。觉有人弄我发辫，一回顾则彼郿瞒者以棉花搓成无数小球系予辫上，以为戏乐。予初不怒，仅婉请其解去。彼交叉两手于胸，若不闻者，一种傲慢之态，令人难堪。予仍不怒，惟申言之。彼忽骤举拳击予颊，势甚猛，特未见血耳。予勃然不复能忍，以彼伟岸，予长才及其肩，斗腕力宁有幸者？然当时不暇计胜负，即以其人所施者反之，遽以拳冲其面。拳出至迅，且有力，彼不及防，受创，唇鼻立破，流血被面。此苏格兰人殆体育家，孔武有力。予之右腕旋被执不能少动。予方思以足力蹴其要害，适公司主人自旁来，极力解散，彼乃自人丛中挤出。时有人大声谓予曰："若欲斗耶？"予即应之曰："否，予固自卫。君友先犯予，伤予颊，殊无赖。"予发此言，声色俱厉，故使众人皆闻之。旋退入别室，任他人之论短长，充耳不听。后有友告予，谓是日英国领事亦在众中，目睹此事，曾发评论，谓："此中国少年，血气太盛。设彼不自由施行法律（指还击）者，固可至英国领事公署控此苏格兰人。今既已报复，且又于众辱之，此其所为为已甚，不能更控人矣。"此苏格兰人者，予前于道中尝数遇之，故能省识。自互殴后，不出现者一星期。人言彼方闭户养伤，殆非事实。盖以被创于一短小之中国人，并受侮辱之辞，故无颜遽出耳。

此事虽琐细无谓，而于租界中颇引起一般人之注意。事阅数日，外人犹引为谈助。更有多数中国人，因闻予为此事，异常推重。盖自外人辟租界于上海以来，侵夺我治外法权。凡寄居租界之中国人，处外人势力范围之内，受彼族凌侮，时有所闻。然从未有一人敢与抵抗，能以赤手空拳，自卫其权利者。此实由于中国人赋性柔和，每受外人无礼之待遇，辄隐忍退让，不敢与较。致养成一般无意识外人之骄恣，喧宾夺主，不复以平等遇我同胞也。予意他日中国教育普及，人人咸解公权、私权之意义，尔时无论何人，有敢侵害其权利者，必有胆力起而自卫矣。近如日人之战胜俄国，亦足使中国人眼界为之一广，不再忍受无礼之待遇。即外人之以强权蚕食我边疆，扩充其势力，我国人亦岂能常听其自由行动乎？国人夜郎自大，顽固性成，致有今日受人侮辱之结果。欧洲各强国，甚且倡瓜分中国之议，幸美政府出而干涉，乃不得实行。今中国人已稍稍知其前此之非，力图自振，且自慈禧太后及光绪帝逝世后，时局又为之一变。究竟中国前途若何，此时尚难逆料也。

自公司闭歇后，予乃为第四次失业之人。第予本不希望以商业终身者，故虽失业，亦不甚措意。予自归国以来，二年中于汉文一道，已略窥门径，遂不汲汲于谋事；此后惟译书自食，以度此优游之岁月，无拘无束，亦殊自由。纵不得多金，固大可借此以多识商学界上流人物，推广交游，以遂予之第一目的。予借译书之机会，遂得识一洋公司中之华经理。此公司在上海实为首屈一指，其行主亦极负一时之盛名。中外商人，无不与之契洽。1857 年，行主不幸逝世，一时商界中人无不深为哀悼，乃撰一长篇诔文，详述死者一生事业，以为纪念。该公司中人得此诔文，则聘二人以译成英文。任此译事者，一为英国领事公署中书记官，其兄即曾著《中国内乱记》者，其一则予也。予之得获此职，实赖该公司华经理之推荐。初不意予所为文，竟博外人之称许，谓较英署书记所译者为佳也。予为此事，不独为公司经理所赏识，即中国商界中人，闻同胞中有人能以长篇诔辞译成精确之英文，优胜于英人手笔，咸引以为荣誉。自予文入选为墓铭，勒之碑石，而本国人中，遂稍稍知予之微名。第此番之博声誉，与前次迥乎不同。前以殴人称，今则人人知予为曾受西国教育之中国学生也。

　　未几，又有一事，需予臂助。其时黄河决口，江苏北境竟成泽国，人民失业无家可归者，无虑千万，咸来上海就食。沪上绅商界中负时誉者，闻予名，乃倩予撰一西文募捐启，向旅沪外人劝募。不数日，竟得西人捐款二万元。中国慈善会董事，见成效之速，乐乃无极。后复由董事具名，予为作函，报告外人以收到捐款之数目，并谢其慷慨解囊之谊。此函旋经沪上某某两西报登出。故予为译事三阅月，而上海之中国人，几无一不知予为美国毕业生矣。予之译事，所以能奏此成效而博此名誉者，皆予友曾继甫[①]之力也。曾君文学极佳。人咸敬而重之。因其在公司日久，故信用尤著。其所往来皆国中名儒硕学，又以身居商界，故凡中国大资本家及殷实之商家，无论在申或居他埠，亦无不与之相识。予前此所译之诔文及募捐启，皆彼所绍介者。曾君后又介予于中国之著名大算学家李君壬叔，予因李君又得识曾公国藩。曾公盖中国之军事家及政治

─────────

　　① 曾继甫：当为曾寄圃，广东香山县吉大村人。下同。

1869年5月5日容闳与鲍留云之子（R. N. Brown）在上海下棋

家，予之教育计画，后亦卒赖曾公力为提倡，乃得实行。予尝谓世上之事，殆如蛛网之牵丝，不能预定交友之中，究何人能解吾毕生之结。即如予之因曾（继甫）而识李，因李而识曾（文正），因曾而予之教育计划乃得告成；又因予之教育计画告成，而中西学术萃于一堂；充类至义之尽，将来世界成为一家，不可谓非由此滥觞。则又如蛛网之到处牵连，不知以何处为止境也。

予因曾继甫，旋识宝顺公司（Dent & Co.）之西经理。经理遇予颇厚，欲命予至日本长崎为其分公司之买办，时日本与各国通商尚未久也。予则婉辞不就此职，且实告以故，谓："买办之俸虽优，然操业近卑鄙。予固美国领袖学校之毕业生，故予极重视母校，尊之敬之，不敢使予之所为于母校之名誉少有辱没。以买办之身份，不过洋行中奴隶之首领耳。以予而为洋行中奴隶之首领，则使予之母校及诸同学闻之，对予将生如何之感情耶？人虽有时困于经济，不得不屈就贱役，为稻粱谋，第予之贫乏尚未至此。设君果任予以事者，则予甚愿为公司代表，至内地一行。如是则予不至以金钱之故而牺牲尊贵之身份。予苟得代表公司以收买丝茶，无论或给常薪，或给用费，似较任奴隶首领为佳也。"予言时，予友曾君亦在座。曾君粗解英语，于予言虽知之不详，固已得其概略。予语毕，乃先辞出，以待彼二人协商。曾君后出语予，谓绘白（Webb）[①]（即该公司之经理）评予曰："容某虽贫，傲骨殊稜稜。"天下贫骨之与傲骨，乃往往长相伴而不相离也。谈判后数日，曾君告予，谓绘白已决计派予至产茶区域，调查装茶之情形云。

---

① 　绘白（Webb）：通译作韦伯。

第九章 产茶区域之初次调查

　　1859 年 3 月 11 日，予等乘一小艇，俗名"无锡快"者，由沪出发，从事于产茶各区域之调查。所谓"无锡快"，乃一种快艇之名，因在运河流域中无锡县所创造，故有是称。无锡距苏州甚近。苏州为名胜之区，与杭州齐名，居民繁庶，物产丰饶，而以丝织品为尤著。苏属城乡市镇间居民往来，咸借"无锡快"为交通利器。其制大小不一，舟中装设颇佳，便利安适，使乘客无风尘之苦。又有一种专供官绅富商雇乘者，则船身较大，装饰尤华丽。此种舟皆平底，值顺风时，其行甚速。惟遇逆风，则或系绳于桅，令人于岸上牵之，或摇橹以进。摇橹为中国人长技，寻常之舟，后舵两旁有橹，左右舷有铁枢纽，橹著其上。摇时一橹需四人，橹身为平面之板，于船尾处在水中左右摇曳，借水力以推舟，速率极大。惟近年中国通行汽船，操此业者为汽船所夺，故江苏一带河面上，民船已渐归淘汰。从前美国1850 年及 1860 年间，向有帆船驶至东印度及中国，往来装运货物。今则海面航业，已为邮船所夺，其事如一辙也。

　　予等舟行三日，至杭州。杭州为浙江省垣，地势颇不平，正西及西南、东北，皆有高山。全城面积，可三四英方里。南北较长于东西，为长方形。城之西有湖曰西湖，为著名名胜。湖面平如镜，底为沙泥，水澄碧，游鱼可数。由城脚迄西山之麓，皆西湖范围。傍湖之山，高入霄汉，绵亘直至城北，有若天然堡垒为城屏障者。钱塘江亦在城西，去城约二英里。江水发源于徽州东南高山中，蜿蜒而下，以趋入杭州湾。去城东约四十英里之处，山水由高处下冲入河中，水势湍激，波涛澎湃；声如万马奔腾。钱塘江中于一定之时间，有所谓"钱塘潮"者，潮头高至八九英尺，亦巨观也。当十二、十三世纪时，宋代君主曾建都于此，故杭州之名著于历史。风景绝佳，有多数之公私建筑物，如巨寺、高塔、桥梁、陵寝等，能令此特别之天然景物益增其灵秀。独惜自宋以后，历时既久，美丽之建筑物多半颓废失修，致令杭州昔日之荣誉渐以湮没。国家多难，恐未易遽复旧观也。

3月15日，予等离杭州，溯钱塘江而上。有地名江口，去杭城东约二英里，亦甚繁盛。河中帆樯林立，商船无虑千数，大小不一，长约五十尺至百尺，阔约十尺至十五尺，吃水不过二三尺，亦皆平底，咸取极坚致易弯曲之木材为之。因钱塘江之潮流曲折纡回，其底又多礁石，无[①]逆流顺水，恒遇极猛烈之激湍，时虞颠覆。故非有极坚固之质，不克经久受冲击也。舟中以板隔成小室，室各设床榻以备乘客之需。若遇装货时，则此隔扇及床榻可以拆卸，腾出空地以容货物。全舟若装配完全，上盖以穹形之篷，乃成圆筒式，状如一大雪茄。此类船多航行杭州、常山间。浙江与江西接壤处，交通多水道，其装运货物，大半即用此船。常山为浙省繁盛商埠。江西境亦有巨埠曰玉山，与常山相去仅五十华里。二埠间有广道，坦坦荡荡，阔约三十英尺，花岗石所铺，两旁砌以碧色之卵石，中国最佳路也。两省分界处，有石制牌坊，横跨路中，即以是为界石。两面俱镌有四大字曰"两省通衢"，以鲜明之蓝色涂之。此坊盖亦著名之古物，可见其商务之盛，由来旧也。当予等自常山至玉山时，

---

① 此处疑脱一"论"字。

汉口、九江、芜湖、镇江等处，犹未辟为通商口岸，汽船之运货至内地者绝少。而此两省通衢，苦力运货，项背相望，耶许相应答也，每日不下数千人。自游历家之眼光观之，饶有趣味。而在中国爱国之士见之，亦足引起其怀古之思。

于扬子江中，行舟可直达四川边境之荆州。全航路之长，约三千英里，六七省之商务赖以交通。设中国无欧西各国之干涉，得完全行使其主权，则扬子江开浚后，其利益实未可限量，予敢云全世界中人必有三分之一分此幸福也。彼西人者何不与中国以时机，俾得自行解决其国内问题耶？又如工人问题，自有欧西之汽船、电气及各种机械输入中国以来，中国工界乃大受其影响，生计事业几已十夺其九。非谓不当输入中国，第当逐渐推行，假以时日，俾人民得徐图他项事业，以恢复元气，不宜骤然尽夺其所业也。

3月15日晨五时①，予等自江口起碇。适值顺风，扬帆而下，一日间几行一百英里。暮十时，舟泊七龙②。遥望钱塘江之东岸，其露出水面者，岩石层次，历历可辨，殆全为红砂岩所砌成。岸上随处皆见有红砂岩所造之屋。四围山岭，晚景尤佳。浙江多佳山水，故随处皆入画。

翌日由七龙首途，值大雨如注，舟仍前进不息。下午泊于兰溪，是日约行四十英里。兰溪亦浙省大市场，两湖所产之"工夫茶"，咸集此间，由此经杭州以至上海。城中只有一街，长至六英里。其著名土产，为极佳之火腿，全国图名。予等因阻雨，在兰溪小住半日。日落后，天色渐霁，遂于夜半十二钟时复行，至衢州。衢州为浙省之州城，去年③3月间，为太平军所困，历

① 此处原文尚有一句置前，略云"今更回述予此次出发之情形："。
② 七龙：浙省无地名七龙者，或为七里泷之误。
③ 去年：指1858年。

四月，围乃解，幸尚无大损失云。在衢州旅馆中一宿，即趱赴萧山[1]。萧山去此可三十英里，因关役查验繁苛，舆人脚夫亦难骤觅多人，登岸至不便。抵萧山后，旋复乘肩舆赴玉山。当晚预雇渔舟，备翌晨赴广信。广信去玉山，亦三十英里。既过玉山，已行入江西境界。此新航路乃向西北行，顺流而下，掠鄱阳湖南岸而至南昌。南昌为江西省会，城垣外观颇壮丽，惜予无暇游览，且不及调查太平军战后之状况若何也。

既过南昌，航路则转向西南，趋湘潭。湘潭即予等最后之目的地。途中历数城，以于历史及商业上无大关系，故略之。湖南之省会曰长沙。予过长沙时，适在夜间。迨 4 月 15 日之晨，乃抵湘潭。湘潭亦中国内地商埠之巨者。凡外国运来货物，至广东上岸后，必先集湘潭，由湘潭再分运至内地。又非独进口货为然，中国丝、茶之运往外国者，必先在湘潭装箱，然后再运广东放洋。以故湘潭及广州间，商务异常繁盛。交通皆以陆，劳动工人肩货往来于南风岭者，不下十万人。南风岭地处湘潭与广州之中央，为往来必经之孔道。道旁居民，咸借肩挑背负以为生，安居乐业，各得其所。迨后外洋机械输入，复经国际战争及通商立约等事，而中国劳动界情势，乃为之一变。此不仅扰乱中国工业制度，且于将来全国之经济、实业、政治上，皆有莫大影响也。

予等乃各依其所指定之地点，分往各处收买生茶，以备运往上海装箱。留湘潭约十日。十日后，拟更赴湖北之荆州，以调查华容地方所产之黄丝。

4 月 26 日，离湘潭北行，趋予等所欲赴地点。翌晨八时至湖南长沙。是日适空气潮湿，同人中咸觉烦懑不欢，乃相约入

---

[1]　萧山：当作常山。下同。

城游览。城中情形，与他处略同，建筑街衢等，皆粗劣秽污，无可观者。明日乘舟复行，遂过洞庭湖，渡扬子江，入荆河口，以达华容。计离湘潭后，水程十日，所经处尚有太平景象。居民各安农业，禾黍满望，叱犊时闻。予于此见二村童，共骑一驴，沿途笑语，意志欢乐，他处未见有此也。抵华容后，因觅旅馆不得，遂寄榻于某丝行中。行装甫卸，即有地方保甲二人，来询旅客姓名职业。行主知其故，即为予等代述来意。彼闻为诚实商人，非为匪徒作侦探者，遂满意而去，任予等自由动作，不复来相扰矣。予既宣布来意，旋有无数商人，送种种黄丝来，以备选购。是日得各种丝样，约六十五磅，装运上海。

两星期后，各收拾行装，准备归计。经汉口后，又赴聂家市。聂家市属长沙①，亦产茶区域也。自5月26日离华容，于6月5日抵汉口，寓一中国旅馆中。天气既炎热潮湿，所居复湫隘异常，殊少清新空气，至为不适。三日后，有委员三人来查询，一如在华容时。示以在华容所购之黄丝，及其包皮上所盖由华容至汉口沿途税卡之戳。彼等见此，知非匪徒侦探，遂去，不复相扰。

汉口当时尚未通商，惟此事已经提议，不久且实行。当太平军未起事之前，汉口本一中国最重要之商埠。1856年，太平军占据武昌时，汉口、汉阳亦同时失陷。以是汉口之一部，尽被焚毁，顿成一片焦土。当予至时，商业已渐恢复，被焚之区，亦从新建筑。第所建房屋，类皆草率急就。若以今日（1909年）之汉口言之，沿岸一带，货栈林立，居屋栉比，类皆壮丽之西式建筑，大有欧西景象，非昔比矣。故在今日中国之有汉口，殆如美国之有芝加哥及圣鲁意二城。予知不久汉口之商业发达，

---

① 聂家市属长沙：属岳州府临湘县。

居民繁盛，必将驾芝加哥、圣路易而上之。予等勾留数日，遂重渡扬子江，趋聂家市产黑茶之地。

6月30离汉口，7月4日至聂家市及杨柳洞①，于此二处，勾留月余。于黑茶之制造及其装运出口之方法，知之甚悉。其法简而易学。予虽未知印度茶之制法如何，第以意度之，印茶既以机器制造，其法当亦甚简。自1850年以后，中国人颇思振兴茶业，挽回利权，故于人工之制茶法，亦已改良不少。究印度所以夺我茶业利权之故，初非以印茶用机器制造，而华茶用人工制造之相差。盖产茶之土地不同，茶之性质，遂亦因之而异。印茶之性质极烈，较中国茶味为浓，烈亦倍之。论叶之嫩及味之香，则华茶又胜过印茶一倍也。总之印茶烈而浓，华茶香而美。故美国、俄国及欧洲各国上流社会之善品茶者，皆嗜中国茶叶；惟劳动工人及寻常百姓，乃好印茶，味浓亦值廉也。

8月下旬，所事既毕，共乘一湖南民船以归。船中满载装箱之茶，以备运沪。于8月29日，重临汉口，计去初次离汉时且两月矣。此行不复过湘潭，经汉口后，即自扬子江顺流而下，至九江，过鄱阳湖。鄱阳湖之南岸，有地曰河口。自河口以往，乃遵3月间所经之原路，9月21日抵杭州。由杭州复乘"无锡快"，于9月30日抵上海。溯自3月以迄10月，凡历七阅月之旅行，借此机缘，予得略知内地人民经太平军乱后之状况。凡所历沿途各地，大半皆为太平军或官军所驻扎者，外状似尚平静。至于各地人民，经太平军及官军抢掠之后，究竟受何影响，则无人能知其真相矣。

惟有一事，令予生无穷之感慨。予素阅中国纪载及旅行日记等书，莫不谓中国人口之众，甲于全球。故予意中国当无地

---

① 杨柳洞：当系羊楼洞，在湖北咸宁境内。

不有人烟稠密之象。乃今所见者，则大抵皆居民稀少，与予夙昔所怀想者，大不相符，是则最足以激刺予之脑筋者也。此种荒凉景象，以予所经之浙江、江西、湖南、湖北四省为尤甚。当予游历时，为春夏两季，正五谷播种、农事方殷之际，田间陌上，理应有多数之驴马牛畜，曳锄相接。乃情形反是，良可怪也。

予自内地归后，10月间复有英友某君，倩予至绍兴收买生丝。绍兴去杭州西南约二十英里，所产丝颇著名。予在绍兴收丝约两月，忽患疟，不得已中途辍业。绍兴城内污秽，不适于卫生，与中国他处相仿佛。城中河道，水黑如墨。以城处于山坳低湿之地，雨水咸潴蓄河内，能流入而不能泄出。故历年堆积，竟无法使之清除。总绍兴之情形，殆不能名之为城，实含垢纳污之大沟渠，为一切微生物繁殖之地耳，故疟疾极多。予幸不久即愈，甫能离榻，即急急去之。

第十章　太平军中之访察

1860年，有二美教士，不忆其名，一中国人曰曾兰生[①]，拟作金陵游，探太平军内幕，邀予与偕。予欣然诺之。太平军中人物若何？其举动志趣若何？果胜任创造新政府以代满洲乎？此余所亟欲知也。是年11月6日，予等共乘一"无锡快"，自上海首途。时适东北风大作，船顺风行颇速，天气复晴朗。同行诸人，兴致殊高。适携有美国国旗，众人乘兴，遂以插船首，迎风招飐，顾而乐之。既念此举殊疏，或误认吾舟谓有国际关系，而加以盘诘，则徒生枝节，乃急卷而藏之。吾侪此行，拟先至苏州，本应道出松江。因闻松江方驻有官军炮艇，恐为所拦阻，不听向前，或被递送还上海，亦殊不便，乃绕道避之。舟离上海三十英里中，沿途居民安堵，不显有政治上扰乱情状。田家操作自若，方收获也。然予赴内地调查产茶时，苏州已为

----

① 曾兰生（1826—1895），亦有误作"来顺、礼逊"，字恒忠、芝亭，英文写作 Tseng Laisun、Chan Laisun 或 Zeng Laisun。祖籍广东潮州海阳（今潮安），生于新加坡。1843年，由教会资助前往美国读书，1846年就读于纽约汉密尔顿学院。1848年，回国后，在香港、广州等地工作。1850年娶毕业于教会学校的华巫混血儿（即娘惹）Ruth Ati 为妻，育有三子三女，Annie Laisun（1851—?）、Lena Laisun（1853—1914）、曾溥（1854—1889）、曾笃恭（1857—1917）、Amy Hanbury Laisun（1865—1886）。1853年，辞职往上海营商。1866年曾在福建船政学堂任职，担任后学堂航海教授英人嘉乐尔（James Carroll）的助手和翻译。1871年任留美幼童英文教习，1872年全家随陈兰彬携带第一批幼童赴美。1875年经欧洲回国后任天津海军公所翻译。1892年曾兼任亨达利洋行（Vrard & Co., L.）翻译。

曾兰生（1826—1895）

太平军占领。苏沪密迩，故上海租界中西人咸惴惴，惟恐太平军来占据租界，乃严为戒备。松江各河中亦炮艇密布，西人守卫队亦远出租界界线之外严密巡逻矣。

11月9日之晨，船抵苏州。沿途畅行无阻，绝未遇一官军，或一太平军。当此战争紧急之际，而巡逻疏略如是，中国人事事不经意，于此可见一斑。予等抵苏州之娄门，先至一军站。站中有护照，欲赴城内者，必先于此领照，乃得入，出城时仍须缴还之。予等欲入城谒其主将，乞介绍书，俾得直赴金陵，沿途无阻。乃以二人留站守候，先遣二人面军站长，问四人可否同时入城。二人去时，有该地警察长，特派一人伴之行。去一小时而返，谓站长已允所请。于是予等同入城。

时城中民政长方公出，遂往谒军事首领刘某。其人躯干高大，身着红衣，有骄矜气，望而可知为浅陋无根柢者。彼询予等赴南京目的，虽返复盘诘，礼遇尚优，旋授一函介绍予等于丹阳主将，并缮一护照，谓持此畅行于无锡常州间，可无留难。刘复绍介予等唔四西人。四人中二美人，一英人，一法人。法人自谓为法国贵族，因在本国丧失其资财，故来中国以图恢复。英人则自称系英国副将。其二美国人，一为医士，一则贩卖枪弹者，因索值过昂，尚未成议云。之数人者，其所谓贵族、副将、医士、商人云云，初莫辨其真伪。其为冒险而来，各怀所欲，则无疑也。予闻刘颂赞美歌，口齿颇伶俐。日暮返舟，复遣人以鸡、羊等物相馈遗，以故此行食品颇充裕。11月11日晨抵无锡。既至，出护照示关吏，果得彼等礼遇。其地之主将某，设筵相款。宴罢，复赠种种干鲜水果，且亲至舟中送行。予等与谈论甚久，后亦颂赞美歌作终结，与苏州刘某所颂者同。

11 月 12 日，离无锡赴常州。自苏至丹阳，舟皆行运河中。河之两岸，道路犹完好。途中所见皆太平军。运河中船只颇少，有时经日不遇一舟。运河两旁之田，皆已荒芜，草长盈尺，满目蒿莱，绝不见有稻秧麦穗。旅行过此者，设不知其中真象，必且以是归咎于太平军之残暴。殊不知官军之残暴，实无以愈于太平军。以予等沿途所见，太平军之对于人民，皆甚和平，又能竭力保护，以收拾人心。其有焚掠肆虐者，治以极严之军法。非如纣之不善，盗跖之率徒为暴，然则仁与不仁，其成败之代名词欤？抵常州，日已暮。自无锡至此，沿途房屋，皆空无人居。偶遇一二老叟，提小筐售物。筐中所贮橘、蛋、糕饼、菜蔬、鱼、肉等零星食品。见舟来，辄追呼求售。观其状，似因年老不能远逃，故借此以延喘息。然皆愁苦万状，穷蹙无生趣矣。13 日晨六钟，复解维趋丹阳行。丹阳居民，对于太平军较有信用，商不辍业，农不辍耕，无荒凉景象。而太平军之对于人民，亦未闻有虐遇事，相处甚得也。是日之晨，途中见有兵千人。傍晚已望见丹阳雉堞，因暮色苍茫，故寄宿舟中。翌日破晓入城，谒其地主将。先以苏州所得之介绍书投入。后知此主将亦刘姓，彼适他出，有副官秦某[①]出迎，盖文职也。为人和蔼可亲，礼貌周至。予等与谈，偶询以太平军中宗教信仰。秦君自谓对于耶稣教之观念，皆得诸其首领洪秀全。其言曰：

"吾等所崇拜之天主，即在天之父。天父之外，复有耶稣及圣灵。三位一体，合成真人，是曰上帝。耶稣教分为二派，一

---

① 副官秦某：疑即天官秦日昌。

曰旧派，一曰新派，太平军则弃新派而从旧派。吾等之天王，曾至天上面谒天父。天父命其降世行道，扫除一切罪恶，指引一切迷路，毁灭偶像及其他一切邪教之迷信，晓谕百姓，使人人咸知天主之真体，其责任盖甚重大也。天王之至天上，其为灵魂御空而行，抑为肉体白日飞升，则非吾等所能知。但天王自言，天王之尊，犹不能与天主相提并论。世人之当崇拜天主，乃为宗教上之崇拜；至天王之受世人敬礼，不过犹世上皇帝之尊荣，为臣民者对其君上，当极其尊敬而已。天王之位，锡自天主，与耶稣为兄弟行。此所谓兄弟者，非谓其为同父共母所生；第因天王与耶稣，皆为上帝先后所派之天使，命其至世界上普度众生，为世人赎罪。天王唧此使命在耶稣后，故当兄事耶稣耳。至太平军中之教规，有所谓饮三杯茶者，乃表感谢上帝之心，初不含赎罪意义。其数之以三者，亦与三位一体之教旨无关，即一杯二杯，本无不可。而必舍一舍二而择三者，则以三之为数乃中国人素来崇尚，如古语称天地人为三才等是也。若言赎罪，则无论何等供养祭献，绝不能赎吾人罪孽于毫末。此权盖尽操诸耶稣之手，世人但尽其真心忏悔之忱，则耶稣自能为之救赎，否则虽祭奉亦无益。即天王自己，亦长日兢兢业业，惟恐或得罪于天主云。"

秦某言次，又论及战争时军民必分处之故。谓中国亘古以来，无论何代，依向来之习惯，凡遇战争时，人民必退处田野，军士则驻守城中，所谓攻城略地，能攻克一城则城外之地，可唾手得也。又言自苏至此，运河两旁荒凉之况，其故有三：一为张玉良军队退败时所焚烧，一为土匪所抢掠，一则太平军之自毁也。当忠王（即李秀成）在苏州时，尝竭力欲禁抢掠之风，悬重赏以募奇才。谓有能出力禁绝焚掠之事者，立酬巨金，并颁以爵位。又下令三通：一不许残杀平民，二不许妄杀牛羊，三不许纵烧民居。有犯其一者，杀无赦。迨后忠王至无锡，曾有一该地长官纵任土匪焚毁民居，忠王乃戮此长官以警众。忠王与英王（即陈良玉）[①]之为人，皆极聪颖，不独擅于军旅之事，文学亦极优长云。

秦某又言攻略各地之情形，及1860年春间官军围攻金陵之失败。语次并出一函相示，函为徽州某主将所发，内云曾国藩已受大创，现方为太平军所困，四面受敌。据其函中所言，似曾国藩已战殁阵中矣。秦某复谓张玉良攻金陵败退后，已受伤咯血，现在杭州养疴，一时不能复出。运河一带，居扬子江之北者，皆入太平军掌握。而忠王、英王，则居上游，方谋取湖北。石达开经略四川云贵等省。镇江近方被围，更有西王率军驻扎于此，以指挥江南全境云云。当日太平军势力所及盖如此。

是日于秦处晚餐，入夜归宿舟中。明日复入城，谒刘主将，又不值。仅晤其中军某，因请其设法护送予等至南京。中军允诺，属以所乘舟可暂留丹阳，彼能善为守护，勿使有失。归途出此再乘之，固甚便也。翌晨[②]，予等遂徒步出丹阳。行十五英里，至一镇曰宝堰，其地去句容六英里。镇中觅宿颇不易，土人皆贫苦不支，对于外来之客，尤怀疑惧。费儿许唇舌，仅于隘巷中得空屋，无几案床榻，以稻藁席地而已。次晨，居停老妇以饘粥饷客，濒行酬以银一圆。九钟，抵句容。城门尽闭，不得入。盖此时适有谣传，谓太平军败于镇江，将来此暂避，故句容戒严。予等闻此大失望，美教士至欲折回上海。余意必至南京，持论久之，乃复前进。幸离句容不远，觅得肩舆及骡，乃不复退缩。

11月18日抵南京。予先至，候于南门外，余人齐集，乃

---

① 英王（即陈良玉）：英王乃陈玉成，原注误。

② 翌晨：即16日晨。

同行入城。城中劳白芝教士（Rev. Roberts）^①已遣仆数人，迎候于途，遂至劳君寓所。寓近干王洪仁^②军署。劳白芝，美教士旧友也。既晤劳君后，彼等殷勤话旧，予则先退至己卧室。长途仆仆，颇觉劳顿，因略盥洗，即休息。予晤劳君时，未发一语，亦未尝告以予之姓名。但前在古夫人小学肄业时，曾晤其人，故一见即能识之。渠此时所衣为黄缎官袍，足华式笨履，举步迟缓，益形龙钟。劳氏在南京果身居何职，予实未详。洪秀全之宗教顾问欤？抑太平天国之国务卿耶？

　　翌日，予等谒干王。干王为洪秀全之侄。^③1856年，予在香港曾识其人。当时彼方为伦敦传道会职员，任中国牧师，其主教为莱克博士（Dr. Legge）^④。莱克博士，即著名善译中国古文

---

　　① 劳白芝教士（Rev. Roberts）：即美国传教士罗孝全（Issachar Jacox Roberts，1802—1871），出生于美国田纳西州，基督教新教美南浸信会传教士。1837年自费来中国，初在澳门向麻风病患者传教。1841年加入美国浸信会差会，1842年成为第一位长期居留香港的新教传教士，6月为第一名中国信徒施浸。1844年到广州，是第一个搬到广州商馆区以外居住的新教传教士。1845年美国浸会分裂，改属于美南浸信会差会。1847年3—5月，洪秀全来到罗孝全在广州的礼拜堂，在那里学习《圣经》，曾要求受洗，罗孝全不同意洪秀全对以前大病时所见"异象"的见解，拒绝为他施洗。洪秀全4个月后离开。1860年从南方经上海到苏州，10月到天京，住在干王洪仁玕的府第，出任通事官领袖一职，封接天义。1862年1月乘坐英国船离开天京。

　　② 干王洪仁：疑为洪仁玕之误。洪仁玕（1822—1864），原名洪仁，字益谦，号吉甫，广东花县人。

　　③ 干王洪仁玕与洪仁达同辈，与洪秀全为兄弟行，此处云云恐误。

　　④ 莱克博士（Dr. Legge）：即英国传教士理雅各（James Legge，1815—1897），英国苏格兰人，1839年被英国基督新教派公理宗的伦敦传道会派驻马六甲主持英华书院。1843年将英华书院迁往香港，任香港英华书院第一届校长。1841年从开始着手翻译中国经典。1862年获得王韬协助翻译中国经典。1867年偕带王韬返回苏格兰家乡。1870年获得苏格兰阿伯丁大学文学院博士学位，重返香港主持英华书院。1870—1873年任香港佑宁堂（Union Church Hong Kong）教区牧师。1873年访问上海、天津、北京、山东，再从上海出发，经日本、美国，返回英国。1876—1897年担任牛津大学第一任汉学教授。

者。予曩在香港晤干王时，干语予，将来愿于金陵得再相见，今果然矣。干王本名洪仁，迨至金陵与其叔共事，晋爵至王位，乃曰干王，殆取干城之义欤？干王接见予等，极表欢迎，尤乐于见予。寒暄后，即询予对于太平军之观念若何？亦赞成此举而愿与之共事否？予告以此来初无成见，亦无意投身太平军中，妄思附骥，第来探视故人，以慰数年来晦明风雨之思耳。

干王复固问，余曰："实无他目的，但得略悉金陵实在情形，一释传闻之疑，于愿已足。惟此次自苏至宁，途次颇有所感触，愿贡其千虑一得之愚。因言七事：一、依正当之军事制度，组织一良好军队；二、设立武备学校，以养成多数有学识军官；三、建设海军学校；四、建设善良政府，聘用富有经验之人才，为各部行政顾问；五、创立银行制度，及厘订度量衡标准；六、颁定各级学校教育制度，以耶稣教《圣经》列为主课[①]；七、设立各种实业学校。此其大略。至若何实行，自非立谈所能罄。倘不以为迂缓，而采纳予言，愿为马前走卒。"余之此言，盖度德量力，自谓能尽力于太平军者只此耳。

越二日，干王复邀予等为第二次谈判。既入见，干王乃以予所言七事，逐条讨论。谓何者最佳，何者最要，侃侃而谈，殊中肯綮。盖干王居外久，见闻稍广，故较各王略悉外情。即较洪秀全之识见，亦略高一筹。凡欧洲各大强国所以富强之故，亦能知其秘钥所在。故对于予所提议之七事，极知其关系重要。第善善不能用，盖一薛居州无能为役，且此时诸要人皆统兵于外，故必俟协议，经多数赞成，乃可实行也。

又数日，干王忽遣使来，赠予一小包袱。拆而视之，则中裹一小印，长四英寸，宽一英寸，上镌予名。又有黄缎一

---

①　原文为"以圣经为课程之一"。

幅，钤印十三，上书予官阶，曰"义"字。按太平军官制，王一等爵，义字四等爵。予睹此大惑不解，干王以此授予，意果何居？其以是为干旄之逮欤？然未先期得予同意，不可谓招以其道。岂谓四等荣衔，遂足令人感激知己，抑亦隘矣。予每见太平军领袖人物，其行为品格与所筹划，实未敢信其必成。乃商之同伴诸人，决计返璧。更亲至干王府，面谢其特别之知遇。且告之曰："无论何时，太平军领袖诸君，苟决计实行予第一次谈判时提出之计划，则予必效奔走。无功之赏，则不敢受。君果不忘故人，愿乞一护照，俾予于太平军势力范围中，无论何时得自由来去，则受赐多矣。"干王知不可强，卒从予请。遂于12月24日发出护照，并为予等代备粮食舆马，送至丹阳。予等共乘原舟遄归，于翌年1月初旬安抵上海。途中追忆太平军起事情形，及彼中人物之举动，以为与中国极有关系，当于下章详之。

第十一章　对于太平军战争之观感

革命之在中国，固数见不鲜。闻者疑吾言乎？则试一翻中国历史。其中所谓二十四朝，非即二十四次革命写真耶？顾虽如此，战国而外，中国之所谓革命，类不过一姓之废兴，于国体及政治上，无重大改革之效果。以故中国二千年历史，如其文化，常陈陈相因，乏新颖趣味。亦无英雄豪杰，创立不世伟业，以增历史精神。太平军战争之起，则视中国前此鼎革，有特异之点。非谓彼果英雄豪杰，以含有宗教性质耳。其魄力至伟，能自僻远之广西，由西南蔓延东北，而达精华荟萃之金陵，历时至十五年之久，亦惟宗教之故。此十五年中，满洲政府几无日不处于飘摇风雨之中。然于历史上究有若何精神，则未易轻许也。

太平军之大战争，以宗教观念为原质。此观念来自欧西，耶稣教徒实传播之。其输此种子于中国之第一人，为英人玛礼孙氏，盖伦敦传道会所派出者。其后十年，复有美教士劳氏继踵而起。二氏者，开浚洪秀全知识之功臣也。玛礼孙善著述，曾译耶教《圣经》为汉文，而译《康熙字典》为英文。虽其书未必当，而后之西人来中国传教者，咸借为津梁。玛氏所译《圣经》，旋经后人加以润色，汉英字典后亦经多人修正，如梅博士（Dr. Medhurst）[①]、文主教（Bishop Boone）[②]、雷博士（Dr. Legge）

[①]　梅博士（Dr. Medhurst）：即英国传教士麦都思（Walter Henry Medhurst，1796—1857）。

[②]　文主教（Bishop Boone）：即文惠廉（William Jones Boone，1811—1864），美国基督教新教圣公会传教士。1840年来中国，在澳门活动。曾任马礼逊学校代理校长。

及勃礼区文（Bridgeman）[①]、威廉姆司（Williams）[②]诸人。先后增订，经过多人之手，要不能不借玛氏所译者为蓝本也。玛礼孙于中国有一最著名之事业，曾于中国得第一耶教信徒，名梁亚发。其人能本耶教宗旨，著成传道书数种。洪秀全求道时，即以玛氏所译《圣经》，及梁氏所著书，诵习研究。第此等书中，微言奥义，非得人善为解释，殊难悟彻。时值美国米苏厘省教士劳白芝君在粤传道，洪秀全乃时至其处请业，二人遂为莫逆交。迨太平军起，洪既雄踞金陵，劳氏亦居此处，大抵友而兼师者，故甚清贵。劳苦功高，固宜有此不次之赏。1864年，官军既克复金陵，劳氏遂不知所终。

洪秀全为耶稣教徒时，尚醉心科举之虚荣。曾应小试，不幸镣羽。乃专心传道，往来两粤，宣扬福音于客家（Hakkas）族中。所谓"客家"者，两广间一种客民，迁徙无常，故俗称为客家云。洪秀全一生之功业，此时传道，不过为其宗教经验之起点；其后革命事业，乃其宗教经验之结果。

洪秀全于应试落第后，得失心盛，殆成一种神经病。神志昏聩中，自谓曾至天上，蒙天主授以极重要之职，命其毁灭世界上崇拜之偶像，指引迷途，晓谕世人，使人人咸知天主，信仰耶稣，俾耶稣得为世人赎罪。洪秀全既自以为在天主之前受此重任，故自命为天主之子，与耶稣平等，称耶稣为兄。盖昏聩中构成之幻想，乃自信为真。日至客家中，历叙其所遭如是。谓世人必须信仰一己，乃能获上帝之福佑。遂以崇拜上帝之事。

---

① 勃礼区文（Bridgeman）：即裨治文（Elijah Coleman Bridgman，1801—1861），美国传教士。1829年受美国公理会派遣，于次年2月到达广州。1832年5月起创办并主编《中国丛报》（*Chinese Repository*）。

② 威廉姆司（Williams）：即卫三畏（Samuel Wells Williams，1812—1884），美国传教士兼外交官，编有《简易汉语教程》《官方方言中的英汉用词》等。

蹈狐鸣篝火之嫌，每日瞻礼祈祷，高诵赞美之歌。广西四境人民闻之，乃大歆动。每日必有多人入教，号召即至。及后人数日增，声势日广。地方官吏对于此一般耶稣教徒，目为异端邪说，妖言惑人，然亦无如之何。

此种人所具耶教之知识，半为西来教士所传播，半为本地中国信徒所讲授。故无论如何，其宗教知识，皆甚浅陋而简单。顾虽浅陋简单，而宗教中真实之势力，则已甚大，足使一般无识愚民，皆成为草野英雄，人人能冒危险，视死如归。此种特性之潜蓄，于政府欲实行解散该教时，乃大发现。彼等揭竿而起，以抵抗官军之压迫。初无枪弹军火之利器，所持者櫌锄棘矜耳。以此粗笨之农具，而能所向无敌，逐北追奔，如疾风之扫秋叶，皆由宗教上所得之勇敢精神为之。

虽然，太平军之起，固宗教上之逼迫使然。实则亦非真因，不过爆发之导火线耳。即使当时政府，无此等逼迫之举动，洪秀全及其属下诸人，亦未必能安居于中国内地，而专以传布宗教为事也。予意当时即无洪秀全，中国亦必不能免于革命。设有人以耶稣教之关系及清政府之操切，为1850年革命之原因，则其所见浅陋实甚。恶根实种于满洲政府之政治，最大之真因为行政机关之腐败，政以贿成。上下官吏，即无人不中贿赂之毒。美其名曰馈遗，黄金累累，无非暮夜苞苴。官吏既人人欲饱其贪囊，遂日以愚弄人民为能事。于是所谓政府者，乃完全成一极大之欺诈机关矣。

革命事业之开幕于中国，殆如埃及之石人，见者莫不惊奇。埃及石人首有二面，太平军中亦含有两种性质，如石人之有二面。凡崇拜天主，信仰救主圣灵，毁灭偶像庙宇，禁止鸦片，守安息日，饭前后战争时均祈祷，种种耶教中重大之要旨，太平天国无不毕具。遂使全世界耶教中人，咸逆料满洲政府必为推翻，洪秀全所称之太平天国行且建设成立。此天意或将使中国立一震古烁今之世业，而为全世界人所惊心动魄也。耶教中人此种幻想，亦未免感情用事，过于信任太平军矣。彼曷不细为分析，一研究太平军之内容耶？

洪秀全之起兵广西也，马首东向，沿途收集流亡，声势甚壮。中途曾移师直指北京，至天津为官军所败，乃折回迳趋南京。所过湖南、湖北、江西、安徽等省，旌旗所至，无坚不摧。第自天津败北，兵力缩减。良由其所招抚，皆无业游民，为社会中最无知识之人。以此加入太平军，非独不能增加实力，且足为太平军之重累，而使其兵力转弱。盖此等无赖之尤，既无军人纪律，复无宗教信仰。即使齐之以刑，不足禁其抢掠杀人之过恶。其所以受创于天津，亦此等人实尸其咎。锐气既挫，迨占据扬州、苏州、杭州等城，财产富而多美色，而太平军之道德乃每下而愈况。盖繁华富丽，固足以销磨壮志，而促其灭亡也。

此次革命，虽经十五年剧烈之战争，乃不久而雾散烟消，于历史上曾未留一足为纪念之盛迹。后之读史至此者，亦不过以为一时狂热，徒令耶教中人为之失望，于宗教上毫无裨补。即如南京占据至十年之久，亦不见留有若何之耶教事迹。广西为其起事之地，亦复如是。至若于中国政治上，则更绝无革新之影响。简而言之，太平军一役，中国全国于宗教及政治上，皆未受丝毫之利益也。其可称为良好结果者惟有一事，即天假此役，以破中国顽固之积习，使全国人民皆由梦中警觉，而有新国家之思想。观于此后 1894、1895、1898、1900、1901、1904、1905 等年种种事实之发生，足以证予言之不谬矣。

第十二章　太平县产茶地之旅行

　　南京之行，本希望遂予夙志，素所主张之教育计划，与夫改良政治之赞助，二者有所借手，可以为中国福也。不图此行结果，毫无所得。曩之对于太平军颇抱积极希望，庶几此新政府者能除旧布新，至是顿悟其全不足恃。以予观察所及，太平军之行为，殆无有造新中国之能力，可断言也。于是不得不变计，欲从贸易入手。以为有极巨资财，则借雄厚财力，未必不可图成。然毕竟营何种商业，以为致富之资乎？

　　某日予方徜徉某茶肆，值素识之茶商某某亦在品茗，遂相与闲话。谈次及予前至两湖江西各省调查产茶事，已复及南京之行，议论纷歧，语乃愈引而愈远。已而众茶商言安徽太平县茶，或谓该处有绿茶百余万，已装箱准备出口，不幸尽落太平军之手。此时设有人能冒险向彼军取回者，巨富可立致。予闻言若有所触，心识之。众人旋散，予亦徐步归寓。且行且思，适间茶商之言，宁非绝好时机乎。第处此乱离时势，前途之危险与困难，不问可知。又况盗贼横行，随在而是。稍有经验之商人，谁复肯以金钱冒奇险，图此毫无凭借之事业耶。然予以为事有可图，不愿坐失时机。因商之予友曾苗（当即第八章所述之曾继甫[①]），即一年前介绍予往内地采茶者。其人商业经验极富，交游亦多，且于我亦非泛泛。曾曰："此事当深长思之，

----

　　① 曾继甫即曾寄圃。

未敢贸然遽答。君苟能少待者，数日后当有以报命。"已而果然。曾谓："予已与公司主人讨论至再。"予所提议之策，已决定实行矣。

此事进行之初步，为余受公司委任赴太平调查，毕竟有无此项茶叶？设有此茶，以巨金向太平军中购出，有无危险？购得茶叶后，雇民船运出，更以汽船载之来申，其间有无困难？盖必如是先期筹备，然后亿则屡中也。自上海赴太平有二途：一由芜湖直达，一在芜湖上游百英里处有地曰大通。当时芜湖至太平县，在太平军势力范围中；大通则为官军所驻。由芜湖入内地，舟行二百五十英里。大通虽较近，然须陆行，殊不便，旅费亦巨。且经大通，沿途有重税，芜湖则否。权衡利害，遂决计取道芜湖。濒行邀四人为伴。此四人亦业茶，皆太平县人，故乡在劫火中已两年，因避乱来上海者。既首途，溯江上行。途中经大城三，尽为太平军所占据。居民甚少，田园荒芜，芦苇高且过人。多数市镇，亦寂无居人。惨淡情状，不堪属目。若在平时，此长途所经地方，至少当有五十万户。今则不知流离何所，存者才数十人耳。亦复形容枯槁，衣裳垢敝，憧憧往来，生气萧索，远望之几疑骷髅人行也。

舟行一星期，抵一镇曰山口。于此复遇茶商三人，亦四年前在上海相识者。此三茶商者，在漫天烽火中，可谓硕果仅存。见予等至，如他乡遇旧，愉快之情，不可言喻。盖当此时此地而有余等，不啻空山中闻足音也。于是于焚毁未尽诸屋中，择一最完善者居之，作为办事地点，以从事调查，并邀所遇三茶商相助为理。渠乃示予某处某处，有存茶若干。并谓山口地方，至少必有绿茶五十万箱。合太平县全境计之，当不下百五十万箱，每箱装茶重可六十磅云。予居此一星期，遂返芜湖，函上海报告调查情形。略谓："由太平县至芜湖，水程尚平安。以予意度之，当不至有生命财产之危险。予在太平县境内，曾亲见有无数之绿茶。但能携款至芜湖，并雇用数人护送以往，款至太平县，茶即不难运归。"函外并附茶样多种。已而上海复书来，谓茶种良佳，命予速往购办。谓能得几许者，尽量收购，不厌多也。

公司汇钱既至，予偕同伴诸人，运资赴山口，复由山口装茶返芜湖。仆仆道途，往返不知几次。犹忆某日伴予行者十二人，中有欧洲人六，亦素业茶者，有银八箱，共四万两。尔时市价，每银一两，约易墨银一圆三角三分。故予所携者，殆合墨银五万三千圆。予雇运茶之舟八，分所携银为二，择二大舟之最坚固者载之。同行之人，亦分为两组。每载银舟，以三西人三华人守之，并将手枪、腰刀及消防具，所以防意外者。吾侪并舟人计之，人数可四十余。然虽多，皆不习武事，设遇警实不足恃。可为缓急之助，惟此数西人耳。虽然，此辈大半皆冒险之徒，或为逃亡之水手，不过在上海受公司佣雇，遂来此为护送之人。究竟能否临难不避，此时亦殊不可必。就中有一英人自言为兽医，身高六英尺，状貌雄伟，望之精神烨然。后乃知此人之心志，亦不坚定，则知人之难也。

予既部署粗定，遂解维趋芜湖。舟中诸人，咸鼓其冒险精神，有陈元龙气概。芜湖山口适中处，有城曰泾县，某日至此而泊。城中驻太平军，其主将曾验予在南京时所得之护照，并知予曾识彼中权要者。予舟泊于湖之小湾，小湾面积，适可容数舟。载银二大舟居中，余舟环之。入夜，以枪械分予众人，令皆实子弹。又另增佣金，每舟各派一人行夜。分布既毕，始各就寝。就中一年老之茶商及予，睡不成寐。余人因日间劳倦，头着枕，已鼾声动矣。予心既悬悬，不能安寝。卧观天际，见黑云片片，飞行甚速。一弯新月，时从云隙窥人。既而云益浓厚，月不可见，夜色乃益昏沉，黑暗中一无所睹。倚枕无聊，长夜将半，耳际忽闻隐隐有呼啸声，由远渐近。乃大惊，披衣起，醒各舟人。此时声益近，听之历历可辨，似有数千人，同时呐喊。深夜静野中有此，益觉凄厉。数分钟后，已见对岸火光熊熊，有无数火捻，闪烁于昏黑可怖之世界中。幸此群匪与予舟，尚隔一河。又幸夜黑，予舟尚未为所见。

予等咸知危险即在目前，向同伴商抵御之策，如临时会议然。咸谓众寡悬殊，果对垒者，当以一当千，竟无一人主战。彼为兽医之英人，创议尽献所有勿与抗，发言时已面无人色，战慄不止，此公可谓虚有其表者。余人议论歧出，莫衷一是。予等诚不值为此区区四万两之银而牺牲生命。但此金系受他人委托，奈何不设法保护之？慷他人之慨，资寇盗之粮，人且鄙予等为无勇懦夫，谁复以一钱相托者。计必临难不苟，庶几扪心自安。乃谓众："诸君且勿自扰，匪果来劫，予请挺身与其酋开谈判。君等第执枪械，守卫银箱。鄙意匪众苟知吾侪为何等人物，并示黄缎护照，明告若辈，脱果取吾金者，当诉之南京。必追还原物，不虞有丝毫损失。如此或竟幸免，亦未可知。"予发言毕，众人勇气得稍振，共坐船头，静待其来。默念数分钟后，不知当得若何结果。人人自危，咸注目对岸火光不少瞬。久之，呼啸声渐低，火捻渐分作无数小队。背予舟方向，徐徐引去。行时每一队皆小作停顿，乃复前行。如是者约历两小时。予莫解其意，或谓殆对岸备有船只，此群盗匪分队登舟也。时已向晓三钟，天忽雨，果见有无数盗舟纷纷驶去，有数舟且掠予舟旁而过。直至四钟，乃不复见盗舟踪迹。予等遇此奇险，竟安然无恙，可谓天幸。设非黑夜天雨，或舟不停泊于湾僻处，则不堪设想矣。迨五钟后，一切恐惧焦灼之念，尽归乌有，人人额手相庆，感谢上帝。

更二日，遂安抵山口。予于两星期内，得绿茶十六船，六西人监送至芜湖，更由芜湖易舟运上海，是为第一批。其第二批复十二船，予自护送之。时值盛夏，河水乃干浅。有数处舟不能行，必掘深河底，乃得通过。予命舟人挖泥，舟人难之。予以身作则，躬自入水掘河，水及予腰。众乃不复观望，踊跃将事，河道遂通。

予从事贩茶之事，凡六阅月，前后共得绿茶六万五千箱，然尚不及太平县所有者十之一。乃予忽膺重疾，芜湖不得良医，则就医上海，缠绵病榻，历两月之久始愈。愈后自知体弱不胜劳剧，遂弃所业，不复为茶商。泾县夜中遇险事，过后思量，犹为心悸。当时予虽持镇静态度，然神经系已受非常震动。意此二月之病，未始不种因于此。吾人处世，以生命为基本。倘果为土匪所得，则一死真等于鸿毛。且余既志在维新中国，自宜大处落墨。若仅仅贸迁有无，事业终等于捞月。太平军当时因茶叶畅销，昂其价格。为此手续繁重之事，以博微利，即多金亦属奢愿难偿。静言思之，顿觉前此之非计。不如善自珍摄，留此有用之身。盖至此而余前此之金钱思想，为二竖子破坏无余矣。

予于太平县之役，虽无所获，然任难事而能坚忍，遇危险而能镇定，颇受中西商人疾风劲草之知。以故余因病辞职，病愈即为某公司聘予至九江，为茶叶经理人。虽非所愿，亦姑就之。半年后辞职，自营商业。计在九江三年，境况殊不恶。而余魂梦不忘之教育计划，亦于此时获一机会，有实行之希望焉。

第十三章　与曾文正之谈话

　　1863年，余营业于九江。某日，忽有自安徽省城致书于余者，署名张世贵[①]。张宁波人，余于1857年于上海识之，当时为中国第一炮舰之统带，该舰属上海某会馆者，嗣升迁得入曾文正幕中。余得此书，意殊惊诧。盖此人于我初无若何交谊，仅人海中泛泛相值耳。地则劳燕，风则马牛，相隔数年，忽通尺素，而书中所言，尤属可疑。彼自言承总督之命，邀余至安庆一行，总督闻余名，亟思一见，故特作此书云。当时总督为曾公国藩，私念此大人物者，初无所需于予，急欲一见胡为？予前赴南京，识太平军中渠帅。后在太平县，向革军购茶，岂彼已有所闻欤？忆一年前湘乡驻徽州，为太平军所败，谣言总督已阵亡。时予身近战地，彼遂疑予为奸细，欲置予于法，故以甘言相诱耶？虽张君为人，或不至卖友，然何能无疑。踌躇再三，拟姑复一函，婉辞谢却。余意暂不应召，俟探悉文正意旨，再决从违。故余书中，但云辱荷总督宠召，无任荣幸，深谢总督礼贤下士之盛意；独惜此时新茶甫上市，各处订货者

----

　　① 张世贵：应为张斯桂（1817—1888），字景颜，号鲁生，浙江慈溪人（今宁波）。咸丰元年（1851）被美国传教士丁韪良聘为中文教师。五年（1855）任宝顺轮管带。七年（1857）与容闳在上海相识。同治二年（1863）入两江总督曾国藩幕。三年（1864）在宁波和上海两地经商。十年（1871）入福建船政大臣沈葆桢幕。光绪三年（1877）以即选知府充任出使日本副大臣。七年（1881）任满回京，以知府即选。十二年（1886）任广平知府，两年后卒于任。

多，以商业关系，一时骤难舍去，方命罪甚，他日总当晋谒，云云。

两阅月后，张君之第二函至，嘱予速往，并附李君善兰（即壬叔）[1] 一书。李君亦予在沪时所识者。此君为中国算学大家，曾助伦敦传道会中教士惠来（Rev. Wiley）[2] 翻译算学书甚夥。中有微积学，即予前在耶路大学二年级时，所视为畏途，而每试不能及格者也。予于各科学中，惟算学始终为门外汉，此予所不必深讳者。李君不仅精算学，且深通天文，此时亦在曾文正幕府中，因极力揄扬予于文正，谓曾受美国教育，1857 年赖予力捐得巨款赈饥；且谓其人抱负不凡，常欲效力政府，使中国得致富强。凡此云云，来书中皆详述之。书末谓总督方有一极重要事，欲委予专任，故劝驾速往。并谓某某二君，以研究机器学有素，今亦受总督之聘，居安庆云。

予得此书，疑团尽释，知前此之浅之乎测丈夫也。遂复书，谓更数月后，准来安庆。乃曾文正欲见予之心甚急，七月间予

---

① 李善兰（1811—1882），原名李心兰，字竟芳，号秋纫，别号壬叔，浙江海宁人。道光二十五年（1845）前后在嘉兴陆费家设馆授徒。咸丰二年（1852）夏到上海墨海书馆。咸丰十年（1860）在江苏巡抚徐有壬幕下作幕宾。十一年（1861）秋成为两江总督曾国藩幕僚。同治五年（1866）被广东巡抚郭嵩焘举荐为京师同文馆天文算学总教习，两年后（1868）北上就任。八年（1869）被"钦赐中书科中书"（从七品卿衔）。十年（1871）年加内阁侍读衔，1874 年升户部主事，加六品卿员外衔，1876 年升员外郎（五品卿衔），十八年（1879）加四品卿衔。光绪八年（1882）授三品卿衔户部正郎、广东司行走、总理各国事务衙门章京。

② 惠来（Wiley）：即伟烈亚力（Alexander Wylie，1815—1887），英国基督教新教传教士。1847 年来华，在上海为伦敦会负责印制《圣经》，后参加墨海书馆编辑和翻译工作，编辑《六合丛谈》月刊，筹建"皇家亚洲文会北中国支会"。1860 年休假回国，辞伦敦会职。次年返上海，任大英圣书公会驻华代理人。曾任上海《教务杂志》编辑。1877 年回国。平生著译很多，除与李善兰合译《几何原本》后九卷、《代数学谈天》等介绍西方科技书籍外，亦向西方介绍中国的著作多种，如《中国文献记略》《中国研究录》等。

复得张君之第三函及李君之第二函。两函述文正之意，言之甚悉。谓总督欲予弃商业而入政界，居其属下任事。予初不意得此机缘，有文正其人为余助力，予之教育计划当不患无实行之时。若再因循不往，必致坐失事机。乃立复一书，谓感总督盛意，予已熟思至再，决计应召来安庆。惟经手未完事件，必须理楚。种种手续，当需一月之摒挡。最迟至 8 月间，必可首途矣。此书发后，张李二君遂不复来书相催。是为予预备入政界之第一步。

曾文正为中国历史上最著名人物，同辈莫不奉为泰山北斗。太平军起事后，不久即蔓延数省。曾文正乃于湖南招练团勇，更有数湘人佐之。湘人素勇敢，能耐劳苦，实为良好军人资格，以故文正得练成极有纪律之军队。佐曾之数湘人，后亦皆著名一时，尝组织一长江水师舰队，此舰队后于扬子江上，大著成效。当时太平军蔓延于扬子江两岸，据地极广。而能隔绝其声援，使之首尾不相顾者，则舰队之功为多也。不数年，失陷诸省，渐次克复。太平军势力渐衰，范围日缩，后乃仅余江苏之一省，继且仅余江苏一省中南京一城。迨 1864 年，南京亦卒为曾文正军队所克复。平定此大乱，为事良不易。文正所以能指挥若定，全境肃清者，良以其才识道德，均有不可及者。当时七八省政权，皆在掌握。凡设官任职、国课军需，悉听调度，几若全国听命于一人。顾虽如是，而从不滥用其无限之威权。财权在握，绝不闻其侵吞涓滴以自肥，或肥其亲族。以视后来彼所举以自代之李文忠（鸿章），不可同日语矣。文忠绝命时，有私产四千万以遗子孙。文正则身后萧条，家人之清贫如故也。总文正一生之政绩，实无一污点。其正直廉洁忠诚诸德，皆足为后人模范。故其身虽逝，而名足千古。其才大而谦，气宏而凝，可称完全之真君子，而为清代第一流人物，亦旧教育中之特产人物。是即 1863 年秋间，予得良好机缘所欲往谒者也。

予既将九江商业结束后，遂乘民船于 9 月间抵安庆，迳赴文正大营，得晤故人张世贵、李善兰、华若汀[①]、徐雪村[②]等（译音）。此数人皆予上海旧交相识，见予至，意良欣慰。谓总督自闻予历史后，此六阅月之内，殆无日不思见予一面。张、李二君之连发数函，亦即以此。今予既至，则

曾国藩（1811—1872）

彼等之劝驾已为有效，推毂之力，当不无微劳足录云。予问总督之急欲见予，岂因予以中国人而受外国教育，故以为罕异，抑别有故欤？彼等咸笑不言，第谓君晤总督一二次后，自能知之。予察其状，似彼等已知总督之意，特故靳不以告予。或者总督之意，即彼等所条陈，未可知也。

抵安庆之明日，为予初登政治舞台之第一日。早起，予往谒总督曾公。刺入不及一分钟，阍者立即引予入见。寒暄数语

---

① 华若汀：即华蘅芳（1833—1902），又作华衡芳，字若汀，江苏金匮县（今属江苏无锡）人。咸丰十一年（1861）经江苏巡抚薛焕举荐，入曾国藩幕。同治元年（1862）与徐寿制成中国第一台蒸汽机。四年（1865）与徐寿研制出中国第一艘轮船"黄鹄号"。七年（1868）到上海江南制造局翻译馆工作。光绪十五年（1889）在天津武备学堂试制氢气球。

② 徐雪村：即徐寿（1811—1884），字生元，号雪村，江苏无锡人。咸丰十一年（1861）经江苏巡抚薛焕举荐，入曾国藩幕。同治四年（1865）与华蘅芳研制出中国第一艘轮船"黄鹄号"。五年（1866）襄办江南机器制造总局。七年（1868）在江南制造局设立"翻译馆"。十二年（1873）任江南制造总局提调。十三年（1874）与英国传教士傅兰雅倡议创办上海格致书院。

后，总督命予坐其前，含笑不语者约数分钟。予察其笑容，知其心甚忻慰。总督又以锐利之眼光，将予自顶及踵，仔细估量，似欲察予外貌有异常人否。最后乃双眸炯炯，直射予面，若特别注意于予之二目者。予自信此时虽不至忸怩，然亦颇觉坐立不安。已而总督询予曰："若居外国几何年矣？"予曰："以求学故，居彼中八年。"总督复曰："若意亦乐就军官之职否？"予答曰："予志固甚愿为此，第未习军旅之事耳。"总督曰："予观汝貌，决为良好将材。以汝目光威稜，望而知为有胆识之人，必能发号施令，以驾驭军旅。"予曰："总督奖誉逾恒，良用惭悚。予于从军之事，胆或有之，独惜无军事上之学识及经验，恐不能副总督之期许耳。"

文正问予志愿时，予意彼殆欲予在其麾下任一军官以御敌。后闻予友言，乃知实误会。总督言此，第欲探予性情近于军事方面否耳。及闻予言，已知予意别有所在，遂不复更言此事。后乃询予年事几何？曾否授室？以此数语，为第一次谈话之结束。计约历三十分钟。语毕，总督即举茶送客。予亦如礼还报，遂兴辞出。举茶送客，盖中国官场之一种礼节。凡言谈已尽，则举杯示意，俾来客得以兴辞也。予既出，归予室。关怀之旧友，咸来问讯，细询予见总督时作何状。予详告之，诸友意颇愉快。

余见文正时为1863年，文正已年逾花甲，[①]精神奕然，身长约五尺八九英寸，躯格雄伟，肢体大小咸相称。方肩阔胸，首大而正，额阔且高，眼三角有棱，目眦平如直线。凡寻常蒙古种人，眼必斜，颧骨必高。而文正独无此，两颊平直，髭髯甚

---

① 年逾花甲：实为52岁。曾国藩（1811—1872），生于1811年，1863年为52岁。

多，鬑鬑直连颊下，披覆于宽博之胸前，乃益增其威严之态度。目虽不巨，而光极锐利，眸子作榛色，口阔唇薄，是皆足为其有宗旨有决断之表证。凡此形容，乃令予一见即识之不忘。

文正将才，殆非由于天生，而为经验所养成者。其初不过翰林，由翰林而位至统帅，此其间盖不知经历几许阶级，乃克至此。文正初时所募之湘勇，皆未经训练之兵。而卒能以此湘军，克敌致果，不及十年而告成。当革军势力蔓延之时，实据有中国最富庶之三省。后为文正兵力所促，自1850年至1865年，历十五年之凤患，一旦肃清，良非细故。溯自太平军起事以来，中国政府不特耗费无数金钱，且二千五百万人民之生命，亦皆牺牲于此政治祭台之上。自此乱完全肃清后，人民乃稍稍得喘息。中国之得享太平，与满政府之未被推翻，皆曾文正一人之力也。皇太后以曾文正功在国家，乃锡以爵位，为崇德报功之举。然曾文正之高深，实未可以名位虚荣量之。其所以成为大人物，乃在于道德过人，初不关其名位与勋业也。综公生平观之，后人谥以"文正"，可谓名副其实矣。

今更回述予在安庆之事。当时各处军官，聚于曾文正之大营中者，不下二百人，大半皆怀其目的而来。总督幕府中亦有百人左右。幕府外更有候补之官员、怀才之士子，凡法律、算学、天文、机器等等专门家，无不毕集，几于举全国人才之精华，汇集于此。是皆曾文正一人之声望道德，及其所成就之功业，足以吸引之罗致之也。文正对于博学多才之士，尤加敬礼，乐与交游。予来此约两星期，在大营中与旧友四人同居，长日晤谈，颇不寂寞。一日，予偶又询及总督招予入政界之意。诸友乃明白告予，谓彼等曾进言于总督，请于中国设一西式机器厂，总督颇首肯，议已成熟，惟厂之性质若何，则尚未决耳。某夕诸友邀予晚餐，食际即以此机器厂问题为谈论之资。在座诸君，各有所发表，既乃询予之意见。盖诸友逆知总督第二次接见予时，必且垂询及此，故欲先知予之定见若何也。

予乃告之曰："予于此学素非擅长，所见亦无甚价值。第就予普通知识所及，并在美国时随时观察所得者言之，则谓中国今日欲建设机器厂，必以先立普通基础为主，不宜专以供特别之应用。所谓立普通基础者无他，即由此厂可造出种种分厂，更由分厂以专造各种特别之机械。简言之，即此厂当有制造机器之机器，以立一切制造厂之基础也。例如今有一厂，厂中有各式之车床、锥、锉等物；由此车床、锥、锉，可造出各种根本机器；由此根本机器，即可用以制造枪炮、农具、钟表及其他种种有机械之物。以中国幅员如是之大，必须有多数各种之机器厂，乃克敷用。而欲立各种之机器厂，必先有一良好之总厂以为母厂，然后乃可发生多数之子厂。既有多数子厂，乃复并而为一，通力合作。以中国原料之廉，人工之贱，将来自造之机器，必较购之欧美者价廉多矣。是即予个人之鄙见也。"诸友闻言，咸异常欣悦。谓愿予于总督询及此事时，亦能如是以答之。

数日后，总督果遣人召予。此次谈论中，总督询予曰："若以为今日欲为中国谋最有益最重要之事业，当从何处着手？"总督此问，范围至广，颇耐吾人寻味。设予非于数夕前与友谈论，知有建立机器厂之议者，予此时必以教育计划为答，而命之为最有益最重要之事矣。今既明知总督有建立机器厂之意，且以予今日所处之地位，与总督初无旧交，不过承友人介绍而来；此与予个人营业时，情势略有不同，若贸然提议予之教育计划，似嫌冒昧。况予对于予之朋友，尤当以恪守忠信为惟一之天职。予胸中既有成竹，故对于此重大问题，不至举止失措。以予先期预备答辞，能恰合总督之意见，欲实行时即可实行也。于是予乃将教育计划暂束之高阁，而以机器厂为前提。予对总督之言，与前夕对友所言者略同，大致谓应先立一母厂，再由母厂以造出其他各种机器厂。予所注意之机器厂，非专为制造枪炮者，乃能造成制枪炮之各种机械者也。枪炮之各部，配合至为复杂；而以今日之时势言之，枪炮之于中国，较他物尤为重要，故于此三致意焉。总督闻言，谓予曰："此事予不甚了了，徐、华二君研此有素，若其先与二君详细讨论，后再妥筹办法可耳。"

予辞出后，即往晤诸友。诸友亟欲知予此谈之结果，闻予所述情形，咸极满意。自此次讨论后，诸友乃以建立机器厂之事，完全托付于予，命予征求专门机器工程师之意见。二星期后，华君若汀告予，谓总督已传见彼等四人，决计畀予全权，先往外国探询专门机器工程师，调查何种机器于中国最为适用。将来此种机器应往何国采购，亦听予决定之。

建立机器厂之地点，旋决定为高昌庙。高昌庙在上海城之西北约四英里，厂地面积约数十亩。此机器厂，即今日所称"江南制造局"，其中各种紧要机器工程，无不全备者也。自予由美国采购机器归国以来，中国国家已筹备千百万现金，专储此厂，鸠工制造，冀其成为好望角以东之第一良好机器厂。故此厂实乃一永久之碑，可以纪念曾文正之高识远见。世无文正，则中国今日，正不知能有一西式之机器厂否耶？

第十四章　购办机器

　　自予与曾督第二次晤谈，一星期而有委任状，命予购办机器，另有一官札，授予以五品军功。军功为虚衔，得戴蓝翎。盖国家用兵，以此赏从军有功之人，为文职所无。文职官赏戴花翎，必以上谕颁赐，大员不得随意赏其僚属。又有公文二通，命予持以领款。款银共六万八千两，半领于上海道，半领于广东藩司。余筹备既毕，乃禀辞曾督，别诸友而首途。

　　予此行抵上海，为 1863 年 10 月。其时适有一美国机械工程师名哈司金（Haskins）者，为上海某洋行运机器来华；事毕，方欲挈妻孥返美。而予不先不后，适于此时抵沪，得与其人相值，时机之巧，洵非意料所及者。予既识哈司金，遂以购机器事委其主任，与订立合同。二人皆取道香港，经苏彝士地峡以达伦敦，本可同行，惟哈司金偕其眷属乘法公司轮船，而予则乘英公司船。哈以行期已迫，匆匆别，期会于纽约。船既放洋，途中惟至星加坡略一停泊，遂过印度洋，由锡兰地方登陆，易舟更过孟加拉海湾，于埃及之开罗城登陆。尔时苏彝士河之工程，方开凿未竣，于是予乃由开罗乘火车，过苏彝士地峡，赴亚立山大城，复由亚立山大乘舟至法国之马塞。马塞为法国南方第一海口，哈司金已由此乘舟迳赴英国。予则于马塞上岸，乘火车赴巴黎，作十日游。巴黎之公园、教堂及各处繁盛之区，游览殆遍。此世界著名繁华都会，予得大扩眼界，略知其梗概焉。十日后，遂于法国加来司地方，乘舟过英吉利海峡至英国之多尔维（Dover），由多尔维改乘火车抵伦敦。是为予初次身履英伦之一日，借此良好机会，使予得睹世界第一大都会，于愿良足。予在伦敦，曾往惠特维尔司机器厂（Whitworth's Machine Shop）参观，无意中遇一十年前在中国所识之西友，其名曰克里司特（Christy）。予居伦敦一月，乃乘哥拿脱（Cunard）公司之汽船过大西洋，于1864年春初抵纽约。

予毕业耶路大学，于今十年。予之同班诸学友，将于7月暑假时，开十周纪念联合会。此时方在正二月间，离会期尚远。哈司金因须预备机器图样，订货条款及估价单等，故已偕眷先予至纽约。予以哈氏谙练可恃，遂以选择机器等事，畀以全权。当此1864年时，正南北美战争之末年，美国国内多数机器厂，皆承造国家急需之要件，工作忙迫异常，而以新英国省中为尤甚。以故外来购机器者，急切骤难成议。幸得哈司金素识各厂，乃克于马沙朱色得士省非支波克（Fitchberg, Mass）城中，与朴得南公司（Putnane & Co.）订约，承造此项机器。然亦须半年后，方能造成运回中国云。

予乘此六阅月休息之暇，遂至纽海纹赴耶路大学，参与同班所开之十周纪念联合会。旧雨重逢，一堂聚话，人人兴高采烈，欢乐异常。虽自毕业分袂后，十载于兹，

容闳与美国康州州长（Joseph Hawley，前排中间）合影

容闳 1865 年 1 月美国留影

而诸同学之感情，仍不减当年亲密。予乃有缘得躬与其盛，何幸如之！此会宗旨，既专以联络旧情，作赏心之乐事，故予于胸中所怀，只字不道。况此时南北美战争尚未结束，美人以国事方殷，亦无暇他顾。故于予此次来美所任之事，咸未注意，几无一知之者。第予自念今兹所任购办机器之事，殆为一种应经之阶级，或由此将引予日夕怀思之教育计划，以渐趋于实行之地也。高会既终，友朋星散，予亦兴尽而返。

抵非支波克后，对于南北美战争，忽有感触。因余曩曾入美籍，美国实余第二祖国也。因嘱哈司金暂居此，主持一切，告以将赴华盛顿投效美政府，尽六阅月之义务。设于此六月内发生意外事，致予一时不能遽归，则此机器装运回国之事，当若何处置，拟悉以奉托。哈氏欣然允予请，乃以种种应需之要件，如订货单、提货单、机器价值单，以及保险装运等费，一一交付哈氏。并告以若何手续，点交与曾督所派驻申之委员。筹备既毕，旋即束装就道。时有斯不林非尔地方之总兵名彭司（Brigadier General Barnes）者，方在华盛顿任将军之职，专司义勇队事务。总兵有子曰喊林（William），为香港 ① 著名律师，曾与予同时肄业于耶路大学者也。1863 年 ②，彭总兵至纽海纹探视其子时，予于耶路大学图书馆中，与有一面之素。此时探得彭

① 香港：原文为旧金山。
② 1863 年：当系 1853 年。

君之办公处，在威拉旅馆（Willard Hotel）中，予乃迳往谒之，告以来意。因言："虽他无所能，然若任予以军差之职，传递军书于华盛顿及最近之大营间，供六阅月之驰驱，至所幸愿。且此六月内，予当自备资斧，不敢耗美国国帑。"又言曩在耶路曾晤总兵，总兵亦尚能忆之。乃询予现任何事。予告以自耶路毕业后，向居中国。此来因奉曾大帅国藩之命，至美购办机器，以为中国建设机器厂之预备。刻已于非支波克城由朴得南公司订约承造，另有一美国机械工程师，监督其事。因此项机器制造，须六月后方能告竣，故予甚愿借此余暇，得略尽义务，以表予忠爱美国之诚也。彭总兵闻言甚悦，且极重视此事，乃谓予曰："鄙人极感君之美意，但君现受中国国家重任，故鄙意君宜仍回非支波克，调度一切，以免贻误。此间传递军书，以及趋赴前敌，尚不乏健儿也。"予闻总兵言，知其意已决，遂亦不更置辞再以为请。予此意虽未获实行，而自问对于第二祖国之心，可以尽矣。

第十五章　第二次归国

　　予所购办之机器，直至 1865 年春间始成，由轮船装运，自纽约而东，绕好望角直趋上海，予则不复循来时旧路。盖予之愿望，此生至少环游地球一次。今既得有机会，大可借此游历，以扩眼界，以是决计由旧金山西行。此时太平洋铁路公司，筑路由芝加哥过鄂马哈以达旧金山，工程犹未完竣。故予此行，只能绕道，先乘一沿海轮船，由纽约以至巴拿马地峡，过地峡后，更换船沿墨西哥海岸，以达旧金山。

　　抵旧金山后，迟二星期以待船。由此间赴上海，例横过太平洋。惟尔时驶往远东之邮船，尚未组成大公司，且须美国国家津贴，以故东行之船极少。予欲另觅他舟不可得，不得已乃乘一南多克（Nantucket）之三桅船。船资由旧金山至横滨，每人须美金五百元。是行乘客并予凡六人，船名"亚衣得老及司"（Ida de Rogers），年龄颇老大。船身长约一百五十英尺，舱中既未装货，亦无压重之石，所载惟一舱淡水耳。船上人役，为船主及船主夫人并一六龄之幼子，此外更有大副一人、水手三人、厨役及中国侍者各一人。此船即船主所自有。船主名诺登（Norton），为南多克人。南多克地方出产之航海家，目力甚近，所见不出五步。迨一及金钱，则眼光尤小，锚铢必较。又不独于金钱为然，凡与人交涉，无论事事物物，较及锚铢，利人之事，一毛不拔。船主诺登，足为此种人之代表。予于此行，本极乏味，乃有机会得以研究南多克种人之行为，不可谓非阅历也。

有金门口者，为旧金山出口必由之路。当未过金门时，予等每日之佳肴为咸鲭鱼，咸而腥，不堪下箸。而船主视为珍品，若毕生食之不厌者，遂无日不以是饷客。奈予等口之于味，偏不同嗜。而尤劣者为舟中庖人之烹调法，于是余等每饭如仰药矣。庖人为船主于旧金山临时雇来承乏者，其是否素操此业，实未可知。凡烹咸鲭鱼，未入镬时，法当先浸以水，令其味稍淡。今乃无需此繁重手续，而以速成为工。又不独于鲭鱼为然，即所食玉粟粉制之饼，亦多不熟者，故予等每食不饱。而船主家庭之风趣，亦有令人见而作恶者。船主每发言，非最秽亵者不出诸口。船主夫人虽无之，而于其夫之亵辞秽语，亦处之泰然，有若司空见惯。其幼子年可六龄，箕裘克绍，且能跨灶，种种秽辞，习之极纯熟，不顾而唾。其父母闻之则大慰，殆以为能亢宗；时或回顾乘客，冀邀旁观之称誉。乘客中有英人某，一日方口啣烟斗立于旁，闻是儿口出种种秽言，不能复耐，因顾船主夫妇曰："此儿佳哉，口齿玲珑若百舌，微贤夫妇教育不及此。"船主闻言大乐，对客频颔其首，初不知客之嘲己也。其妻亦信以为真，则左右顾盼，大有自矜之色。凡此怪状，无日不触于耳目，即欲逃避，亦苦无术。因舟小舱狭，甲板上竟无六尺余地，容人著足，惟餐室尚凉爽，为全舟最佳处，故予等长日居此中，以观可厌之丑剧，无可如何也。

行程未及半，泊于檀香山极北之小岛，以装淡水，并添备粮食。予等咸乘此机会纷纷登岸，至田野间散步，神气为之一舒。游行竟日，日暮乃返舟。忽见船主购有多数之火鸡及雏鸡，畜之前舱。予等见此，以为船主购此享客；是殆前此长食盐鲭鱼，船主或亦抱歉，故备此盖愆者，不觉食指之动。迨明日就食，餐桌之上，果有嫩鸡，深幸期望之不虚。乃异味之尝，只此一次，翌晨即复原状；火鸡之肉，则永不出现。怪之，私询厨役，始知此鸡船主之贩卖品，以备售之横滨云。船主之计划良得，但众鸡不惯风涛，于未抵横滨之前数日，无一存者，船主逐利之术犹未工也。长途困顿，度日如年。抵横滨后，亟换英公司汽船以赴上海。

予至上海后，始知一切机器，已于一月前运到，幸皆完全无损。计予离中国年余，大陆已一度沧桑，曾文正已与其弟国荃，克复南京，肃清太平军之大乱矣。时文正方驻徐州，调度诸军以平捻匪。徐州在运河上游，为江苏最北之地。捻匪乃当日安徽之一股土匪也。

余往徐州谒文正，同行者为华君若汀。舟自扬子江仙女庙地方入运河而抵扬州，弃舟陆行，乘骡车，经三日达徐州。曾督对于予之报告，极为嘉许。乃以予购办机器之事，专摺请奖。中国官场之常例，专奏之效力极大。以予毫无官职之人，遂得特授五品实官，此亦特例。其奏章略言："容某为留学西洋之中国学生，精通英文。此行历途万里，为时经年，备历艰辛，不负委托，庶几宏毅之选，不仅通译之材。拟请特授以候补同知，指省江苏，尽先补用，以示优异，而励有功。"

曾督幕府中办奏稿者，于予未离徐州前，即录此稿示予，以得曾督识拔为贺。故予于禀辞时，即面谢曾督之提携，谓愿将来有所成就，不敢以不舞鹤遗羊公羞也。

予留徐三日，即来上海。十月间奉到曾督札文，谓保奏五品实官，已蒙核准。于是予以候补同知之资格，在江苏省行政署为译员，月薪二百五十金。若以官阶论，当日之四品衔候补道，无此厚俸也。

此时任上海道者为丁日昌，与予交颇投契。丁之居官，升迁甚速，由上海道而盐运司，而藩司，未几竟升为江苏巡抚。予亦借丁之力，旋得加衔而戴花翎。当丁任盐运司时，予曾随至扬州。在扬州六个月，译哥尔顿所著之《地文学》(*Colton's Geography*) 一书。6 月后仍回上海，就译员之旧职。公余多暇，复译派森著之《契约论》(*Parsons on Contracts*)，予以为此书与中国甚有用也。此时予幸得一中国文士，助予译事。其人不独长于文墨，精于算学，且于中国政界事务亦甚谙练。彼旋劝予勿译此书，谓纵译毕，亦恐销路不广。因在中国法庭中，因契约而兴诉讼者极少；即或有之，而违背契约之案件，亦自有中国法律可援，外国之法律，实不合于中国情势云。

1867 年，文正得李文忠襄助，平定捻匪，乃至南京就任两江总督。未抵任前，先于所辖境内巡行一周，以视察民情风俗。而尤注意者，则其亲创之江南制造局也。文正来沪视察此局时，似觉有非常兴趣。予知其于机器为创见，因导其历观由美购回各物，并试验自行运动之机，明示以应用之方法。文正见之大乐。予遂乘此机会，复劝其于厂旁立一兵工学校，招中国学生肄业其中，授以机器工程上之理论与实验，以期中国将来不必需用外国机械及外国工程师。文正极赞许，不久遂得实行。今日制造局之兵工学校，已造就无数机械工程师矣。

第十六章　予之教育计划

予自得请于曾文正，于江南制造局内附设兵工学校，向所怀教育计划，可谓小试其锋。既略著成效，前者视为奢愿难偿者，遂跃跃欲试。曾文正者，于余有知己之感，而其识量能力，足以谋中国进化者也。当日政界中重要人物，而与余志同道合者，又有老友丁日昌。丁为人有血性，好任事，凡所措施，皆勇往不缩。当丁升任江苏巡抚，予即谒之于苏州公署，语以所谓教育计划。丁大赞许，且甚注意此事，命予速具详细说帖，彼当上之文相国，请其代奏。文祥满人，时方入相，权力极伟也。予闻丁言，惊喜交集，初不意苏州之行，效力如是，于是亟亟返沪，邀前助予译书之老友（南京人），倩其捉刀，将予之计划，撰为条陈四则，寄呈丁抚，由丁抚转寄北京。略谓：

一、中国宜组织一合资汽船公司。公司须为纯粹之华股，不许外人为股东。即公司中经理、职员，亦概用中国人。欲巩固公司之地位，并谋其营业之发达，拟请政府每年拨款若干以津贴之。其款可由上海镇江及其他各处运往北京之漕米项下，略抽拨数成充之。漕运旧例，皆运米而不解银；每年以平底船装运，由运河驶赴北京。故运河中专为运漕而设之船，不下数千艘。运河两岸之居民，大半皆借运漕为生。但因运法不善，遂致弊端百出。水程迢迢，舟行纡缓，沿途侵蚀，不知凡几。值天气炎热，且有生蛀之患。以故漕米抵京，不独量数不足，米亦朽败不可食。官厅旋亦知其弊，后乃有改用宁波船，由海运至天津，更由天津易平底船以运京。然宁波船之行驶亦甚缓，损失之数，与用平底船等。愚意若汽船公司成立，则平底船及宁波船皆可不用，将来漕米即迳以汽船装运。不独可免沿途之损失，即北方数百万人民仰漕米以为炊者，亦不至常食朽粮也。（此后招商局轮船，即师此法以运漕）

二、政府宜选派颖秀青年，送之出洋留学，以为国家储蓄人材。派遣之法，初次可先定一百二十名学额以试行之。此百二十人中，又分为四批，按年递派，每年派送三十人。留学期限定为十五年。学生年龄，须以十二岁至十四岁为度。视第一、第二批学生出洋留学著有成效，则以后即永定为例，每年派出此数。派出时并须以汉文教习同往，庶幼年学生在美，仍可兼习汉文。至学生在外国膳宿入学等事，当另设留学生监督二人以管理之。此项留学经费，可于上海关税项下，提拨数成以充之。

三、政府宜设法开采矿产以尽地利。矿产既经开采，则必兼谋运输之便利。凡由内地各处以达通商口岸，不可不筑铁路以利交通。故直接以提倡开采矿产，即间接以提倡铁路事业也。（按中国当时尚无良好矿师，足以自行开采。人民尤迷信风水之说，阻力多端。予之此策，第姑列之，使政府知中国实有无穷厚利，不须患贫。且以表示予之计划远大，冀政府能信任予言也）

四、宜禁止教会干涉人民词讼，以防外力之侵入。盖今日外人势力之放恣，已渐有入中国越俎代谋之象。苟留心一察天主教情形，即可知予言之非谬。彼天主教士在中国势力，已不仅限于宗教范围，其对于奉教之中国人，几有管辖全权。教徒遇有民刑诉讼事件，竟由教会自由裁判，不经中国法庭讯理。

是我自有之主权，已于法律上夺去一部分也。是实不正当手段。若不急谋防范，则涓涓不塞，将成江河，故政府当设法禁止。以后无论何国教会，除关于宗教者外，皆不得有权以管理奉教之中国人。

此条陈之第一、三、四，特假以为陪衬；眼光所注而望其必成者，自在第二条。予友谓予，官厅批答公事，例有准驳。吾与以可驳者，而欲得者乃批准矣。且目的所在，列之第二，乃不显有偏重之意也。此条陈上后两阅月，丁抚自苏驰函告予，谓文相国丁内艰。盖中国礼制，凡现任职官，遭父母之丧，谓之“丁艰”。丁艰必退职，居丧三年，不得与闻政事。予得此消息，心意都灰，盖至此而元龙湖海豪气全除矣。抑蹇运之来，天若不厌其酷耶。得第二次噩耗，[①] 希望几绝。盖文祥居丧不三月，亦相继为古人矣。予目的怀之十年，不得一试。才见萌蘖，遽遇严霜，亦安能无怏怏哉！失望久之，烬余复热。自 1868 年至 1870 年，此三年中，无日不悬悬然不得要领。偶因公事谒丁抚，必强聒不已，并恳其常向曾督言此，以免日久淡忘。办事必俟机会，机会苟至，中流自在，否则枉费推移。余非不知此，然时机者，要亦人力所造也。

已而天津人民忽有仇教举动，惨杀多数法国男女僧侣，其结果使中国国家蒙极大之不幸。予乃因此不幸之结果，而引为实行教育计划之机会，洵匪夷所思。然使予之教育计划果得实行，借西方文明之学术以改良东方之文化，必可使此老大帝国，一变而为少年新中国。是因仇教之恶果，而转得维新之善因，在中国国家未始非塞翁失马，因祸得福也。

天津仇教事，发生于 1870 年春间。所以演成此惨剧者，则

---

① 按文义，此句前当加“旋又”二字。

以北方人民，类皆强悍而无识，迷信而顽固，遂因误会以酿成极大之暴动。先是天津有恶俗：贫民无力养其子女者，恒弃之道旁，或沉溺河中。天主教僧侣，悯其无辜，乃专事收育此等弃儿，养之医院，授以教育，稍长则令其执役于教会之中。此实有益之慈善事业，顾蛊蛊者氓，误会其意，造为无稽之说，谓教会中人取此弃儿，藏之医院及教堂中，将其双目挖去，以配药剂，或则作为祭祀之供献品。此等荒唐可哂之谣言，恰合于天津愚民之心理，故一时谣传极广。因市虎之讹，竟激起人心之愤。久之又久，祸机乃不可遏，遂不恤孤注一掷，取快一朝，虽铸错而不悔也。计是役焚毁天主教医院及教堂各一所，杀毙教中法国男女僧侣无数。

此暴动发生之际，崇厚[①]适为直隶总督。此人前曾任俄国公使，今甫督直而即值此暴动，可谓大不幸。盖中国律例，凡地方有变故者，长官须负其责，故崇厚遂因此革职，发配边远地方充军。迨后中国政府，允以巨款赔偿被害人之家族，并建还所焚毁之医院、教堂，更以政府名义发正式公函，向法国道歉，事乃得寝。幸尔时普法战争未已，法政府在恐慌中，故未遑以全力对付中国。否则必且借题发挥，肆意诛求，以履其贪饕，交涉恐未易就范。但此次虽无难堪之要索，然后来中国属地安南东京之一片土，卒因是不我属矣。

---

① 崇厚（1826—1893），完颜氏，字地山，号子谦。内务府镶黄旗人。河道总督麟庆之子，署盛京将军崇实之弟。道光二十九年（1849）举人，选任阶州知州。历任长芦盐运使，大理寺卿。咸丰十年（1860）协助恭亲王奕䜣与英、法议和。次年升任三口通商大臣。后署直隶总督，在天津组织洋枪队，与捻军对抗。同治六年（1867）创办军火机器总局。九年（1870）天津教案后，被派为钦差大臣赴法国"谢罪"。光绪四年（1878）充出使俄国大臣，谈判交还伊犁问题，因擅自签订《里瓦几亚条约》，受到舆论谴责，被捕入狱，定为斩监候。十年（1884）输银 30 万两获释，以原官降二级使用。

中国政府当日曾派大臣四人调停，四人为曾文正、丁日昌、毛昶熙、其一人刘姓忘其名①。是时捻匪虽渐平，尚未肃清。李文忠身在戎行，未与闻斯役。丁奉派后，电招予为译员。电至略晚，不及与同行，予乃兼程赴津。抵津后，尚得与闻末后数次之谈判。此交涉了结后，钦派之诸大臣，留天津未即散。而予乃乘此时会，十余年梦想所期者，得告成功焉。

---

　　① 刘姓忘其名：可能是刘铭传，天津教案发生后，曾国藩将驻守山东张秋的淮军刘铭传部调至天津附近的沧州防御，刘铭传并非办案大臣。清政府派出的四位办案大臣分别是：工部尚书兼总理衙门大臣毛昶熙、浙江巡抚丁日昌、三口通商大臣崇厚和直隶总督曾国藩。

第十七章　经理留学事务所（派送第一批留学生）

　　钦派四大臣中，曾文正实为领袖。当诸人未散时，予乃乘机进言于丁抚，请其向曾督重提教育事，并商诸其他二人。予知丁于三年前已向曾督及此，故曾当已略知此中梗概，丁又素表同情于予，得此二公力助，余二人当无不赞成矣。一夕，丁抚归甚晚，予已寝。丁就予室，呼予起，谓此事已得曾公同意，将四人联衔入奏，请政府采择君所条陈而实行之。予闻此消息，乃喜而不寐，竟夜开眼如夜鹰，觉此身飘飘然如凌云步虚，忘其为偃卧床笫间。两日后，奏折拜发，文正领衔，余三人皆署名，由驿站加紧快骑，飞递入京。此时曾督及余人皆尚在津沽也。

丁抚旋荐陈兰彬[①]于予，谓将来可副予为中国留学生监督[②]。陈乃中国翰林，在刑部任主事垂二十年。丁抚之荐陈，盖有深意。尝谓余："君所主张，与中国旧学说显然反对。时政府又甚守旧，以个人身当其冲，恐不足以抵抗反动力，或竟事败于垂成。故欲利用陈之翰林资格，得旧学派人共事，可以稍杀阻力也。"予闻丁抚此议，极佩其思虑周密。丁抚旋发函召陈，

① 陈兰彬（1816—1895），字荔秋（丽秋），号均暾，广东高州府吴川县黄坡村人（今属湛江吴川市）。道光十五年（1835）廪膳生。十七年（1837）获优贡生，授翁源训导不就，入京师国子监。二十六年（1846）再度赴京求学，并游历西北。咸丰元年（1851）参加顺天府恩科乡试，考中举人。三年（1853）参加恩科会试，考中进士，改翰林院庶吉士，充国史馆纂修。旋蒙直隶总督桂良奏调，赴直隶军营，奖给六品翎顶。六年（1856）改刑部主事江西司行走、山东清吏司主稿。八年（1858）由两广总督黄宗汉奏调办理外务。十年（1860）丁母忧还乡，聘为高文书院山长，并参与剿灭陈金釭。同治二年（1863）守制满，入京补原官；又以军功，升四品衔，赏戴花翎。三年（1864）丁父忧回籍。六年（1867）守制满，回京供职。八年（1869）由直隶总督曾国藩调用。九年（1870）天津教案后，曾国藩改督两江，奏调陈兰彬出任上海机器局兼上海广方言馆总办。十一年（1872）任出洋肄业局总办，率领第一批官学生赴美肄业。十二年（1873）赴古巴调查华工受奴役与迫害情事。十三年（1874）奉调回国，协助总理各国事务衙门与西班牙的谈判。光绪元年（1875）以三四品京堂候补赏二品顶戴担任出使美日秘三国大臣。二年（1876）授太常寺卿。四年（1878）补宗人府府丞，赴美国履任，设驻华盛顿使署和驻旧金山领事馆。五年（1879）赴西班牙履任，设驻马德里使署和驻古巴岛领事馆，擢都察院左副都御史。六年（1880）设驻夏威夷国商董，代办外交事宜。七年（1881）奏请改驻夏威夷国商董为领事。七年（1881）任满回国，任总理各国事务大臣，先后署兵部右侍郎、充壬午科乡试较射大臣。九年（1883）先后任癸未科会试复试阅卷大臣、武会试较射大臣、署礼部左侍郎。十年（1884）因病开缺回籍，讲学高文书院，先后参与纂修《高州府志》《吴川县志》《石城县志》等。光绪二十年十二月十四日（1895年1月9日）在吴川家中去世，谥号"文毅"，葬于化州笪桥镇水碓洞村瓦面岭。

② 将来可副予为中国留学生监督：原文意为"决定由丁抚举荐陈兰彬，与予共同负责留学事务"。

陈兰彬（1816—1895，字荔秋）

数日后，津中有为曾、丁诸公祖饯者，予及陈兰彬均在座，丁抚遂为余等介绍。予之与陈，素未识面，今则将为共事之人矣。陈居刑部二十年，久屈于主事末秩，不得升迁，以故颇侘傺不自得，甚愿离去北京。居京除刑曹外，亦未任他事，故于世途之经验甚浅。其为人持躬谦抑，平易近人，品行亦端正无邪，所惜者胆怯而乏责任心耳。即一羽之轻，陈君视之，不啻泰山，不敢谓吾力足以举之。

1870年冬，曾文正办天津教案事毕，回任两江。抵南京后，奉到前所上封奏硃批，着照所请。曾督即驰书召予，商此事之进行。至此予之教育计划，方成为确有之事实，将于中国二千年历史中，特开新纪元矣。既抵南京，所商定者凡四事：曰派送出洋学生之额数；曰设立预备学校；曰筹定此项留学经费；曰酌定出洋留学年限。有种种应办事宜，势不能无办事机关，于是乃有事务所之组织，酌设监督二人、汉文教习二人、翻译一人。监督即陈兰彬及予任之。二人之责任，亦复划清权限。陈君专司监视学生留美时汉文有无进步，予则监视学生之各种科学，并为学生预备寄宿舍等事。至关于经费之出纳，则由予二人共主之。此外所聘汉文教员二人，一名叶绪东^①，一名容云甫^②（译音），翻译则为曾兰生。此当日留学事务所组织情形也。

既稍有头绪，乃议派送之学额并招考章程。旋决定学生人数，照予前次所拟，暂定为百二十人，分四批，每批三十人，按年分送出洋。学生年龄，定为十二岁以上，十五岁以下，须身家清白，有殷实保证，体质经医士检验，方为合格。考试科目为汉文之写读；其曾入学校已习英文者，则并须试验其英文。应考及格后，当先入预备学校，肄习中西文字，至少一年，方可派赴美国留学。当未出洋之先，学生之父兄须签名于志愿书，书中载明自愿听其子弟出洋留学十五年（自抵美入学之日起，至学成止）；十五年中如有疾病死亡及意外灾害，政府皆不负责。至于学生留学经费及出洋之服装等，皆由政府出资供给。每批学生放洋时，并派一汉文教习随同偕往，此规定学额及招考章程之大略也。

予与曾督筹议甚久。议定后乃返上海，为第一步之进行。先于上海设立一预备学校，此校至少须能容学生三十人；因必有此数，方能足第一批派送之定额也。时有久居曾督幕府之刘

---

① 叶绪东：即叶源浚（？—1879），字绪东，江苏江宁人（今南京）。同治十一年（1872）随陈兰彬携带首批幼童赴美，任肄业局教习。十三年（1874）随陈兰彬赴古巴调查华工情况。光绪元年（1875）与陈兰彬回国，协助总理衙门与西班牙商定古巴华工条款。次年陈兰彬奏调为出使美日秘随员。四年（1878）随陈兰彬出使美国，任参赞。五年（1879）随陈兰彬赴西班牙，因病殁于巴黎。

② 容云甫：即容增祥，原名家杰，族名瑞龙，字世膺，号元甫，广东新会人。同治六年（1867）丁卯科乡试举人，捐内阁中书。同治十一年（1872）任出洋肄业局汉文教习。光绪四年（1878）调任驻美使馆参赞，兼任出洋肄业局总办。次年丁忧回籍，未再出仕。

开成^①者，奉派为该校校长。刘在曾督幕府，专司奏稿，为曾督第一信任之人，故任以此职。予接见刘君，觉其人实予良好之臂助，即平常相处，亦可称为益友，对于予之教育计划，尤抱热心。后此四批学生，预备期满，陆续派送，皆由刘君一手料量，始终其事焉。

当 1871 年之夏，予因所招学生未满第一批定额，乃亲赴香港，于英政府所设学校中，遴选少年聪颖而于中西文略有根柢者数人，以足其数。时中国尚无报纸以传播新闻，北方人民多未知中政府有此教育计划，故预备学校招考时，北人应者极少。来者皆粤人，粤人中又多半为香山籍。百二十名官费生中，南人十居八九，职是故也。

1871 年冬间，曾文正公薨于南京，寿七十有一。曾之逝世，国家不啻坏其栋梁，无论若何，无此损失巨也。时预备学校开学才数月，设天假以年，使文正更增一龄者，则第一批学生已出洋，犹得见其手植桃李，欣欣向荣。惜夫世之创大业者，造化往往不锡以永年，使得亲见手创事业之收效。此种缺憾，自古如斯。然创业之人，既播其种子于世，则其人虽逝，而此种子之孳生繁殖，固已绵绵不绝。故文正种因虽未获亲睹其结果，而中国教育之前途，实已永远蒙其嘉惠。今日莘莘学子，得受文明教育，当知是文正之遗泽，勿忘所自来矣。文正一生之政绩、忠心、人格，皆远过于侪辈，殆如埃浮立司脱（Mt. Everest）高峰，独耸于喜马拉耶诸峰之上，令人望而生景仰之思。予闻文正临危时，犹念念不忘教育事业，深望继己之李文

---

① 刘开成：应为刘开生，即刘翰清（1824—1882），字开孙、开生，江苏常州府武进人。道光二十六年（1846）顺天府举人，候选主事。咸丰十一年（1861）以军功保举知府。同治元年（1862）加入曾国藩幕府。同治十年（1871）协办留美幼童事宜。

忠，有以竟其未竟之志云。

李文忠虽为曾文正所荐举以自代之人，顾其性情品格，与文正迥不相侔。其为人感情用事，喜怒无常，行事好变迁，无一定宗旨。而生平大病，尤在好闻人之誉己。其外貌似甚卤莽，实则胸中城府甚深。政治之才，固远不逮文正；即其人之忠诚与人格，亦有不可同日而语者。设有燃犀史笔传之，则其一生行为，如探海灯烛物，秋毫无遁形矣。（铁樵谨按：文忠事迹俱在，功罪自有定评，不必因此数言，遂累盛德。昔眉山、伊川意见不合，遂以君子而互相水火。是容先生此语，亦未必便为失言。此书悉照原本意思，不敢稍有出入，致失真相，阅者鉴之）

1872 年夏季之末，第一批学生三十人，渡太平洋而赴美国。予先期行，抵美后，即乘火车过华盛顿而至纽约，再由纽约赴斯不林非尔，将于此预先布置学生住宿诸事。盖予与彼等，约于此处期会也。当由纽约赴斯不林非尔时，道经纽海纹，遇海德列先生（Prof. James Hadley）。海闻予任此重职，复来美国，班荆道故，不胜欢欣。予告以一人先至之故，海君嘱予往谒康纳特克省之教育司，谓渠当能代予筹划。予如言谒教育司拿德

1872 年 9 月，第一批留美幼童中的六人在旧金山的合影（从左向右：钟文耀、梁敦彦、不详、史锦镛、不详、牛尚周）

鲁布（Northrop）君，告以来意，请其指示。拿谓当将学生分处于新英国省之各人家，每家二三人，但须相去不远，庶便于监视。俟将来学生程度已能入校直接听讲时，乃更为区处。予如其教，即至斯不林非尔觅一适宜之所，以为办事处。盖斯不林非尔地处新英国省中心点，居此易于分配学生，使各去予不远也。况予于 1854 年所识之好友麦克林夫妇（Dr. and Mrs. A. S. McCLean）亦居此，公余之暇，得常与良友把晤，亦人生乐事。后因从教育司拿德鲁布及他友之言，乃迁居于哈特福德地方，其地即康纳特克之省城。此后二年，办事处皆在哈特福德之森孟纳街（Sumner Street）。予虽迁居哈特福德，顾未愬置斯不林非尔，仍以其处为分派学生之中心点。后之学生来美者，皆先至斯不林非尔，然后再分派各处，直至 1875 年乃已。

1874 年，李文忠从留学事务所之请，命予于哈特福德之克林街（Collins Street）监造一坚固壮丽之屋，以为中国留学事务所永久办公之地。次年春正月，予即迁入此新居。有楼三层，极其宏敞，可容监督、教员及学生七十五人同居。屋中有一大课堂，专备教授汉文之用。此外则有餐室一、厨室一，及学生之卧室、浴室等。予之请于中国政府，出资造此坚固之屋以为办公地点，初非为徒壮观瞻，盖欲使留学事务所在美国根深蒂固，以冀将来中政府不易变计以取销此事，此则区区之过虑也。而讵知后来之事，乃有与予意背道而驰者。

1872 年 9 月钟文耀（左）和牛尚周（右）在美国旧金山合影

美国康州哈特福德出
洋肄业局大楼

出洋肄业局会客厅

出洋肄业局大楼教室

出洋肄业局教习讲授
汉学情形

第十八章　秘鲁华工之调查

1873 年春，予以谋输入一种新式军械于中国，曾归国一行。此行程途迅速，不敢少延，盖此时予固有教育职务在身也。予所谓新式军械，乃格特林（Gatling，人名）新发明之物，为战争中利器，炮亦即名"格特林"。予甚愿中国有最新式之军械，犹望中国有新学问之人材也。故特至格特林公司，欲与商订合同，予愿为之经理，专销此种军械于中国。初时颇为困难，公司中因未识予之为人，故于予商业上之经验，未敢遽信。彼盖未知予于 1860 及 1861 两年在太平县贩茶之事，固尝大著成效，冒众人所不敢冒之险者。后费种种手续，亲谒其总理格特林（即创此新炮之人），与之谈论此事，几于唇焦舌敝，始得总理之允诺，托予为中国之经理人，为之推广新炮销路。予既归国，抵天津甫一月，即致电该公司，订购格特林新炮五十尊，价约十万美金。公司初颇轻予，今初次即成此大宗交易，实彼等意料所不及。后复陆续订购不少，于是公司对于予所经理之事业，大为满意；而对予之态度，遂不复如前之落漠矣。

予在津经理军械贸易时，直督告予，谓有秘鲁专使来此，拟与中国订约，招募华工赴秘鲁。命予往谒专使，与之谈判此事。予奉命往见，秘鲁专使颜色极和霁，历言华工在秘鲁营业若何发达，秘鲁政府若何优待，工资之厚为中国所绝无。故彼甚愿中政府速与秘鲁订约，鼓励多数华工赴秘鲁，俾此贫困之华人，咸得获此良好机会，以各谋其生活云云。此种币重言甘之辞，在他人闻之，鲜不堕其术中，顾予则非其人也。予于华工之事，所见已多，深知此中真相。因以质直之辞告之曰："贩卖华工，在澳门为一极寻常之事，予已数见不鲜。此多数同胞之受人凌虐，予固常目击其惨状。当其被人拐诱，即被禁囚室中不令出。及运奴之船至，乃释出驱之登船。登船后即迫其签字，订作工之约，或赴古巴，或赴秘鲁。抵埠登岸后，列华工于市场，若货物之拍卖，出价高者得之。既被卖去，则当对其新主人，再签字另立一合同，订明作工年限。表面上虽曰订年限，实则此限乃永无满期。盖每届年限将满时，主人必强迫其重签新约，直欲令华工终身为其奴隶而后已。以故行时，每于中途演出可骇之惨剧。华工被诱后，既悟受人之愚，复受虐待之苦，不胜悲愤，辄于船至大洋四无涯际时，群起暴动以反抗。力即不足，宁全体投海以自尽。设或竟以人多而战胜，则尽杀贩猪仔之人及船主水手等，一一投尸海中以泄忿。纵船中无把舵之人，亦不复顾，听天由命，任其飘流。凡此可惊可怖之事，皆予所亲闻亲见者。予今明白告君，君幸毋希望予能助君订此野蛮之条约。不惟不能助君，且当力阻总督，劝其毋与秘鲁订约，而为此大背人道之贸易也。"

秘鲁专使闻予言，大为失望，初时和颜悦色之假面具，猝然收去，代以满面怒容。即予亦自觉悻悻之色，不可遏止。盖述此惨无人理之往事，不期而发指也。因亦不顾秘使之喜怒若何，语毕，遽兴辞而出。予对秘使所言，在未曾目击者，或疑予言不无过甚。不知语语皆真确，无一字虚妄。当1855年，予初次归国时，甫抵澳门，第一遇见之事，即为无数华工，以辫相连，结成一串，牵往囚室。其一种奴隶牛马之惨状，及今思之，犹为酸鼻。又某次予在广州时，曾亲获贩猪仔之拐匪数人，送之官厅，拘禁狱中，罚其肩荷四十磅重大木枷两月，亦令其稍受苦楚也。予即报命直督，告以与秘使①谈判之言。总督谓予曰："汝此次返国大佳，否则予亦将电召汝归矣。今予即命汝至秘鲁一行，以调查彼中华工实在之情形。汝其速返哈特福德，部署一切，以备启行。

予勉奉命返至哈特福德，陈兰彬亦适奉政府之电，派其赴古巴调查华工情形。此双方进行之举，盖亦出于李文忠之意。予乃先陈兰彬而启行。行时有二友为予伴，一为吐依曲尔牧师（Rev. Twitchell），一为开洛克博士（Dr. Kellogg），开君即予后日之妻兄。予至秘鲁，以迅速之手段，三阅月内即调查完竣，一切报告皆已造齐。返美时，陈兰彬犹未首途。直俟陈自古巴返，造齐报告后，予之报告书乃与之一并封寄李文忠，以文忠时方掌外交事务也。

予之报告书中，另附有二十四张摄影。凡华工背部受笞、被烙斑斑之伤痕，令人不忍目睹者，予乃借此摄影，一一呈现于世人之目中。予摄此影，皆于夜中秘密为之。除此身受其虐之数华工外，无一人知之者。此数名可怜之华工，亦由予密告以故，私约之来也。秘鲁华工之工场，直一牲畜场。场中种种野蛮之举动，残暴无复人理，摄影特其一斑耳。有此确凿证据，无论口若悬河，当亦无辩护之余地。

彼秘鲁所派之专使，欲与李

杜渣牧师（Rev. Twichell, 1838—1918）

---

① 秘使，指秘鲁专使。

文忠订约招募华工者，仍久滞天津，专俟予之调查报告到津，以决订约之成否。后有友人发函告予，述秘使在津之行为，谓彼初犹坚不承认予之报告，斥为空中楼阁，毫无事实可据。然予已预防其出此，故于报告中密请总督暂秘摄影之片，勿示秘使。俟彼理穷词遁，专以"无证据"为言时，然后再出此影以示之，使彼更无一辞之可措。总督果从予言，秘使出不意睹此真确可据之摄影，乃嗫不能声，垂头丧气而去。自予报告秘鲁调查情形，政府遂以华工出洋著为禁令。"猪仔"之祸，乃不如前此甚矣。

美国康州哈特福德容闳家

美国康州哈特福德容闳晚年故居

第十九章　留学事务所之终局

最后一批学生，于 1875 年秋间抵美。同时偕来者，有新监督区岳良[①]、新翻译邝其照，更有汉文教习二人，皆为李文忠所派者。兹数人予曩在中国亦皆识之，而于区、邝二君交尤熟。此次更动之原因，出于陈兰彬一人之意。陈以急欲请假回国，遂请政府另派新监督以代其职。又陈于古巴调查华工之役，深得汉文教习叶绪东之臂助；故此次归国，并欲携叶偕行。而旧日翻译曾兰生，亦以他故，政府命其交卸回国。予于数月前已知有此更动，不以为意也。

自陈归北京三月，中政府忽派陈兰彬并予同为驻美公使，叶绪东亦得参赞。以常理论，是为迁擢，事属可喜，然予则不以为荣以为忧。予友皆贺予升迁，盖亦未就全局之关系一着想。若专就予一身言，以区区留学生监督，一跃而为全权公使，是政府以国士遇我，受知遇而不感激，非人情；但以教育计划言，是予视为最大事业，亦报国之惟一政策。今发轫伊始，植基未

---

① 区岳良：当为区谔良（1839—？），字黼猷，号海峰，广东南海人。同治六年（1867）举人。十年（1871）进士，改翰林院庶吉士。十三年（1874）散馆以部属用，签分工部。光绪元年（1875）携带第四批幼童赴美，任驻洋肄业局总办。四年（1878）任满回国，仍回工部任职，奉旨免补主事以员外郎即补。次年补虞衡司员外郎。六年（1880）回京销差。次年补行验放。九年（1883）与康有为在广东南海创立不裹足会。十七年（1891）补都水司郎中。十九年（1893）俸满截取，经工部堂官保送堪胜繁缺知府。二十年（1894）经工部堂官保送，以知府分发补用指省江西。余事不详。

区谔良（1839—？）

固，一旦舍之他去，则继予后者，谁复能如予之热心，为学生谋幸福耶？况予与诸学生相处既久，感情之亲不啻家人父子；予去，则此诸生且如孤儿失怙，是恶可者？默揣再四，乃上书总督，略谓："过蒙逾格擢升，铭感无既。第公使责任重大，自顾庸朽不堪负荷。拟乞转请政府收回成命，俾得仍为学生监督，以期始终其事。俟将来留学诸生，学成种种专门学术，毕业归来，能为祖国尽力，予乃卸此仔肩。如是量而后入，予个人对于祖国，得略尽其天职。且此学生皆文正手植，譬之召伯甘棠，尤愿自我灌溉之，俾得告无罪于文正。况政府既已派陈兰彬为公使，则外交事务以陈独当一面，必能胜任，固无需予之襄助也。"是书予倩容云甫属稿缮就，寄之中国。容云甫即偕第一批学生来美，与叶绪东同为汉文教习者也。书上后四月，总督有覆函来，不准不驳，亦允亦否。盖命予为副公使而兼监督之任，俾予于留学生方面，仍得有权调度一切也。

新监督区岳良，大约即陈兰彬所举荐，此行与一妻二子俱来。区君较陈兰彬为年少，虽非翰林，出身固亦中国饱学之文士。其人沉默静穆，对于一切事物，皆持哲学观念，不为已甚。其于前人布置已定之局，绝不愿纷更破坏之。观其所言所行，胸中盖颇有见地。惜此君任事未久，于1876年即辞职归国。

1876年，陈兰彬以全权公使之资格，重履美土，一时携

1878 年留美幼童组成的棒球队合影
（后排左起：蔡绍基、钟俊成、吴仲贤、詹天佑、黄开甲）
（前排左起：陈巨溶、李桂攀、梁敦彦、邝咏钟）

来僚属极多。中有一人曰吴子登[①]，予约于二十年前曾在上海识之。其人亦为翰林，第不知何故从未指分各部授职，亦从未得政府之特别差委。闻其人好研究化学，顾所研究亦殊未见其进步。凡与吴交者，咸赠吴以"性情怪僻"四字之考语。当区岳良辞监督职时，陈兰彬乃荐此性情怪僻者以继任，李文忠亦竟贸然允陈之请，于是留学界之大敌至矣。吴子登本为反对党之一派[②]，其视中国学生之留学外洋，素目为离经叛道之举；又因前与曾文正、丁日昌二人不睦，故于曾、丁二公所创之事业，尤思破坏，不遗余力。凡此行径，予初不之知，乃陈兰彬属下代理秘鲁公使某君告予者。然则陈兰彬之荐吴继区，可知陈亦极顽固之旧学派，其心中殆早不以遣派留学为然矣。陈之此举，

----

①　吴嘉善（1820—1885），字子登，江西南丰人。咸丰二年（1852）进士，散馆授翰林院编修。同治二年（1863）任广州同文馆汉文总教。光绪三年（1877）陈兰彬奏调出使。次年随使美国。五年（1879）任驻西班牙参赞。次年任肄业局总办。七年（1881）回国。著有《翻译小补》《测圆密率》《尖锥变法解》《算学二十一种》等书籍。

②　反对党之一派：按文意为"反对派之一员"。

不啻表示其自居反对党代表地位，揎拳掳袖，准备破坏新政，以阻中国前途之进步。甚矣，知人之难也。

陈既挟此成见，故当其任监督时，与予共事，时有龃龉。每遇极正当之事，大可著为定律，以期永久遵行者，陈辄故为反对以阻挠之。例如学生在校中或假期中之正杂各费，又如学生寄居美人寓中随美人而同为祈祷之事，或星期日至教堂瞻礼，以及平日之游戏、运动、改装等问题，凡此琐琐细事，随时发生。每值解决此等问题时，陈与学生常生冲突，予恒居间为调停人。但遇学生为正当之请求，而陈故靳不允，则予每代学生略为辩护。以是陈疑予为偏袒学生，不无怏怏。虽未至形诸词色，而芥蒂之见，固所不免。盖陈之为人，当未至美国以前，足迹不出国门一步。故于揣度物情，评衡事理，其心中所依据为标准者，仍完全为中国人之见解。即其毕生所见所闻，亦以久处专制压力之下，习于服从性质，故绝无自由之精神与活泼之思想。而此多数青年之学生，既至新英国省，日受新英国教育之淘镕，且习与美人交际，故学识乃随年龄而俱长。其一切言行举止，受美人之同化而渐改其故态，固有不期然而然者，此不足为学生责也。况彼等既离去故国而来此，终日饱吸自由空气，其平昔性灵上所受极重之压力，一旦排空飞去，言论思想，悉与旧教育不侔，好为种种健身之运动，跳踯驰骋，不复安行矩步，此皆必然之势，何足深怪。但在陈兰彬辈眼光观之，则又目为不正当矣。

陈兰彬自赴华盛顿后，与哈特福德永远断绝关系。因有以上种种原因，故其平素对于留学事务所，感情极恶。即彼身所曾任之监督职务，亦久存厌恶之心。推彼意想，必以为其一己所受纯洁无瑕之中国教育，自经来美与外国教育接触，亦几为其所污染。盖陈对于外国教育之观念，实存一极端鄙夷之思也。

虽然，陈之此种观念，亦未免自忘其本矣。独不思彼一生之发迹，固由于此素所厌弃之事业耶？设无此留学事务所，则彼亦安能以二十年刑部老主事，一旦而为留学生监督？更安得由留学生监督，一跃而为华盛顿公使？是则此留学事务所者，固大有造于陈兰彬，不啻为其升官发财之阶梯。陈苟能稍稍念木本水源，则不当登高而撤梯。乃不谓其尽忘前事，极力欲破坏予之教育计划，而特荐吴子登为留学生监督。吴之为陈傀儡，又恰合其身份。盖舍吴而外，固无人能受陈黑幕中之指挥也。吴既任监督，而留学事务所乃无宁岁矣。

　　1876 年秋间，吴既任事，对于从前已定之成规，处处吹毛求疵，苛求其短。顾有所不满意，又不明以告予，惟日通消息于北京，造为种种谣言：谓予若何不尽职，若何纵容学生，任其放荡淫佚，并授学生以种种不应得之权利，实毫无裨益；学生在美国，专好学美国人为运动游戏之事，读书时少而游戏时

陈兰彬使团于 1878—1881 年间在华盛顿租用的使馆大楼

107

多；或且效尤美人，入各种秘密社会，此种社会有为宗教者，有为政治者，要皆有不正当之行为；坐是之故，学生绝无敬师之礼，对于新监督之训言，若东风之过耳；又因习耶教科学，或入星期学校，故学生已多半入耶稣教；此等学生，若更令其久居美国，必致全失其爱国之心，他日纵能学成回国，非特无益于国家，亦且有害于社会；欲为中国国家谋幸福计，当从速解散留学事务所，撤回留美学生，能早一日施行，即国家早获一日之福云云。

吴子登日毁予于北京友人及李文忠前，予初毫无闻知。后文忠有书来，以吴报告之言转告，命予注意。予乃知吴媒孽予短，因亦作书报文忠。书中略谓："凡此捕风捉影之谈，皆挟私恨者，欲造谣生事，以耸听闻。予固知造此言者，其人性情乖张，举止谬妄，往往好为损人不利己之事。似此荒谬之人，而任以重职，实属大误。今彼且极力思破坏从前曾文正所创之事业。夫文正之创此留学事务所，其意固将为国家谋极大幸福也。吴子登苟非丧心病狂，亦何至欲破坏此有益于国之事？愚以为若吴子登其人者，只宜置之疯人院或废病院中，恶足以任留学生监督？且举荐吴者实为陈兰彬，陈亦怯懦鄙夫，生平胆小如鼠，即极细微之事，亦不敢担负丝毫责任。予之与陈共事，无论外交方面，教育方面，意见咸相左。予今试略举一事：1873年政府派陈赴古巴调查华工情形，陈奉命不敢遽往，迟至三月后乃首途。且于未行之先，先遣他人为之试探。所遣者为叶绪东及一教员，并有美国律师及通译各一人。迨诸人调查既竣，事事完备，陈乃至古巴略一周旋，即返美呈报销差矣。凡冒炎暑任艰巨之事，皆叶绪东一人当之，陈兰彬特坐享其成耳。今则陈兰彬已升迁公使，而叶绪东乃仅得参赞。予之为此言，非有所私憾于陈兰彬而德叶绪东，第见政界中往往有此不平之事，无功受禄转来不虞之誉，劳苦功高反有求全之毁。总督明察，当知予之所言，非有所掩著。盖予固甚愿辞公使之职，仍退处于监督旧任，俾得专心于教育事业，冀将来收良好之效果。即如某日因事致书于美国国务院，予与陈兰彬意见不合，致有争论。尔时予曾语陈谓：无论副使公使若何尊荣，皆不在予心目中，予已预备随时辞职，以便足下独断独行。斯言也，亦足以表明予之心迹矣。"

予为此详细之报告以覆总督，欲其知予之历史及陈、吴二人之行为也。至于总督以何言告陈兰彬，则非予所得知矣。第此后公使馆及留学事务所两处，表面上似觉暂时平静，并无何等冲突。会有数学生程度已高，予意欲送其入陆海军学校肄业，乃致书美国国务院，求其允准。美国国务院复书，则以极轻藐之词，简单拒绝予请。其言曰：此间无地可容中国学生也。嗟夫，中国之见轻于美人，其由来也渐矣。先是有美国工党首领某某二人，创议反对华工。太平洋沿海一带人民咸受其煽惑，即美政府及行政各部亦在其催眠术中，而以美国国会为尤甚。当时有上议院议员名白伦（Blaine）者，最为兴高采烈，首先创议反对华人。推白伦之心理，亦非与华人有深仇夙恨，不过其时脑中有欲作总统之妄想，遂假此题目以博誉于工党，冀得太平洋沿海一带之选举票也。自有此议以来，美人种族之见日深，仇视华人之心亦日盛。不独此次予之请求为其直捷拒绝，即从前1868年中政府与美政府所订之勃林加姆（Burlingame）条约①

---

① 勃林加姆（Burlingame）条约：即蒲安臣条约。同治七年（1868）7月28日，美国前驻华公使蒲安臣利用被清政府委派为出使各国大臣的名义，擅自与美国国务卿西华德（William Henry Seward, 1801—1872）在华盛顿签订。共8款。主要内容：两国人民往来居住，听其自便，不得禁阻；可以往来游学并在指定地点设立学校；两国侨民不得因宗教信仰不同，而受到欺侮凌虐、屈抑苛待。

亦无端遭其蹂躏，视如无物。此种完全违背公理之举动，实为外交界从来所未有。而美国国会中人，乃不惮蔑视条约，以为区别种族之预备。故后来禁止华工之议案一经提出，即由国会通过，立见实行。予此次请求之被拒，乃蔑视中国之小焉者耳。

予之所请既被拒绝，遂以此事函告总督。迨接读总督覆书，予即知留学事务所前途之无望矣。总督覆书，亦言美政府拒绝中国学生入陆海军学校，实违背 1868 年之条约，惟亦无如之何云。

自 1870 年至 1878 年，留学事务所已过之历史，予已略述如前状。而此致美政府请求学生入陆海军学校之一函，亦即为予任学生监督最后所办之公牍。1878 年以后，则予身之职务，乃专在公使馆中矣。

予向美政府请求之事未成，总督意似不怿。吴监督子登闻之，遂又乘风兴浪，思设法以破坏此留学事务所。顾吴一人之力犹有未逮，因暗中与陈兰彬密商，设为种种謷言，以极细微之事，造成一绝大文章，寄之北京。适此时反对党中有一御史，因美国华工禁约之举，遂乘机上一封奏，请即解散留学事务所，撤回留学生，以报复美人之恶感。政府阅之，亦未敢贸然准其所奏，乃以此事质之总督李文忠、公使陈兰彬与监督吴子登三人，询其意见。李文忠此时不愿为学生援手，即顺反对党之意而赞成其议。陈兰彬因曾任留学生监督，此中真相理应洞彻，故政府亦垂询及之。陈乃以极圆滑之词答政府，谓学生居美已久，在理亦当召回。其措词之妙，可谓至极。吴子登则更无犹豫之词，直捷痛快以告政府，谓此等学生当立即撤回，归国后并须交地方官严加管束云。此三人各陈所见，初无一语询予。予于此事，已无发言之权。盖彼等咸疑予怀私见，即有所言，亦不足信也。留学事务所之运命，于是告终，更无术可以挽回矣。此百二十名之学生，遂皆于1881年凄然返国。

美国人中，理想高尚，热心教育，关怀于东西人种之进步者，正复不少。其对于中国解散留学事务所召回留学生之举动，未尝不竭全力以争之，爰即联名上书于总理衙门（即外务部）反对此事，惟措词极其和平，态度始终镇静耳。其中主张最力者，为予毕生之良友吐依曲尔君及蓝恩（Lane）君。赖彼二人提倡，联络多数之大教育家及大学校校长，签名书中，思有以阻止中国为此退化之事。此书为耶路大学校长朴德（President Porter）手笔，虽后来未获收效，顾其词严义正、磊落光明，诚不愧为文明人口吻。爰录其文如下：

总理衙门（即外务部）鉴：

予等与贵国留美学生之关系，或师或友，或则为其保人。今闻其将被召回国，且闻贵国政府即欲解散留学事务所，予等咸规规自失，且为贵国忧之。今请以某等观察所及，及得之外界评论者，为贵衙门一陈之。

贵国派遣之青年学生，自抵美以来，人人能善用其光阴，以研究学术。以故于各种科学之进步，成绩极佳。即文学、品行、技术，以及平日与美人往来一切之交际，亦咸能令人满意无间言。论其道德，尤无一人不优美高尚。其礼貌之周至，持躬之谦抑，尤为外人所乐道。职是之故，贵国学生无论在校内肄业，或赴乡村游历，所至之处，咸受美人之欢迎，而引为良友。凡此诸生言行之尽善尽美，实不愧为大国国民之代表，足为贵国增荣誉也。盖诸生年虽幼稚，然已能知彼等在美国之一举一动，皆与祖国国家之名誉极有关系，故能谨言慎行，过于成人。学生既有此良好之行为，遂亦收良好之效果。美国少数无识之人，其平日对于贵国人之偏见，至此逐渐消灭。而美国国人对华之感情，已日趋于欢洽之地位。今乃忽有召令回国之举，不亦重可惜耶？夫在学生方面，今日正为最关重要时期。曩之所受者，犹不过为预备教育，今则将进而求学问之精华矣。譬之于物，学生犹树也，教育学生之人犹农也。农人之辛勤灌溉，胼手胝足，固将以求后日之收获。今学生如树木之久受灌溉培养，发芽滋长，行且开花结果矣，顾欲摧残于一旦而尽弃前功耶？

至某等授于贵国学生之学问，与授与敝国学生者不少异，绝无歧视之心。某等因身为师保，故常请贵国所派之监督或其代表来校参观，使其恍然于某等教授中国学生之方法。惜贵国所派之监督轻视其事，每遇此种邀请，或不亲临，或竟无代表派来也。贵衙门须知此等学生，乃当日由贵政府请求美国国务卿，特别咨送至予等校中，欲其学习美国之语言、文字、学术、技艺，以及善良之礼俗，以冀将来有益于祖国。今学生于科学、文艺等，皆未受有完全教育，是所学未成。予等对于贵国之责任，犹未尽也。乃贵政府不加详细调查，亦无正式照会，遽由予等校中召之返国。此等举动，于贵国国体，无乃有亏乎？

某等对于贵国，固深望其日跻富强。即美国国人平日待遇贵国学生，亦未尝失礼。贵政府乃出此种态度以为酬报，揆之情理，亦当有所不安。至于他人之造谣诬蔑，谓中国学生在校中肄业，未得其益反受其损等言，此则某等绝对不能承认。何也？苟所谓无益有损者，指其荒芜中学而言，则某等固不任咎。以某等对于此事，从未负丝毫职务也。况贵政府当日派送学生来美时，原期其得受美国教育，岂欲其缘木求鱼，至美国以习中学？今某等所希望之教育虽未告成，然已大有机会可竟全功。当此事业未竟、功过未定之日，乃预作种种谣言以为诬蔑，是亦某等所不乐闻也。某等因对于素所敬爱之贵国学生，见其忽受此极大之损失，既不能不代为戚戚；且敝国无端蒙此教育不良之恶名，遂使美利坚大国之名誉亦受莫大之影响，此某等所以不能安缄默也。愿贵衙门三复此言，于未解散留学事务所之前，简派诚实可恃、声望素著之人，将此关于学生智育德育上诬蔑之言，更从实地调查，以期水落石出，则幸甚幸甚。

1881年容闳和吐依曲尔牧师在康州合影

第二十章　北京之行与悼亡

　　学生既被召回国，以中国官场之待遇，代在美时学校生活，脑中骤感变迁，不堪回首可知。以故人人心中咸谓东西文化，判若天渊；而于中国根本上之改革，认为不容稍缓之事。此种观念，深入脑筋，无论身经若何变迁，皆不能或忘也。今此百十名学生，强半列身显要，名重一时。而今日政府，似亦稍稍醒悟，悔昔日解散留学事务所之非计，此则余所用以自慰者。自中日、日俄两次战争，中国学生陆续至美留学者，已达数百人。是1870年曾文正所植桃李，虽经蹂躏，不啻阅二十五年而枯株复生也。

　　当诸学生撤回未久，予亦出使任满，去美返国。时陈兰彬已先予一年归。故事，凡外交官任满归国，必向政府报告一次，谓之销差。予亦循例入都，道出天津，谒直督李文忠。谈次及撤回留学生事，文忠忽转诘予曰："汝何亦任学生归国乎？"予闻言，莫知其命意所在，答曰："此事乃由公使陈兰彬奉上谕而行，鄙意以为总督及陈兰彬与吴子登，皆赞成此举也。予纵欲挽回此事，亦何

李鸿章（1823—1901）

能为役。且违抗谕旨，则人且目为叛逆，捕而戮之。"文忠曰："否，予当日亦甚愿学生勿归，仍留美以求学，故颇属望于汝，谓汝当能阻止学生勿使归也。"予曰："当日此举，总督既未有反对之表示？身居四万五千里外，安能遥度总督心事？设总督能以一函示予，令勿解散，自当谨遵意旨，惜当日未奉此训示耳。"文忠怒形于色，忿然曰："予已知此事之戎首为谁矣。"于是吴子登亦自京来津，约予往晤，以理不可却，访之。吴语予，渠在北京，京人士遇之极冷淡；此次谒李文忠，不知何故逢怒，命此后勿再来见，甚怪事也。予察吴状，似甚狼狈。此为予与彼末次晤谈。嗣后此人销声匿迹，不复相闻问矣。

既抵京，循例谒政府中各重要人物，如恭亲王、庆亲王及六部尚书等，耗时几一月，乃得尽谒诸大老。北京地方辽阔，各达官所居，相去夐远。往来代步惟骡车，既重且笨。车中坐处，状类衣箱，其底即轮轴。轮与箱间无弹簧，故行时震动极烈，行亦甚缓。街衢复不平，车辙深至数寸。行路之难，可想而知。道中浊尘扑衣，秽气刺鼻。漫空涨天者，初非泥砂，乃骡马粪为车轮马蹄捣研而成细末，陈陈相因，变为黑色，似尘土也。飞入耳鼻毛孔中，一时不易擦净。行人皆戴眼纱，头及两手，亦有风帽手套等物，以为抵御。水含盐质，洗濯尤不易去秽。不图首善之区，而令人难堪如此。

予居京三月，颇欲设法禁止鸦片之输入，灭绝中国境内之罂粟。乃上条陈于政府，请其采择施行。旋总理衙门大臣王文韶告予，谓目前殊乏办理此事之人材，故一时未能实行。于是予此计划，束之高阁者垂二十五年。直至近数年来，始见此问题于万国公会中提出讨论焉。

1882年，去京赴沪，居沪者四阅月。得予妻自美来书，谓撄病甚剧，乃急归视。翌年春间抵美，则病者垂危，喉音尽失。

1875年容闳夫人祁洛氏婚纱照
（Mary Louise Kellogg，1851—1886）

予于途次，颇虑不及面。今犹未为失望，不得谓非上帝厚余。一月后，竟得转机。尤幸之幸者，予妻体素荏弱，又因予常漫游，虑或遇不测，恒抑抑不欢。余归国时，适有美教士某君告予妻曰："容君此行，殊为冒险，恐中政府或以留学事务所事，置之于法。"女子善怀，闻此不殊青天之霹雳，所以病也。予之返中国，可一年有半。妇已积思成痗，令人增伉俪之

好。1883年之夏，妇病良已，至诺福克（Norfolk）避暑，归时渐复旧状。医谓宜迁地调养，庶不复病。因于冬间卜居于南部乔治亚省之亚特兰德（Atlanta，Ga.），又曾移居纽约省之亚特朗德（Adirondaks，N. Y.）。但此迁徙之调养，功效亦仅。居亚特朗德久之，1885年冬，复病胃，饮食锐减，复思迁居他处。予重违其意，乃徙于纽求才省之色末维尔（Summerville，N. J.），不幸又感寒疾。居色末维尔约两月，仍返旧居。1886年6月28日，予遂赋哀弦矣。于亚特朗德①西带山公塚（Cedar

祁洛氏与长子容觐形
（1877—1933）

① 亚特朗德：应为哈特福德（Hartford）。

Hill Cemetery）间购地葬之。中年哀乐，人所难堪，吾则尤甚。今老矣，以吾妻留有二子，差幸鳏而非独。然对子思其母，辄复凄咽。吾二子皆能养志，品行亦佳，无忝耶教人格，此则余引以自慰者。

自 1880 年至 1886 年，为余生最不幸时期。毕生志愿，既横被摧残（指教育计划）；同命之人，复无端夭折。顿觉心灰，无复生趣。两儿失母时，一才七龄，一才九龄。计嗣后十年，以严父而兼慈母，心力俱付劬劳鞠育之中。予外姑开洛克夫人，助予理家政、抚幼子者凡二年。最难堪之际，赖能勉强支持焉。

1894 年容闳与耶鲁同学毕业四十周年合影

第二十一章　末次之归国

1894 年，中日因朝鲜问题，遽起衅端。予颇不直日本，非以祖国之故有所偏袒，其实曲在彼也。日人亦非不自知，特欲借此兴戎，以显其海陆军能力耳。战事既开幕，予之爱国心油然而生，乃连发两书寄予友蔡锡勇君，蔡君前在公使馆为予之通译兼参赞者也。每书皆有条陈，规划战事，可使中国与日本继续战争，直至无穷期而力不竭。

第一策：劝中国速向英伦商借一千五百万元，以购已成铁甲三四艘，雇用外兵五千人，由太平洋抄袭日本之后，使之首尾不能相顾。则日本在朝鲜之兵力，必以分而弱。中国乃可乘此暇隙，急练新军，海陆并进，以敌日本。第二策与第一策同时并行：一面由中政府派员将台湾全岛，抵押于欧西无论何强国，借款四万万美金，以为全国海陆军继续战争之军费。时蔡为湖广总督张文襄（之洞）幕府，得书后以予策译为汉文，上之张督。此 1894 年冬间事也。

予初不意张督竟赞成予之第一策，立电来美，派予速赴伦敦借款一千五百万元。此时驻伦敦之中国公使，为李文忠属下之人。彼已先知予来英伦所任之事，故亦无需另备特别公文，有事即可迳往谒公使。予抵伦敦不及一月，筹商借款已就绪，惟担保品尚未指定。予乃托公使转电政府，请以关税为抵押。不意总税务司赫德及直督李文忠不允所请，以为日本此时方要求一极大赔款，此关税指为日本赔款之抵押品，尤且虞其不足云。实则此亦遁辞耳。盖李文忠素与张文襄意见不合，战事起后张李二人尤时有争议。张对于李所提议之和约，极端反对；然李方得慈禧太后宠，内有大援，故竭力主张和议。赫德之依附中央政府，又为必然之趋势。于是张督拟借款一千五百万之议，乃置诸不闻不问之列，此大借款遂以无成。而予之为经手人者，乃处于进退维谷之地位。伦敦承商借款之银行团，几欲以此事控予于法庭也。

予以借款无成归纽约，乃电致张督，请其指示此后进行方针。张覆电亦无他语，但速予立归中国。予之去中国，十三年于兹矣。当1883年归美时，自分此身与中国政府，已永远脱离关系。讵知事竟不然，至今日而犹有人欲招予归国也。但此次招予之人，乃与予素未谋面；其人之学问、品行、政见若何，予除一二得之传闻者外，实毫无所知，而彼转似能深知予者。盖张已上奏清廷，召予归国，奏中褒誉，至无以复加。余因思归中国一探真相，果有机会能容予再作一番事业与否？惟予前在中国时，本属于李文忠门下，今兹则将入文襄幕府，适处于与李反对地位矣。

未首途之前，予所不能不注意者，即对于予之二子，必先为布置妥贴，使得受良好教育。因托予妻兄开洛克博士（Dr. Kellogg）为二子之保护人。长子觐彤，此时已入耶路大学雪费尔专门学院（Sheffield Scientific School），年齿较长，力足自顾。幼子觐槐，尚在哈特福德中学（Hartford High School）预备。予深虑其废学，乃商之予友吐依曲尔夫妇（Rev. and Mrs. Twitchell），令觐槐寄宿其家。吐依曲尔故一国之善士，学行俱优。彼视余子犹子，而余子得亲炙其家庭教育，亦幸事也。屏当既竟，即航海归国。

1895年初夏抵上海，购中国官场礼服，耗费不赀。时文襄已由湖广调署两江，故予迳至南京，往总督署谒之。忆予于1863年，第一次见曾文正于安庆，觉文正之为人，具有一种无形之磁力，能吸引吾人，使心悦诚服。今见张督，则殊无此种吸力。张之为人，目空一世，而又有慵惰不振之态。谈次，于一千五百万借款之决裂，偶一及之即轻轻略过，亦不告予政府不允之故。但予于此中真相，早已了然。盖张李既冰炭，而李在北京政府中之势力，远胜于张。故张所主张借款之策，政府竟不采纳。张自不乐自言其失败，故仅以官话了事。次乃及李文忠，张斥其为贪鄙庸懦之匹夫，谓李水陆两战皆大失败，坐是革职，几不能自保其首领。中国因李一人，乃受此最可耻辱之挫败，言次若有余恨者。旋询予中国新败，当用何策补救？予谓中国不欲富强则已，苟其欲之，则非行一完全之新政策，决不能恢复其原有之荣誉。所谓新政策，政府至少须聘外人四员，以为外交、财政、海军、陆军四部之顾问，与之订立十年合同。十年后若有成效，则更继续聘请。惟所聘之顾问，必须有真确之经验，高深之学识，纯洁之品行而后可。既聘之后，其所陈之嘉言良策，政府当诚意采纳，见诸实行。此外更派青年有才学之中国学生，处于各顾问之下，以资练习。如是行之数年，则中国行政各机关，不难依欧西之成规，从新组织也。

以上所言，乃予对张督所发表之意见。顾张闻予言，始终未置可否，亦不发表其意见，默然静坐，有如已干之海绵，只能吸水入内而不复外吐也者。故此次之谈话，较前与曾文正之晤谈，乃大异其趣。曾文正之招予，将任予以何职，胸中已有成竹；其见予也，不过示予以进行之方针耳。张则对于中国全局，既无一定之宗旨，亦无方针之可言。而于予所献之计划，则又嫌其太新太激烈。不知予此次之回国，因恨中国之败，慨然作积极进行之想，故所言如此。且舍此计划，实无救亡之良策，不能以激烈为予咎也。张而果如曾文正之磊落光明，则一时纵不能实行予言，正不妨略以数语为鼓励，使予知其人有举行新政之决心。予之计划，目前虽不能实施，而对于将来，尚有一线之希望也。乃张则不独无此言语，且无如是之思想。于是予与张之交际，以此处为起点，亦即以此处为终点，以后更无机会再见其人。

张之电招予归国，仅于其未归武昌之前，派予一江南交涉委员差使，聊以敷衍予远来之意。迨后刘忠诚（坤一）实授两江总督抵任后，张仍回武昌原任，去时亦未招予同行。可知张之意见，与予不合，故不欲予之臂助。虽不明言，而其心已昭然若揭矣。在予方面，此次归国，既非谋升官发财而来，则亦何乐与之周旋，以仰其鼻息。予居刘坤一属下，任交涉委员，亦不过三月之久，旋即自行辞职。在中国官场中，必谓予此举为不敬上官，予则不暇计及矣。此三月内，每月领薪百五十元，而无一事可为，不啻一挂名差使。此即予居张、刘两督属下之短期经验也。

1896年，予与江南政界断绝关系，遂至上海。于时脱然无累，颇得自由。已而予又得一策，拟游说中央政府，于北京设

容闳回国后与曾经的留美幼童合影（左起：吴其藻、杨昌龄、容闳、吴仰曾）

立一国家银行。因欲为此条陈之预备，乃先将国家银行律及其他有关系之法律，由1875年美国订正之法律中译为汉文。并聘一中国文士，助予合译。而当时助予者有黄君开甲。黄曾出洋留学，曾为政府任为圣鲁易（St. Louis）博览会之副监督者也。予之译事既毕，乃怀译本入京，并携一中国书记同行。至京，遇予之旧友张荫桓君。其人即于1884至1888年，在华盛顿任中国公使者。张因邀予寓其家，寄榻于此凡数月。此时张荫桓身兼二职，一为总理衙门（即外交部）大臣，一为户部（后改度支部）左侍郎。而户部尚书则为翁同龢，光绪帝之师傅也。张见予之国家银行计划，极为注意。将予译本详细参阅，加以评断。谓其中有若干条，不合于中国国情，难期实行，但择其最紧要而切实可行者，列入足矣。予如其教，斟酌损益后，乃上之户部尚书翁同龢。翁与张意见相同，亦甚以为然，遂以遍示部中同僚，征求意见。数星期后，部中重要之数大员，咸来予寓，对于予之条陈，赞赏不置，谓此事即当奏之清廷云。

不数日，遂以予之国家银行计划，拟成奏折，由张荫桓署名，翁同龢则从中赞助焉。

今试述予之计划：予以为欲立国家银行之基础，必由政府预筹一千万两之资本，以为开办费。中以二百万两购置各种机器，以鼓铸银币、印刷国债券及一切钞票；以二百万两为购地建屋之用；所余六百万两存贮库中，以备购金、银、铜三者，将来铸成各种泉币，以流通全国。此一千万两，只足供国家银行第一年之开办费。将来中国商业发达，则国家银行亦当随商业发达之比例，而逐年增加其资本。此其大略也。

此事既有端绪，旋即着手进行，派委员，购地址。予则受户部之委任，将赴美国，向美国财政部商酌此事，并调查设立国家银行最良之方法。户部奏折，亦邀清廷批准。部署粗定，乃忽横生枝节，有为张荫桓及发起诸人意料所不及者。先是有中国电报局总办兼上海招商局总办盛宣怀其人者，与翁同龢交颇深。此时忽由上海来电，嘱翁同龢暂缓此举，俟两星期彼抵京后，再为区处。翁得电，遂允其请，而垂成之局，乃从此破坏矣。盖盛道台之名，中国无人不知其为巨富，家资累万，无论何种大实业，盛必染指。盛虽身居上海，而北京为之耳目者极多，京中一举一动，无不知之。北京有势力之王公大臣，亦无不与结纳。即慈禧太后最宠幸之太监李莲英，盛亦交结其人。以故盛之势力，在政界中卓卓有声。此次银行计划，遂亦为盛之贿赂所破坏。有人谓盛宣怀此次来京，辇金三十万两，贿买二三亲贵及政府中重大人物，以阻挠其事。于是筹备设立国家银行之一千万两现银，遂为盛一人攫去，以营其私业云。

究国家银行计划失败之原因，亦不外夫中国行政机关之腐败而已。尊自太后，贱及吏胥，自上至下，无一不以贿赂造成。贿赂之为物，予直欲目之为螺钉，一经钻入，即无坚不破也。简言之，吾人之在中国，只需有神通广大之金钱，即无事不可达其目的。事事物物，无非拍卖品，孰以重价购者孰得之。自中日、日俄两次战争之后，东方空气，乃略为之扫荡清洁。中国人对于国家腐败之情形，始稍稍有所觉悟也。

予之国家银行计划，既为盛宣怀所破坏，乃另改方针，拟向政府请求一筑造铁路之特权。予心中所欲造之铁路，为由天津直达镇江。天津居北，镇江居南，在扬子江口，两地相距，以直线计，不过五百英里。若绕山东，过黄河，经安徽，以达湖南[①]，则此路须延长至七百英里。予所规划之路线，则拟取其近者。惟德国政府抗议，不允有他线经过山东。谓山东造路之

---

① 湖南：应为江南，因镇江地处江南之地。

权，为德人所专有，无论何人，不能在山东另造铁路云。此种理由，殊为奇特。任翻遍中国法律或国际法律，皆不能得其根据之所在。但彼时中国国势孱弱，不能提出此问题，以争回固有之主权。而外交部中，亦无人能引证条文，驳斥德国要求之无理，深恐惹起国际交涉，一惟外人之命是听。以故政府只许予造一曲折之铁路，即上所云绕山东过黄河者。予以极力欲成此事，遂拟以此铁路让与外国公司承造。乃政府又命予必招中国资本，不许外人入股，且仅限予六月之期。六月之内，若不能招齐路股者，则将特许状取消。当彼时中国资本家，欲其出资任股以兴造铁路，殆难如登天。予既明知此事势有所不能，遂不得已，复将此铁路计划舍去。予之种种政策，既皆无效。于是予救助中国之心，遂亦至此而止矣。

一年前予在北京时，常遇康有为、梁启超二人。当予筹划银行、铁路等策时，绝不意康、梁等亦正在筹划维新事业也。康、梁等计划进行之极点，即为后来之戊戌政变。其详俟下章言之。

第二十二章　戊戌政变

　　1898 年 9 月之政变，乃清史中一极可纪念之事。因此事光绪帝几被废，所有皇帝之权力，尽为慈禧太后所夺，而己则几成一国事犯，慈禧直以奸细目之。溯光绪即位之初，年才五龄，虽名为继承大位，实则执舵者仍慈禧耳。直至光绪婚礼后，乃将朝政交还。顾光绪虽亲政，而慈禧如电之眼光，仍无时不鉴临，以为监督。皇帝之一举一动，莫不特别留意。总之慈禧之对于光绪，始终不怀善念。盖慈禧当同治在位时（1864 年）曾垂帘听政，故引起其好揽大权之野心。此念一起，不复能制。自是以后，遂无时不思窃取威权，绝不愿安居深宫，百不闻问也。光绪当亲政后，颇思革新庶政，其一种励精图治之决心，足使京内外人士注意，如北斗之见于天空，人人咸为引领。惟慈禧之眼光，则为嫉妒心所蔽，乃视光绪之举动，大不以为然。甚且目之为痴人或狂夫，谓宜幽之冷宫，加以严酷之约束。平心论之，光绪实非痴，尤非狂。后人之读清史者，必将许其为爱国之君，且为爱国之维新党。其聪明睿智，洞悉治理，实为中国自古迄今未有之贤主也。天之诞生光绪于中国，殆特命之为中国革新之先导，故其举措迥异常人，洵伟人也。

　　中国政治上当存亡危急之秋，适维新潮流澎湃而来，侵入北京。光绪帝受此奇异势力之激动，遂奋起提倡维新之事业。全世界人见此，莫不惊奇，以为得未曾有。予睹此状，乃决意留居北京，以觇其究竟。予之寓所，一时几变为维新党领袖之会议场。迨 1898 年秋，遂有政变之事。因此变局，光绪被废，多数维新党之领袖，皆被清廷捕杀。予以素表同情于维新党，寓所又有会议场之目，故亦犯隐匿党人之嫌，不得不迁徙以逃生。乃出北京，赴上海，托迹租界中。即在上海组织一会，名曰中国强学会，以讨论关于维新事业及一切重要问题为宗旨，予竟被选为第一任会长。1899 年，有人劝予，谓上海租界亦非乐土，不如迁地为良。予乃再迁至香港，请英人保护。居香港者二年，后遂归美国。归时幼子觐槐正毕业于耶路大学，予适见其行毕业礼也。

　　1901 年春，予至台湾游历，谒见台湾总督儿玉子爵。子爵盖于日俄战争时，曾为大山大将之参谋长者也。予晤子爵时，因子爵不谙英语，而予又未习日文，乃倩舌人以翻译。子爵曰："久仰大名，又数闻时人盛道君之事业，深以不得把晤为憾。今日识荆，异常欣幸。第惜初次晤面，即有一极恶之消息报君，滋抱歉也。"予闻而大异，急欲知彼所谓恶消息者，究为何事。子爵答曰："中国闽浙总督方有公文来，嘱予留意，谓君设来此者，即倩予捕君送之中政府也。"子爵言时，意颇镇定，无仓皇状，面且有笑容。此恶消息虽出予意料之外，然予初不以是之故惊惶失措，亦以从容镇定之态，答子爵曰："予今在阁下完全治权之下，故无论何时，阁下可从心所欲，捕予送之中政府。予亦甚愿为中国而死，死固得其所也。"子爵闻言，庄重而对曰："容先生幸毋以予为中国之警吏。君今请安居于此，慎无过虑。予决不能听君往中国就戮也。第尚有他事，欲求教于君，不识君肯指示否？"予询以何事，子爵即出一中国报纸，指示予曰："此条陈果为何人所献者？"予见此亦不加思索，立应曰："是予所为也。"且语且以右手拍胸，自示承认之坚。在旁诸人，睹予此状，咸极注意。并有日本军官数人在侧，颇为予言所动。予又续言曰："报纸所载，尚略有错误。君若见允者，予请得为更正之。报纸所云之数目为八万万，予当日所提议则四万万也（按：四万万美金，约合墨银八万万元。报纸所载之数，或照墨银计算耳）。"子爵见予慷慨自承，且更正数目之误，转笑容可掬，异常愉快。盖子爵示予报中所载，乃1894、1895两年间，予所上于张之洞之条陈，请张转奏清廷者也。时在李文忠于对马岛签和约之前半年，予上此条陈，请政府将台湾全岛为抵押品，向欧洲与中国通商之国，借款四万万金元，以九十九年为期。用此借款，中国仍可招练海陆新军，以与日人继续争战。此议虽未实行，而一经报纸揭载，几于举国皆知，子爵亦不知于何处得此报纸。予甫至台湾，即遇此质问，亦可异也。予以有道德上威武不屈之气，故敢于子爵前直承不讳，并更正报纸之误点，更告之曰："设将来中国再有类似于此之事实发生，予仍当抱定此宗旨，上类似于此之条陈于中政府，以与日本抵抗也。"

此次予与日本台湾总督之谈话，实为予一生最可纪念之事。予初闻子爵告予恶消息，以为此日本台湾总督者，必将予交付中政府；予之生命，且丧于其手。迨见其满面笑容，予已知此身所处之地位，安如泰山。于是胆乃益壮，即对日人而谈日本之事，亦毫无顾忌。以予之心地光明，胸无宿物，乃极荷子爵之激赏。

1910年6月21日容闳与美国女孩在康州孟松（Monson）合影

子爵自谓不久将升迁归日，欲邀予偕行，谓将介绍予以觐明治天皇，并结识彼国中重要人物。予此时适患气喘之疾甚剧，不宜于旅行，因掬诚谢之。谓得此宠招，深为荣幸，惜病躯不堪旅行之苦，致力与愿违，辜负盛意也。言毕，遂兴辞而出。出时子爵复告予曰："君之身命，今甚危险。惟若居台湾，在予治权之下，予必极力保护，当派护兵为君防卫，不致有意外之变云。"明日果有护兵四人来，夜间在予寓之四围巡逻。日间逢予外出，无论何时，此四护兵必随行。二居予前，二居予后，加意防护。予居台湾数日，承日人如是待遇，意良可感。迨后予自台湾首途赴香港，乃亲往子爵处，面谢其隆情焉。

评　析

　　长期以来，容闳研究的史料，主要是容闳用英文所作自传 *My life in china and America*，记录了容闳自 1828 年出生至 1902 年离开中国、将近 70 年的人生经历。由于在 20 世纪，研究容闳和留美幼童，容闳自传几乎是唯一的可见史料，因此颇为学界重视，出版和翻译的次数比较多。按语言划分，容闳自传有英、中、日三个版本。容闳自传的中文译本主要有四种：徐凤石和恽铁樵译本、王蓁译本、石霓译本、王志通和左滕慧子译本。各版本的具体情况如下表：

序号	语言	书名	译者	时间	出版社
1	英文	*My life in China and America*	/	1909	New York: Henry Holt And Company
2	中文	西学东渐记	徐凤石 恽铁樵	1915	上海：商务印书馆
3	日文	西学东渐记——容闳自传	百濑弘翻译， 阪野正高解说	1969	东京：平凡社
4	中文	我在美国和在中国生活的追忆	王蓁	1991	北京：中华书局
5	中文	容闳自传——我在中国和美国的生活	石霓	2003	上海：百家出版社
6	中文	耶鲁中国人——容闳自传	王志通 左滕慧子	2018	南京：江苏凤凰文艺出版社

由上表可知，徐凤石和恽铁樵译本、王蓁译本、石霓译本、王志通和左滕慧子译本间隔时间为76年、12年、15年。容闳自传的翻译和重印次数如此之多，足见容闳自传的重要性，又反映出容闳研究史料匮乏，未能有新的容闳著述发现和出版。

在四种译本中，徐凤石和恽铁樵译本是最早的版本，有着非常强烈的时代气息和浓厚的文学风格，也是容闳自传中最经典的译本。该译本受严复和林纾译书风格的影响较大，采用"新民体"，文字简洁流畅，流传最广，影响深远。徐凤石和恽铁樵译本首先在1915年《小说月报》第六卷第1—8号上连载，同年由上海商务印书馆首印成书。截至目前，该译本出版超过20次，具体情况如下：

序号	名称	出版机构	时间
1	西学东渐记——容纯甫先生自述	上海：商务印书馆	1915
2	西学东渐记	上海：商务印书馆	1934
3	西学东渐记	台北：广文书局	1961
4	西学东渐记	台北：学人月刊杂志社	1971
5	西学东渐记——容闳自传	台北：文海出版社	1973
6	西学东渐记	台北：广文书局	1977
7	西学东渐记	台北：广文书局	1981
8	西学东渐记——容纯甫先生自述	武汉：华中师院历史系资料室	不详
9	西学东渐记	长沙：湖南人民出版社	1981
10	西学东渐记	长沙：岳麓书社	1985
11	西学东渐记——容纯甫先生自述	上海：上海书店	1992
12	西学东渐记	北京：美国联合技术公司	1997
13	中国留学生之父的足迹与心迹——西学东渐记	郑州：中州古籍出版社	1998

续表

序号	名称	出版机构	时间
14	容闳自传：我在中国和美国的生活	北京：团结出版社	2005
15	我在中国和美国的生活 ——容闳回忆录	北京：东方出版社	2006
16	西学东渐记	长沙：岳麓书社	2008
17	西学东渐记	北京：生活·读书·新知三联书店	2011
18	西学东渐记——容纯甫先生自叙	广州：新世纪出版社	2011
19	容闳回忆录	北京：东方出版社	2012
20	容闳自述	合肥：安徽文艺出版社	2014
21	西学东渐记	长沙：岳麓书社	2015
22	西学东渐记	北京：朝华出版社	2017

徐凤石和恽铁樵译本虽然经典，然而受时代和史料的限制，也存在不少遗漏和错译等问题。袁鸿林在《容闳述论》中提及"其中文旧译本《西学东渐记》漏误甚多，故本文引文除特别注出外，均译自英文原版"①。美籍华人学者梁伯华亦认为"容闳的自传虽然是第一手史料，参考价值很高，但引用时却要十分小心，一因容闳写这书时离他去世的时间不远，晚年的记忆力衰退，因此自传中的错误地方很多；此外，容闳的自传中经常夸大他自己在历史中扮演的角色，叙事亦流于主观，因此引用该书时要小心及客观地求证及旁证史实。但无可置疑的是，容闳在中国现代化及中西文化交流史上占着重要的地位"②。也许为

① 袁鸿林：《容闳述论》，《近代史研究》1983 年第 3 期。
② 梁伯华：《中外学者对"留美幼童"研究的成果》，《近代中国在世界的崛起：文化、外交与历史的新探索》，武汉大学出版社，2006，第 51 页。

了保持1915年译版的原汁原味，《西学东渐记》版本翻印虽多，对于原文大多未动，只是改头换面，或在篇首序言详述容闳事迹和史实，或在文中添加一些晚清民国时期的图片，或在文末附录容闳的信函和条陈，缺少了对文中史实的考证和错谬的纠正。值得一提的是1981年"走向世界丛书"版本中，编者和校注者对《西学东渐记》中存在的问题大多进行了考证和纠正，如补入容闳自序和为吐依曲尔氏演讲词做跋，补充注释20余处（本书延用部分注释）及《西学东渐记》译文正误表。

除此之外，徐凤石和恽铁樵译本还有一些较为明显的翻译错误，如："容云甫"当为"容元圃（字增祥，广东新会人）"。"曾兰生"译作"曾来顺"，"一八七一年冬间，曾文正公薨于南京，寿七十有一。"曾国藩（1811—1871），逝世时应该是六十一岁。"He said that he remembered me well, having met me in the Yale Library in New Haven, in 1853, on a visit to his son, William Barners, who was in the college at the time I was, and who afterwards became a prominent lawyer in San Francisco."译作"总兵有子曰喊林（William），为香港著名律师，曾与予同时肄业于耶路大学者也。一八六三年，彭总兵至纽海纹探视其子时，予于耶路大学图书馆中，与有一面之素。"其中的"香港"，应该是"旧金山"；"一八六三年"，应该是"一八五三年"。① 诸如此类等等，不一一列举。

由于容闳回忆上的误差，加之"徐凤石和恽铁樵译本"存在的错漏，"王蓁译本""石霓译本""王志通和左滕慧子译本"先后应运而生，三个译本分别出版于1991年、2003年、2018年，

---

① 容闳:《西学东渐记》（走向世界丛书），徐凤石、恽铁樵原译，张叔方补译，杨坚校译、韦圣英补校、钟叔河标点，湖南人民出版社，1981。

相隔时间十年左右，正好反映出容闳研究一直受到学界关注，容闳自传是近代留学史研究的重要史料。

容闳主张通过留学的方式，全面地向西方学习。他在1850年左右在耶鲁求学期间，已经萌发"予意以为予之一身，既受此文明之教育，则当使后予之人，亦享此同等之利益。以西方之学术，灌输于中国，使中国日趋于文明富强之境"的想法。"借西方文明之学术以改良东方之文化"使"老大帝国，一变而为少年新中国。"容闳推动和组织的留美幼童，就是"教育救国"的现实策略，为近代中国培育了一大批人才，容闳也因此被誉为"中国留学生之父"。由于容闳接受了系统的西式教育，对中国传统文化的优缺点还没有足够的认识，所以他对于中西方文化的态度，几乎是"全盘西化"，留学理念也是偏向"美国化"，从而对留美幼童的撤回产生负面影响，这是读者必须加以注意的。

容闳长子容觐彤（Morrison Brown Yung，1877-1933）1898年毕业照　容闳次子容觐槐（Bartlett Golden Yung，1879-1942）1901年毕业照

My Life in China and America[1]

By Yung Wing, A. B. LL. D. (Yale)

To: My Devoted Sons Morrison Brown and Bartlett Golden Yung

These Reminiscences are affectionately dedicated

---

[1] 本部分据 1909 年出版的容闳自传 *My life in China and America*（New York: Henry Holt and Company, 1909）。

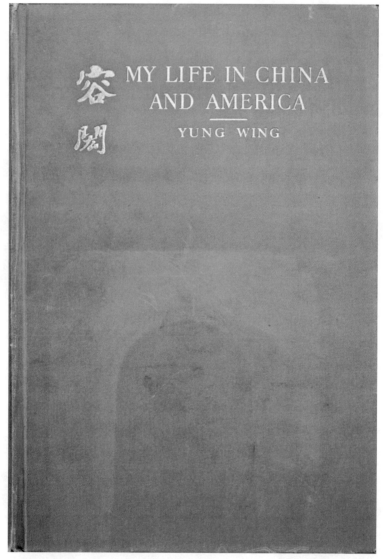

《西学东渐记》(*My Life in China and America*) 1909 年英文原版封面

Preface

The first five chapters of this book give an account of my early education, previous to going to America, where it was continued, first at Monson Academy, in Monson, Massachusetts, and later, at Yale College.

The sixth chapter begins with my reentrance into the Chinese world, after an absence of eight years. Would it not be strange, if an Occidental education, continually exemplified by an Occidental civilization, had not wrought upon an Oriental such a metamorphosis in his inward nature as to make him feel and act as though he were a being coming from a different world, when he confronted one so diametrically different? This was precisely my case, and yet neither my patriotism nor the love of my fellow countrymen had been weakened. On the contrary, they had increased in strength from sympathy. Hence, the succeeding chapters of my book will be found to be devoted to the working out of my educational scheme, as an expression of my undying love for China, and as the most feasible method to my mind, of reformation and regeneration for her.

With the sudden ending of the Educational Commission, and the recall of the one hundred and twenty students who formed the vanguard of the pioneers of modern education in China, my educational work was brought to a close.

Of the survivors of these students of 1872, a few by dint of hard, persistent industry, have at last come forth to stand in the front ranks of leading statesmen of China, and it is through them that the original Chinese Educational Commission has been revived, though in a modified form, so that now, Chinese students are seen flocking to America and Europe from even the distant shores of Sinim for a scientific education.

November, 1909

16 Atwood St., Hartford, Conn.

Chapter I Boyhood

I was born on the 17th of November, 1828, in the village of Nam Ping (South Screen) which is about four miles southwest of the Portuguese Colony of Macao, and is situated on Pedro Island lying west of Macao, from which it is separated by a channel of half a mile wide.

I was one of a family of four children. A brother was the eldest, a sister came next, I was the third, and another brother was the fourth and the youngest of the group. I am the only survivor of them all.

As early as 1834, an English lady, Mrs. Gutzlaff, wife of the Rev. Charles Gutzlaff, a missionary to China, came to Macao and, under the auspices of the Ladies' Association in London for the promotion of female education in India and the East, immediately took up the work of her mission by starting a girls' school for Chinese girls, which was soon followed by the opening of a school for boys also.

Mrs. Gutzlaff's comprador or factotum happened to come from the village I did and was, in fact, my father's friend and neighbor. It was through him that my parents heard about Mrs. Gutzlaff's school and it was doubtless through his influence and means that my father got me admitted into the school. It has always been a mystery to me why my parents should take it into their heads to put me into a foreign school, instead of a regular orthodox Confucian school, where my brother much older than myself was placed. Most assuredly such a step would have

139

been more in play with Chinese public sentiment, taste, and the wants of the country at large, than to allow me to attend an English school; moreover, a Chinese cult is the only avenue in China that leads to political preferment, influence, power and wealth. I can only account for the departure thus taken on the theory that as foreign intercourse with China was just beginning to grow, my parents, anticipating that it might soon assume the proportions of a tidal wave, thought it worth while to take time by the forelock and put one of their sons to learning English that he might become one of the advanced interpreters and have a more advantageous position from which to make his way into the business and diplomatic world. This I take to be the chief aim that influenced my parents to put me into Mrs. Gutzlaff's Mission School. As to what other results or sequences it has eventually brought about in my subsequent life, they were entirely left to Him who has control of all our devising and planning, as they are governed by a complete system of divine laws of antecedents and consequents, or of cause and effect.

In 1835, when I was barely seven years of age, my father took me to Macao. Upon reaching the school, I was brought before Mrs. Gutzlaff. She was the first English lady I had ever seen. On my untutored and unsophisticated mind she made a deep impression. If my memory serves me right, she was somewhat tall and well-built. She had prominent features which were strong and assertive; her eyes were of clear blue lustre, somewhat deep set. She had thin lips, supported by a square chin—both indicative of firmness and authority. She had flaxen hair and eyebrows somewhat heavy. Her features taken collectively indicated great determination and will power.

As she came forward to welcome me in her long full flowing

white dress (the interview took place in the summer), surmounted by two large globe sleeves which were fashionable at the time and which lent her an exaggerated appearance, I remember most vividly I was no less puzzled than stunned. I actually trembled all over with fear at her imposing proportions—having never in my life seen such a peculiar and odd fashion. I clung to my father in fear. Her kindly expression and sympathetic smiles found little appreciative response at the outset, as I stood half dazed at her personality and my new environment. For really, a new world had dawned on me. After a time, when my homesickness was over and the novelty of my surroundings began gradually to wear away, she completely won me over through her kindness and sympathy. I began to look upon her more like a mother. She seemed to take a special interest in me; I suppose, because I was young and helpless, and away from my parents, besides being the youngest pupil in the school. She kept me among her girl pupils and did not allow me to mingle with what few boys there were at the time.

There is one escapade that I can never forget! It happened during the first year in the school, and was an attempt on my part to run away. I was shut up in the third story of the house, which had a wide open terrace on the top—the only place where the girls and myself played and found recreation. We were not allowed to go out of doors to play in the streets. The boy pupils had their quarters on the ground floor and had full liberty to go out for exercise. I used to envy them, their freedom and smuggled down stairs to mingle with them in their sports after school hours. I felt ill at ease to be shut up with the girls all alone way up in the third story. I wanted to see something of the outside world. I occasionally stole down stairs and ventured out to the wharves around which were clustered a number of small ferry boats which had a peculiar fascination to my young fancy. To gain my freedom, I planned to run away. The girls were all much older than I was, and a few sympathized with me in my wild scheme; doubtless, from the same restlessness of being too closely cooped up. I told them of my plan. Six of the older ones fell in with me in the idea. I was to slip out of the house alone, go down to the wharf and engage a covered boat to take us all in.

The next morning after our morning meal, and while Mrs. Gutzlaff was off taking her breakfast, we stole out unbeknown to any one and crowded into the boat and started off in hot haste for the opposite shore of Pedro Island. I was to take the whole party to my home and from there the girls were to disperse to their respective villages. We were half way across the channel when, to my great consternation, I saw a boat chasing us, making fast time and gaining on us all the while. No promise of additional pay was of any avail, because our two oars against their four made it impossible for us to win out; so our boatmen gave up the race at the waving of the handkerchiefs in the other boat and the whole party was captured. Then came the punishment. We were marched through the whole school and placed in a row, standing on a narrow school table placed at one end of the school room facing all the pupils in front of as. I was placed in the center of the row, with a tall foolscap mounted on my head, having three girls on the right and three on the left. I had pinned on my breast a large square placard bearing the inscription, "Head of the Runaways;" there we stood for a whole hour till school was dismissed. I never felt so humiliated in my life as I did when I was undergoing that ordeal. I felt completely crestfallen.

Some of the mischievous fellows would extract a little fun out of this display by taking furtive glances and making wry faces at us. Mrs. Gutzlaff, in order to aggravate our punishment, had ordered ginger snaps and oranges to be distributed among the other pupils right before us.

Mrs. Gutzlaff's school, started in September, 1835, was originally for girls only. Pending the organization and opening of the so-called "Morrison Education Society School", in the interval between 1835 and 1839, a department for boys was temporarily incorporated into her school, and part of the subscription fund belonging to the M. E. S. School was devoted to the maintenance of this one.

This accounts for my entrance into Mrs. Gutzlaff's School, as one of only two boys first admitted. Her school being thus enlarged and modified temporarily, Mrs. Gutzlaff's two nieces—the Misses Parkes, sisters to Mr. Harry Parkes who was afterwards knighted, by reason of the conspicuous part he played in the second Opium War, in 1864, of which he was in fact the originator—came out to China as assistants in the school. I was fortunately placed under their instruction for a short time.

Afterwards the boys' school under Mrs. Gutzlaff and her two nieces, the Misses Parkes, was broken up; that event parted our ways in life in divergent directions. Mrs. Gutzlaff went over to the United States with three blind girls—Laura, Lucy and Jessie. The Misses Parkes were married to missionaries, one to Dr. William Lockhart, a medical missionary; the other to a Rev. Mr. MacClatchy, also a missionary. They labored long in China, under the auspices of the London Missionary Society. The three blind girls whom Mrs. Gutzlaff took with her were taught by me to read on raised letters till they could read from *The Bible* and *Pilgrim's Progress*.

On my return to my home village I resumed my Chinese studies. In the fall of 1840, while the Opium War was still going on, my father died, leaving four children on my mother's hands without means of support.

Fortunately, three of us were old enough to lend a helping hand. My brother was engaged in fishing, my sister helped in housework, and I took to hawking candy through my own village and the neighboring one. I took hold of the business in good earnest, rising at three o'clock every morning, and I did not come home until six o'clock in the evening. My daily earnings netted twenty-five cents, which I turned over to my mother, and with the help given by my brother, who was the main stay of the family, we managed to keep the wolf away from our door. I was engaged in hawking candy for about five months, and when winter was over, when no candy was made, I changed my occupation and went into the rice fields to glean rice after the reapers. My sister usually accompanied me in such excursions. But unlike Ruth of old, I had no Boaz to help me out when I was short in my gleaning. But my knowledge of English came to my rescue. My sister told the head reaper that I could speak, read and write English. This awakened the curiosity of the reaper. He beckoned me to him and asked me whether I wouldn't talk some "Red Hair Men" talk to him. He said he never heard of such talk in his life. I felt bashful and diffident at first, but my sister encouraged me and said "the reaper may give you a large bundle of rice sheaf to take home." This was said as a kind of prompter. The reaper was shrewd enough to take it up, and told me that if I would talk, he would give me a bundle heavier than I could carry. So I began and repeated the alphabet to him. All the reapers as well as the gleaners stood in vacant silence, with mouths wide open, grinning with evident delight. A few minutes after my maiden speech was delivered in the paddy field with water and mud almost knee deep, I was rewarded with several sheaves, and I had to hurry away in order to get two other boys to carry what my sister and I could not lug. Thus I came home loaded with joy and sheaves of golden rice to my mother, little dreaming that my smattering knowledge of English would serve me such a turn so early in my career. I was then about twelve years old. Even Ruth with her six measures of corn did not fare any better than I did.

Soon after the gleaning days, all too few, were over, a neighbor of mine who was a printer in the printing office of a Roman Catholic priest happened to be home from Macao on a vacation. He spoke to my mother about the priest wanting to hire a boy in his office who knew enough English to read the numerals correctly, so as to be able to fold and prepare the papers for the binders. My mother said I could do the work. So I was introduced to the priest and a bargain was struck. I returned home to report myself, and a few days later I was in Macao and entered upon my duty as a folder on a salary of $4.50 a month. My board and lodging came to $1.50— the balance of $3.00 was punctually sent to my mother every month. I did not get rich quickly in this employment, for I had been there but four months when a call for me to quit work came from a quarter I least expected. It had more the sound of heaven in it. It came from a Dr. Benjamin Hobson, a medical missionary in Macao whose hospital was not more than a mile from the printer's office. He sent word that he wanted to see me; that he had been hunting for me for months. I knew Dr. Hobson well, for I saw him a number of times at Mrs. Gutzlaff's. So I called on him. At the outset, I thought he was going to take me in to make a doctor of me, but no, he said he had a promise to fulfill. Mrs. Gutzlaff's last message to him, before she embarked for America with the three blind girls, was to be sure to find out where I was and to put me into the Morrison Education Society School as soon as it was opened for pupils. "This is what I wanted to see you for," said Dr. Hobson, "Before you leave your employment and after you get the consent of your mother to let you go to the Morrison School, I would like to have you come to the hospital and stay with me for a short time so that I may become better acquainted with you, before I take you to the Morrison School, which is already opened for pupils, and introduce you to the teacher."

At the end of the interview, I went home to see my mother who, after some reluctance, gave her consent. I returned to Macao, bade farewell to the priest who, though reticent and reserved, not having said a word to me during all the four months I was in his employ, yet did not find fault with me in my work. I went over to the hospital. Dr. Hobson immediately set me to work with the mortar and pestle, preparing materials for ointments and pills. I used to carry a tray and accompany him in his rounds to visit patients, in the benevolent work of alleviating their pains and sufferings. I was with him about a couple of months in the hospital work, at the end of which time he took me one day and introduced me to the Rev. Samuel Robins Brown, the teacher of the Morrison Education Society School.

Chapter II School Days

The Morrison School was opened on the 1st of November, 1839, under the charge of the Rev. S. R. Brown who, with his wife, Mrs. Brown, landed at Macao on the 19th of February, 1839. Brown, who was afterwards made a D. D., was a graduate of Yale of the class of 1832. From his antecedents, he was eminently fitted to pioneer the first English school in China. I entered the school in 1841. I found that five other boys had entered ahead of me by one year. They were all studying primary arithmetic, geography and reading. I had the start of them only in reading and pronouncing English well. We studied English in the forenoon, and Chinese in the afternoon. The names of the five boys were: 1. Wong Shing; 2. Li Kan; 3. Chow Wan; 4. Tong Chik; 5. Wong Foon. I made the sixth one and was the youngest of all. We formed the first class of the school, and became Brown's oldest pupils throughout, from first to last, till he left China in December, 1846, on account of poor health. Half of our original number accompanied him to this country, on his return.

The Morrison Education Society School came about in this way: Not long after the death of Dr. Robert Morrison, which occurred on the 1st of August, 1834, a circular was issued among the foreign residents on the 26th of January, 1835, calling for the formation of an Association to be named the "Morrison Education Society". Its object was to "improve and promote English education in China by schools

147

and other means". It was called "Morrison" to commemorate the labors and works of that distinguished man who was sent out by the London Missionary Society as the first missionary to China in 1807. He crossed the Atlantic from London to New York where he embarked for China in the sailing vessel "Trident" on the 31st of January, 1807. He tried to land in Macao, but the jealousy of the Jesuits thwarted his purpose. He was obliged to go up to Canton. Finally, on account of the unsettled relations between the Chinese government and the foreign merchants there, he repaired to Malacca, and made that place the basis of his labors. He was the author of the first Anglo-Chinese dictionary, of three quarto volumes. He translated *The Bible* into Chinese; Leang Afah was his first Chinese convert and trained by him to preach. Leang afterwards became a powerful preacher. The importance and bearing of his dictionary, and the translation of *The Bible* into Chinese, on subsequent missionary work in China, were fundamental and paramount. The preaching of his convert, Leang Afah, likewise contributed in no small degree towards opening up a new era in the religious life of China. His memory, therefore, is worthy of being kept alive by the establishment of a school named after him. Indeed, a university ought to have been permanently founded for that purpose instead of a school, whose existence was solely dependent upon the precarious and ephemeral subscriptions of transient foreign merchants in China.

At the close of the Opium War in 1840, and after the Island of Hong Kong had been ceded to the British government, the Morrison school was removed to Hong Kong in 1842. The site chosen for it was on the top of a hill about six hundred feet above the level of the sea.

The hill is situated on the eastern end of the Victoria Colony and was called "Morrison Hill" after the name of the school. It commands a fine view of the harbor, as that stretches from east to west. The harbor alone made Hong Kong the most coveted concession in Southern China. It is spacious and deep enough to hold the Navy of Great Britain, and it is that distinguishing feature and its strategic location that have made it what it is.

On the 12th of March, 1845, Mr. Wm. Allen Macy arrived in Hong Kong as an assistant teacher in the school. His arrival was timely, because the school, since its removal from Macao to Hong Kong, had been much enlarged. Three more classes of new pupils had been formed and the total number of pupils all told was more than forty. This was more than one man could manage. The assistant teacher was much needed. Brown continued his work in the school till the fall of 1846. Macy had a whole year in which to be broken into the work.

Between Brown and Macy there was a marked difference in temperament and character. Brown, on the one hand, showed evidences of a self–made man. He was cool in temperament, versatile in the adaptation of means to ends, gentlemanly and agreeable, and somewhat optimistic. He found no difficulty in endearing himself to his pupils, because he sympathized with them in their efforts to master their studies, and entered heart and soul into his work. He had an innate faculty of making things clear to the pupils and conveying to them his understanding of a subject without circumlocution, and with great directness and facility. This was owing in a great measure to his experience as a pedagogue, before coming out to China, and even before he entered college. He knew how to manage boys, because he knew boys' nature well, whether Chinese, Japanese, or American. He impressed his pupils as being a fine teacher and one eminently fitted from inborn tact and temperament to be a successful school master, as he proved himself to be in his subsequent career in Auburn, N. Y. , and in Japan.

Macy, the assistant teacher, was likewise a Yale man. He had never taught school before in his life, and had no occasion to do so. He possessed no previous experience to guide him in his new work of pedagogy in China. He was evidently well brought up and was a man of sensitive nature, and of fine moral sensibilities—a soul full of earnestness and lofty ideals.

After the Morrison School was broken up in 1850, he returned to this country with his mother and took up theology in the Yale Theological Seminary. In 1854, he went back to China as a missionary under the American Board. I had graduated from Yale College then and was returning to China with him. We were the only passengers in that long, wearisome and most trying passage of 154 days from Sandy Hook to Hong Kong.

Brown left China in the winter of 1846. Four months before he left, he one day sprang a surprise upon the whole school. He told of his contemplated return to America on account of his health and the health of his family. Before closing his remarks by telling us of his deep interest in the school, he said he would like to take a few of his old pupils home with him to finish their education in the United States, and that those who wished to accompany him would signify it by rising. This announcement, together with his decision to return to America, cast a deep gloom over the whole school. A dead silence came over all of us.

And then for several days afterwards the burden of our conversation was about Brown's leaving the school for good. The only cheerful ones among us were those who had decided to accompany him home. These were Wong Shing, Wong Foon and myself. When he requested those who wished to accompany him to the States to signify it by rising, I was the first one on my feet. Wong Foon was second, followed by Wong Shing. But before regarding our cases as permanently settled, we were told to go home and ask the consent of our respective parents. My mother gave her consent with great reluctance, but after my earnest persuasion she yielded, though not without tears and sorrow. I consoled her with the fact that she had two more sons besides myself, and a daughter to look after her comfort. Besides, she was going to have a daughter—in—law to take care of her, as my elder brother was engaged to be married.

It may not be out of place to say that if it had depended on our own resources, we never could have come to America to finish our education, for we were all poor. Doubtless Brown must have had the project well discussed among the trustees of the school months before he broached the subject to his pupils.

It was also through his influence that due provision was made for the support of our parents for at least two years, during our absence in America. Our patrons who bore all our expenses did not intend that we should stay in this country longer than two years. They treated us nobly. They did a great work for us. Among those who bore a conspicuous part in defraying our expenses while in America, besides providing for the support of our aged parents, I can recall the names of Andrew Shortrede, proprietor and editor of the "Hong Kong China Mail" (he was a Scotchman, an old bachelor, and a noble and handsome specimen of humanity), A. A. Ritchie, an American merchant, and A. A. Campbell, another Scotchman. There were others unknown to me. The Olyphant Sons, David, Talbot and Robert, three brothers, leading merchants of New York, gave us a free passage from Hong Kong to New York in their sailing vessel, the "Huntress", which brought a cargo of tea at the same time. Though late in the day for me to mention the names of these benefactors who from pure motives of Christian philanthropy aided me in my education, yet it may be a source of satisfaction to their descendants, if there are any living in different parts of the world, to know that their sires took a prominent part in the education of three Chinese youths—Wong Shing, Wong Foon and myself.

Chapter III   Journey to America and First Experiences There

Being thus generously provided for, we embarked at Whampoa on the 4th of January, 1847, in the good ship "Huntress" under Captain Gillespie. As stated above, she belonged to the Olyphant Brothers and was loaded with a full cargo of tea. We had the northeast trade wind in our favor, which blew strong and steady all the way from Whampoa to St. Helena. There was no accident of any kind, excepting a gale as we doubled the Cape of Good Hope. The tops of the masts and ends of the yards were tipped with balls electricity. The strong wind was howling and whistling behind us like a host of invisible Furies. The night was pitch dark and the electric balls dancing on the tips of the yards and tops of the masts, back and forth and from side to side like so many infernal lanterns in the black night, presented a spectacle never to be forgotten by me. I realized no danger, although the ships pitched and groaned, but enjoyed the wild and weird scene hugely. After the Cape was doubled, our vessel ploughed through the comparatively smooth waters of the Atlantic until we reached the Island of St. Helena where we were obliged to stop for fresh water and provisions. Most sailing vessels that were bound from the East for the Atlantic board were accustomed to make St. Helena their stopping place. St. Helena, as viewed from the shipboard, presented an outward appearance of a barren volcanic rock, as though freshly emerged from the baptism of fire and brimstone. Not a blade of grass could be seen on its burnt and charred surface. We landed at Jamestown, which is a small village in the valley of the Island. In this valley there was rich and beautiful vegetation. We found among the sparse inhabitants a few Chinese who were brought there by the East India Company's ships. They were middle-aged people, and had their families there. While there, we went over to Longwood where was Napoleon's empty tomb. A large weeping willow hung and swept over it. We cut a few twigs, and kept them alive till we reached this country and they were brought to Auburn, N. Y. , by Mr. Brown, who planted them near his residence when he was teaching in the Auburn Academy for several years before his departure for Japan. These willows proved to be fine, handsome trees when I visited Auburn in 1854.

From St. Helena we took a northwesterly course and struck the Gulf Stream, which, with the wind still fair and favorable, carried us to New York in a short time. We landed in New York on the 12th of April, 1847, after a passage of ninety-eight days of unprecedented fair weather. The New York of 1847 was altogether a different city from the New York of 1909. It was a city of only 250000 or 300000 inhabitants; now it is a metropolis rivaling London in population, wealth and commerce. The whole of Manhattan Island is turned into a city of skyscrapers, churches, and palatial residences.

Little did I realize when in 1845 I wrote, while in the Morrison School, a composition on "An Imaginary Voyage to New York and up the Hudson", that I was to see New York in reality. This incident leads me to the reflection that sometimes our imagination foreshadows what lies uppermost in our minds and brings possibilities within the sphere of realities. The Chinese Education Scheme is another example of the realities that came out of my day dreams a year before I graduated. So was my marrying an American wife. Still there are other day dreams yet to be realized; whether or not they will ever come to pass the future will determine.

Our stay in New York was brief. The first friends we had the good fortune to make in the new world, were Prof. David E. Bartlett and his wife. He was a professor in the New York Asylum for the Deaf and Dumb, and was afterwards connected with a like institution in Hartford. The Professor died in 1879. His wife, Mrs. Fanny P. Bartlett, survived him for nearly thirty years and passed away in the spring of 1907. She was a woman highly respected and beloved for her high Christian character and unceasing activities for good in the community in which she lived. Her influence was even extended to China by the few students who happened to enjoy her care and instruction. I count her as one of my most valued friends in America.

From New York we proceeded by boat to New Haven where we had an opportunity to see Yale College and were introduced to President Day. I had not then the remotest idea of becoming a graduate of one of the finest colleges of the country, as I did a few years afterwards. We went by rail from New Haven to Warehouse Point and from there to East Windsor, the home of Mrs. Elizabeth Brown, wife of Dr. Brown. Her parents were then living. Her father, the Rev. Shubael Bartlett, was the pastor of the East Windsor Congregational Church. I well remember the first Sabbath we attended his church. We three Chinese boys sat in the pastor's pew which was on the left of the pulpit, having a side view of the minister, but in full view of the whole congregation. We were the cynosure of the whole church. I doubt whether much attention was paid to the sermon that day.

The Rev. Shubael Bartlett was a genuine type of the old New England Puritan. He was exact and precise in all his manners and ways. He spoke in a deliberate and solemn tone, but full of sincerity and earnestness. He conducted himself as though he was treading on thin ice, cautiously and circumspectly. One would suppose from his appearance that he was austere and exacting, but he was gentle and thoughtful. He would have his family Bible and hymn book placed one on top of the other, squared and in straight lines, on the same spot on the table every morning for morning prayers. He always sat in the same spot for morning prayers. In other words, you always knew where to find him. His habits and daily life were as regular as clock work. I never heard him crack a joke or burst out in open laughter.

Mrs. Bartlett, Mrs. Brown's mother, was of a different makeup. She was always cheerful. A smile lighted up her features nearly all the time and for everyone she had a kind and cheerful word, while the sweet tone of her voice always carried with it cheerfulness and good will. Her genial temperament and her hospitality made the parsonage a favorite resort to all the friends and relatives of the family, who were quite numerous. It was always a puzzle to me how the old lady managed to make ends meet when her husband's salary was not over $400 a year. To be sure, the farm annually realized something, but Daniel, the youngest son, who was the staff of the old couple, had to work hard to keep up the prestige of the parsonage. It was in this parsonage that I found a temporary home while at school in Monson, and also in Yale.

Chapter IV At Monson Academy

We were in East Windsor for about a week; then we went up to Monson, Mass., to enter the Academy there. Monson Academy was, at one time, quite a noted preparatory school in New England, before high schools sprang into existence. Young men from all parts of the country were found here, undergoing preparation for colleges. It was its fortune, at different periods of its history, to have had men of character and experience for its principals. The Rev. Charles Hammond was one of them. He was in every sense a self—made man. He was a graduate of Yale; he was enthusiastically fond of the classics, and a great admirer of English literature. He was a man of liberal views and broad sympathies. He was well—known in New England as an educator and a champion of temperance and New England virtues. His high character gave the Academy a wide reputation and the school was never in a more prosperous condition than when he was principal. He took a special interest in us, the three Chinese students—Wong Shing, Woon Foon and myself—no so much from the novelty of having Chinese in the school as from his interest in China, and the possible good that might come out of our education.

In our first year in the Academy, we were placed in the English department. Greenleaf's Arithmetic, English Grammar, Physiology, and Upham's Mental Philosophy were our studies. In the last two studies we recited to the new preceptress, Miss Rebekah Brown, a graduate of Mt. Holyoke, the valedictorian of her class. She afterwards became the wife of Doctor A. S. McClean of Springfield, Mass. She was a fine teacher and a woman of exceptional Christian virtues. She had an even and sweet temper, and was full of good will and good works. She and her husband, the good Doctor, took a genuine interest in me; they gave me a home during some of my college vacations, and helped me in various ways in my struggle through Yale. I kept up my correspondence with them after my return to China, and upon coming back to this country, I was always cordially invited to their home in Springfield. It was on account of such a genuine friendship that I made Springfield my headquarters in 1872, when I brought the first installment of Government students to this country.

Brown placed us under the care of his mother, Mrs. Phoebe H. Brown. We boarded with her, but had a separate room assigned us in a dwelling right across the road, opposite to her cottage. Her widowed daughter with her three boys had taken up all the spare rooms in the cottage, which accounts for the want of accommodation for us.

In those primitive days, board and lodging in the country were very reasonable. Indigent students had a fair chance to work their way for an education. I remember we paid for board and lodging, including fuel, light and washing, only $1.25 a week for each, but we had to take care of our own rooms and, in the winter, saw and split our own wood, which we found to be capital exercise.

Our lodging was about half a mile from the academy. We had to walk three times a day to school and back, in the dead of winter when the snow was three feet deep; that gave us plenty of exercise, keen appetites and kept us in fine condition.

I look back upon my acquaintance with Mrs. Phoebe H. Brown with a mingled feeling of respect and admiration. She certainly was a remarkable New England woman—a woman of surpassing strength of moral and religious character. Those who have had the rare privilege of reading her stirring biography, will, I am sure, bear me out in this statement. She went through the crucible of unprecedented adversities and trials of life and came out one of the rare shining lights that beautify the New England sky. She is the authoress of the well-known hymn, "I love to steal awhile away from every cumbering care", etc., which breathes the calm spirit of contentment and resignation wherever sung.

The Rev. Charles Hammond, the principal of the academy when we joined it, was a graduate of Yale, as I stated before, and a man of fine cultivated taste. He was an enthusiastic admirer of Shakespeare, who was his favorite poet; among orators, he was partial to Daniel Webster. He had the faculty of inspiring his pupils with the love of the beautiful, both in ancient and modern literature. In our daily recitations, he laid a greater stress on pointing out the beauties of a sentence and its construction, than he did on grammatical rules, moods and tenses. He was a fine writer. His addresses and sermons were pointed and full of life. Like Dr. Arnold of Rugby, he aimed to build character in his pupils and not to convert them into walking encyclopedias, or intelligent parrots. It was through him that I was introduced to Addison, Goldsmith, Dickens, Sir Walter Scott, the

Edinburgh Reviews, Macaulay and Shakespeare, which formed the bulk of my reading while in Monson.

During my first year in the Monson Academy, I had no idea of taking a collegiate course. It was well understood that I was to return to China at the end of 1849, and the appropriation was made to suit such a plan. In the fall of 1848, after Wong Shing—the eldest of the three of us— had returned to China on account of his poor health, Wong Foon and myself, who were left behind to continue our studies for another year, frequently met to talk over future plans for the end of the prescribed time. We both decided finally to stay in this country to continue our studies, but the question arose, who was going to back us financially after 1849? This was the Gordian Knot. We concluded to consult Mr. Hammond and Mr. Brown on the subject. They both decided to have the matter referred to our patrons in Hong Kong. Reply came that if we wished to prosecute our studies after 1849, they would be willing to continue their support through a professional course, if we were willing to go over to Scotland to go through the University of Edinburgh. This was a generous and noble-hearted proposal.

Wong Foon, on his part, after much deliberation, decided to accept the offer and go over to Scotland at the end of 1849, while, on my part, I preferred to remain in this country to continue my studies here with the view of going to Yale. Wong Foon's decision had relieved him of all financial anxieties, while the problem of how I was to pay my education bills after 1849, still remained to be solved. But I did not allow the perplexities of the future to disturb my peace of mind. I threw all my anxieties to the wind, trusting to a wise Providence to care for my future, as it had done for my past.

Wong Foon and I, having taken our decisive steps, dropped our English studies at the close of the school year of 1849, and in the fall of the same year we began the A B C's of our classical course. In the summer of 1850, we graduated from the academy. Wong Foon, by previous arrangements, went over to Scotland and entered the University of Edinburgh. I remained in this country and finally entered Yale. It was fully a decade since we had met for the first time in the Morrison School in Macao, in 1840, to become school-mates as well as classmates. Now that link was broken.

Wong was in the University seven years. After completing his professional studies as a doctor, he returned to China in 1857. He was a fine scholar. He graduated the third man in his medical class. He also distinguished himself in his profession. His ability and skill secured for him an enviable reputation as one of the ablest surgeons east of the Cape of Good Hope at that time. He had a fine practice in Canton, where the foreign residents retained him as their physician in preference to European doctors. He was very successful and made quite a fortune before his death, which took place in 1879. Both the native and foreign communities felt his loss. He was highly respected and honored by Chinese and foreigners for his Christian character and the purity of his life.

Chapter V My College Days

Before entering Yale, I had not solved the problem of how I was to be carried through the collegiate course without financial backing of a definite and well–assured character. It was an easy matter to talk about getting an education by working for it, and there is a kind of romance in it that captivates the imagination, but it is altogether a different thing to face it in a business and practical way. So it proved to me, after I had put my foot into it. I had no one except Brown, who had already done so much for me in bringing me to this country, and Hammond, who fitted me for college. To them I appealed for advice and counsel. I was advised to avail myself of the contingent fund provided for indigent students. It was in the hands of the trustees of the academy and so well guarded that it could not be appropriated without the recipient's signing a written pledge that he would study for the ministry and afterwards become a missionary. Such being the case, I made up my mind that it would be utterly useless for me to apply for the fund.

However, a day was appointed for me to meet the trustees in the parsonage, to talk over the subject. They said they would be too glad to have me avail myself of the fund, provided I was willing to sign a pledge that after graduation I should go back to China as a missionary. I gave the trustees to understand that I would never give such a pledge for the following reasons: First, it would handicap and circumscribe my usefulness. I wanted the utmost freedom of action to avail myself of every opportunity to do the greatest good in China. If necessary, I might be obliged to create new conditions, if I found old ones were not favorable to any plan I might have for promoting her highest welfare.

In the second place, the calling of a missionary is not the only sphere in life where one can do the most good in China or elsewhere. In such a vast empire, there can be hardly any limit put upon one's ambition to do good, if one is possessed of the Christ-spirit; on the other hand, if one has not such a spirit, no pledge in the world could melt his ice-bound soul.

In the third place, a pledge of that character would prevent me from taking advantage of any circumstance of event that might arise in the life of a nation like China, to do her a great service.

"For these reasons," I said, "I must decline to give the pledge and at the same time decline to accept your kind offer to help me. I thank you, gentlemen, very much, for your good wishes."

Both Brown and Hammond afterwards agreed that I took the right view on the subject and sustained me in my position. To be sure, I was poor, but I would not allow my poverty to gain the upper hand and compel me to barter away my inward convictions of duty for a temporary mess of pottage.

During the summer of 1850, it seems that Brown who had been making a visit in the South to see his sister, while there had occasion to call on some of the members of "The Ladies' Association" in Savannah, Ga., to whom he mentioned my case. He returned home in the nick of time, just after I had the interview with the board of trustees of the academy. I told him of the outcome, when, as stated above, he approved of my position, and told me what he had done. He said that members of the association agreed to help me in college. On the strength of that I gathered fresh courage, and went down to New Haven to pass my examination for entrance. How I got in, I do not know, as I had had only fifteen months of Latin and twelve months of Greek, and ten months of mathematics. My preparation had been interrupted because the academy had been broken up by the Palmer & New London R. R. that was being built close by. As compared with the college preparations of nine–tenths of my classmates, I was far behind. However, I passed without condition. But I was convinced I was not sufficiently prepared, as my recitations in the classroom clearly proved. Between the struggle of how to make ends meet financially and how to keep up with the class in my studies, I had a pretty tough time of it. I used to sweat over my studies till twelve o'clock every night the whole Freshman year. I took little or no exercise and my health and strength began to fail and I was obliged to ask for a leave of absence of a week. I went to East Windsor to get rested and came back refreshed.

In the Sophomore year, from my utter aversion to mathematics, especially to differential and integral calculus, which I abhorred and detested, and which did me little or no good in the way of mental discipline, I used to fizzle and flunk so often that I really thought I was going to be dropped from the class, or dismissed from college. But for some unexplained reasons I was saved from such a catastrophe, and I squeezed through the second year in college with so low a mark that I was afraid to ask my division tutor, who happened to be Tutor Blodget, who had me in Greek, about it. The only redeeming feature that saved me as a student in the class of 1854, was the fortunate circumstance that I happened to be a successful competitor on two occasions in English composition in my division. I was awarded the first prize in the second term, and the first prize in the third term of the year. These prizes gave me quite an éclat in the college as well as in the outside world, but I was not at all elated over them on account of my poor scholarship which I felt keenly through the whole college course.

Before the close of my second year, I succeeded in securing the stewardship of a boarding club consisting of sophomores and juniors. There were altogether twenty members. I did all the marketing and served at the table. In this way, I earned my board through the latter half of my college course. In money matters, I was supplied with remittances from "The Ladies' Association" in Savannah, and also contributions from the Olyphant Brothers of New York. In addition to these sources of supply, I was paid for being an assistant librarian to the "Brothers in Unity," which was one of the two college debating societies that owned a library, and of which I was a member.

In my senior year I was again elected librarian to the same Society and got $30.00. These combined sums were large enough to meet all my cash bills, since my wants had to be finely trimmed to suit the cloth. If most of the country parsons of that period could get along with a salary of $200 or $300 a year (supplemented, of course, with an annual donation party, which sometimes carried away more than it donated), having as a general thing a large family to look after, I certainly ought to have been able to get through college with gifts of nearly a like amount, supplemented with donations of shirts and stockings from ladies who took an interest in my education.

The class of 1854, to which I had the honor and the good fortune to belong, graduated ninety–eight all told. Being the first Chinaman who had ever been known to go through a first–class American college, I naturally attracted considerable attention; and from the fact that I was librarian for one of the college debating societies (Linonia was the other) for two years, I was known by members of the three classes above, and members of the three classes below me. This fact had contributed toward familiarizing me with the college world at large, and my nationality, of course, added piquancy to my popularity.

As an undergraduate, I had already acquired a factitious reputation within the walls of Yale. But that was ephemeral and soon passed out of existence after graduation.

All through my college course, especially in the closing year, the lamentable condition of China was before my mind constantly and weighed on my spirits. In my despondency, I often wished I had never been educated, as education had unmistakable enlarged my mental and moral horizon, and revealed to me responsibilities which the sealed eye of ignorance can never see, and sufferings and wrongs of humanity to which an uncultivated and callous nature can never be made sensitive. The more one knows, the more he suffers and is consequently less happy; the less one knows, the less he suffers, and hence is more happy. But this is a low view of life, a cowardly feeling and unworthy of a being bearing the impress of divinity. I had started out to get an education. By dint of hard work and self–denial I had finally secured the coveted prize and although it might not be so complete and symmetrical a thing as could be desired, yet I had come right up to the conventional standard and idea of a liberal education. I could, therefore, call myself an educated man and, as such, it behooved me to ask, "What am I going to do with my education?" Before the close of my last year in college I had already sketched out what I should do. I was determined that the rising generation of China should enjoy the same educational advantages that I had enjoyed; that through western education China might be regenerated, become enlightened and powerful. To accomplish that object became the guiding star of my ambition. Towards such a goal, I directed all my mental resources and energy. Through thick and thin, and the vicissitudes of a checkered life from 1854 to 1872, I labored and waited for its consummation.

Chapter VI Return to China

In entering upon my life's work which to me was so full of meaning and earnestness, the first episode was a voyage back to the old country, which I had not seen for nearly ten years, but which had never escaped my mind's eye nor my heart's yearning for her welfare. I wanted very much to stay a few years longer in order to take a scientific course. I had taken up surveying in the Sheffield Scientific School just as that department was starting into existence under Professor Norton. Had I had the means to prosecute a practical profession, that might have helped to shorten and facilitate the way to the goal I had in view; but as I was poor and my friends thought that a longer stay in this country might keep me here for good, and China would lose me altogether, I was for this and other reasons induced to return. The scientific course was accordingly abandoned. The persons who were most interested in my return to China were Pelatiah Perit of Messrs. Goodhue & Co., merchants in the China trade, and the Olyphant Brothers, who had taken such a lively interest eight years before in helping me to come over in their ship, the "Huntress". These gentlemen had no other motive in desiring me to return to China than that of hoping to see me useful in Christianizing the Chinese, which was harmony with their well-known broad and benevolent characters.

On the 13th of November, 1854, the Rev. William Allen Macy,

who went out to Hong Kong to take the place of the Rev. Dr. Brown, as teacher in the Morrison Education Society School in 1845, went back to China as a missionary under the American Board, and we were fellow-passengers on board the sailing clipper ship "Eureka," under Captain Whipple, of Messrs. Chamber, Heisser & Co., of New York.

Winter is the worst season of the year to go on an eastern voyage in a sailing vessel, via the Cape of Good Hope. The northeast trade winds prevail then and one is sure to have head winds all the way. The "Eureka," in which Macy and myself were the only passengers, took that route to Hong Kong. We embarked on board of her as she rode in midstream of the East River. The day was bleak and bitingly cold. No handkerchiefs were fluttering in the air, waving a good voyage; no sound from the shore cheered us as the anchor was weighed, and as the tug toward us out as far as Sandy Hook. There we were left to our own resources. The sails were not furled to their full extent, but were reefed for tacking, as the wind was nearly dead ahead and quite strong. We found the "Eureka" to be empty of cargo, and empty even of ballast of any kind; for that reason she acted like a sailor who had just had his nip before he went out to sea. She tossed up and down and twisted from right to left, just as though she had a little too much to keep her balance. It was in such a fashion that she reeled her way from Sandy Hook to Hong Kong—a distance of nearly 13000 nautical miles, which took her 154 days to accomplish. It was decidedly the most uninteresting and wearisome voyage I ever took in my life. The skipper was a Philadelphian. He had the unfortunate habit of stuttering badly, which tended to irritate a temper naturally quick and fiery. He was certainly a ludicrous object to look at. It was particularly in the morning that he might be seen pacing the quarter deck, scanning the sky. This, by the spectator, was deemed necessary for the skipper to work himself up to the right pitch, preliminary to his pantomimic performances in his battle with the head wind. All at once, he halted, stared at the quarter of the sky from whence the malicious head wind came. With a face all bloated and reddened by intense excitement, his eyes almost standing out of their sockets, and all ablaze with uncontrollable rage, with arms uplifted, he would clutch his hair as if plucking it out by the roots, gnash his teeth, and simultaneously he would jump up and down, stamping on the deck, and swear at the Almighty for sending him head winds. The air for the moment was split with his revolting imprecations and blasphemous oaths that were ejaculated through the laborious process of stammering and stuttering, which made him a most pitiable object to behold. In the early part of the voyage it was a painful sight to see him working himself up to that pitch of contortion and paroxysm of rage which made him appear more like an insane than a sane man, but as these exhibitions were of daily occurrence for the greater part of the voyage, we came to regard him as no longer deserving of sympathy and pity, but rather with contempt. After his passion had spent its force, and he subsided into his calmer and normal mood, he would drop limply into a cane chair, where he would sit for hours all by himself. For the sake of diversion, he would rub his hands together, and soliloquize quietly to himself, an occasional smile breaking over his face, which made him look like an innocent idiot. Before the voyage was half through, the skipper had made such a fool of himself through his silly and insane conduct about the wind, that he became the laughing stock of the whole crew, who, of course, did not dare to show any outward

171

signs of insubordination. The sailing of the vessel was entirely in the hands of the first mate, who was literally a sea-tyrant. The crew was composed of Swedes and Norwegians. If it had been made up of Americans, the inhuman treatment by the officers might have driven them to desperate extremities, because the men were over-worked night and day in incessant tacking. The only time that they found a resting spell was when the ship was becalmed in the tropics when not a breath of wind was to be had for several days at a time. Referring to my diary kept in that memorable voyage—it took us nearly two weeks to beat up the Macassar straits. This event tried our patience sorely. After it was passed, the skipper made the remark within the hearing of the Rev. Macy that the reason he had bad luck was because he had a Jonah on board. My friend Macy took the remark in a good-natured way and gave me a significant smile. We were just then discussing the feat of going through the Macassar straits and I remarked in a tone just loud enough to be heard by the old skipper that if I had charge of the vessel, I could take her through in less than ten days. This was meant as a direct reflection on the poor seamanship of the old fellow (for he really was a miserable sailor), as well as to serve as a retaliation for what he said a few minutes before, that there was a Jonah on board.

In the dead of winter, the passage to the East should have been taken around Cape Horn instead of the Cape of Good Hope, in which case we would no doubt have had strong and fair wind all the way from New York to Hong Kong, which would not only have shortened the voyage but also saved the captain a world of swearing and an incalculable amount of wear and tear on his nervous system. But as a passenger only, I had no idea of the financial motive back of the move to send the ship perfectly empty and unballasted, right in the teeth of the northeast monsoon. I would have been glad to go around Cape Horn, as that would have added a new route to my journeying around the world, and furnished me with new incidents as well.

As we approached Hong Kong, a Chinese pilot boarded us. The captain wanted me to ask him whether there were any dangerous rocks and shoals nearby. I could not for the life of me recall my Chinese in order to interpret him; the pilot himself understood English, and he was the first Chinese teacher to give me the terms in Chinese for dangerous rocks and shoals. So the skipper and Macy, and a few other persons who were present at the time, had the laugh on me, who, being a Chinese, yet was not able to speak the language.

My first thought upon landing was to walk up to the office of the "China Mail," to pay my respects to Andrew Shortrede, the proprietor and editor of the paper, and the friend who supported me for over a year, while I was in Monson Academy. After seeing him and accepting his hospitality by way of an invitation to take up my quarters in his house, I lost no time in hastening over to Macao to see my aged and beloved mother, who, I knew, yearned to see her long–absent boy. Our meeting was arranged a day beforehand. I was in citizen's dress and could not conveniently change the same for my Chinese costume. I had also allowed a pair of mustaches to grow, which according to Chinese custom, was not becoming for an unmarried young man to do. We met with tears of joy, gratitude and thanksgiving. Our hearts were too full even to speak at first. We gave way to our emotions. As soon as we were fairly composed, she began to stroke me all over, as expressive of her maternal endearment which had been held in patient suspense for at least ten years. As we sat close to each other, I gave her a brief recital of my life in America, for I knew she would be deeply interested in the account. I told her that I had just finished a long and wearisome voyage of five months' duration, but had met with no danger of any kind; that during my eight years of sojourn in the United States, I was very kindly treated by the good people everywhere; that I had had good health and never been seriously sick, and that my chief object during the eight years was to study and prepare myself for my life work in China. I explained to her that I had to go through a preparatory school before entering college; that the college I entered was Yale—one of the leading colleges of the United States, and that the course was four years, which accounted for my long stay and delayed my return to China. I told her that at the end of four years I had graduated with the degree of A. B.—analogous to the Chinese title of Siu Tsai, which is interpreted "Elegant Talent"; that it was inscribed on a parchment of sheep skin and that to graduate from Yale College was considered a great honor, even to a native American, and much more so to a Chinese. She asked me naively how much money it conferred. I said it did not confer any money at once, but it enabled one to make money quicker and easier than one can who has not been educated; that it gave one greater influence and power among men if he built on his college education, he would be more likely to become the leader of men, especially if he had a well-established character. I told her my college education was worth more to me than money, and that I was confident of making plenty of money.

"Knowledge," I said, "is power, and power is greater than riches. I am the first Chinese to graduate from Yale College, and that being the case, you have the honor of being the first and only mother out of the countless millions of mothers in China at this time, who can claim the honor of having a son who is the first Chinese graduate of a first—class American college. Such an honor is a rare thing to posses." I also assured her that as long as I lived all her comforts and wants would be scrupulously and sedulously looked after, and that nothing would be neglected to make her contented and happy. This interview seemed to give her great comfort and satisfaction. She seemed very happy over it. After it was ended, she looked at me with a significant smile and said, "I see you have already raised your mustaches. You know you have a brother who is much older than you are; he hasn't grown his mustaches yet. You must have yours off." I promptly obeyed her mandate, and as I entered the room with a clean face, she smiled with intense satisfaction, evidently thinking that with all my foreign education, I had not lost my early training of being obedient to my mother. And if she could only have read my heart, she would have found how every throb palpitated with the most tender love for her. During the remaining years of her life, I had the rare privilege of seeing her often and ministered to her every comfort that it was in my power to bestow. She passed away in 1858, at the age of sixty—four, twenty—four years after the death of my father. I was in Shanghai at the time of her death. I returned to my native village in time to attend her funeral.

In the summer of 1855, I took up my residence in Canton, with the Rev. Mr. Vrooman, a missionary under the American Board. His headquarters were in Ham Ha Lan, in the vicinity of the government execution ground, which is in the southwestern outskirts of the city, close to the bank of the Pearl River. While there, I began my Chinese studies and commenced to regain the dialect of Canton, which I had forgotten during my stay in the United States. In less than six months, the language came back to me readily, although I was still a little rusty in it. I was also making slow progress in recovering the written language, in which I was not well-grounded before leaving China, in 1846. I had studied it only four years, which was considered a short time in which to master the written language. There is a greater difference between the written and the spoken language of China than there is between the written and spoken English language. The Chinese written language is stilted and full of conventional forms. It is understood throughout the whole empire, but differently pronounced in different provinces and localities. The spoken language is cut up into endless dialects and in certain provinces like Fuhkien, Anhui and Kiangsu, the people are as foreigners to each other in the matter of dialects. Such are the peculiar characteristics of the ideographic and spoken languages of China.

During the six months of my residence in Canton, while trying to recover both the written and spoken languages, Kwang Tung province was thrown into a somewhat disorganized condition. The people of Canton attempted to raise a provincial insurrection or rebellion entirely distinct from the Taiping rebellion which was being carried on in the interior of China with marked success. To suppress and nip it in the bud, drastic measures were resorted to by Viceroy Yeh Ming Hsin, who, in the summer of 1855, decapitated seventy-five thousand people, most of whom, I was told, were innocent. My residence was within half a mile of the execution ground, as stated above, and one day, out of curiosity, I ventured to walk over to the place. But, oh! what a sight! The ground was perfectly drenched with human blood. On both sides of the driveway were to be seen headless human trunks, piled up in heaps, waiting to be taken away for burial. But no provision had been made to facilitate their removal.

The execution was carried on on a larger scale than had been expected, and no provision had been made to find a place large enough to bury all the bodies. There they were, left exposed to a burning sun. The temperature stood from morning to night in midsummer steadily at 90° Fahrenheit, and sometimes higher. The atmosphere within a radius of two thousand yards of the execution ground was heavily charged with the poisonous and pestilential vapor that was reeking from the ground already over–saturated with blood and from the heaps of corpses which had been left behind for at least two days, and which showed signs of rapid decomposition. It was a wonder to me that no virulent epidemic had sprung up from such an infectious spot to decimate the compact population of the city of Canton. It was a fortunate circumstance that at least a deep and extensive ravine, located in the far–off outskirts of the western part of the city, was found, which was at once converted into a sepulchral receptacle into which this vast human hecatomb was dumped. It was said that no earth was needed to be thrown over these corpses to cover them up; the work was accomplished by countless swarms of worms of a reddish hue and of an appearance that was perfectly hideous and revolting.

I was told that during the months of June, July and August, of 1855, seventy–five thousand people had been decapitated; that more than half of that number were declared to be innocent of the charge of rebellion, but that the accusation was made as pretext to exact money from them. This wholesale slaughter, unparalleled in the annals

of modern civilization, eclipsing even the enormities and blood-
thirstiness of Caligula and Nero, or even the French Revolution, was
perpetrated by Yeh Ming Hsin, who was appointed viceroy of Kwang
Tung and Kwangsi in 1854.

Yeh Ming Hsin was a native of Han–Yang. Han–Yang is a part of
the port of Hankau, and was destroyed with it when the Taiping rebels
took possession of it. It was said that Yeh Ming Hsin had immense
estates in Han–Yang, which were completely destroyed by fire. This
circumstance embittered him towards the Taiping rebels and as the
Taiping leaders hailed from Kwang Tung and Kwangsi, he naturally
transferred his hatred to the people of those two provinces. It was in
the lofty position of a viceroy that he found his opportunity to wreak his
private and personal vengeance upon the Canton people. This accounts
for his indiscriminate slaughter of them, and for the fact that he did not
deign to give them even the semblance of a trial, but hurried them from
life to death like packs of cattle to the shambles.

But this human monster did not dream that his day of reckoning
was fast approaching. Several years after this appalling sacrifice of
human life, in 1855, he got into trouble with the British government.
He was captured by the British forces and banished to some obscure
and remote corner in India where he led a most ignominious life, hated
by the whole Chinese nation, and despised by the world at large.

On my return to headquarters, after my visit to the execution
ground, I felt faint–hearted and depressed in spirit. I had no appetite
for food, and when night came, I was too nervous for sleep. The scene
I had looked upon during the day had stirred me up. I thought then
that the Taiping rebels had ample grounds to justify their attempt to

overthrow the Manchu regime. My sympathies were thoroughly enlisted in their favor and I thought seriously of making preparations to join the Taiping rebels, but upon a calmer reflection, I fell back on the original plan of doing my best to recover the Chinese language as fast as I possibly could and of following the logical course of things, in order to accomplish the object I had at heart.

Chapter VII Effort to Find a Position

Having at last succeeded in mastering the spoken language sufficiently to speak it quite fluently, I at once set to work to find a position in which I could not only support myself and mother, but also form a plan for working out my ideas of reform in China.

Doctor Peter Parker, who had been a medical missionary under the American Board for many years in Canton, was at the time made United States Commissioner as a temporary expedient, to take the place of an accredited minister plenipotentiary—a diplomatic appointment not yet come into existence, because the question of a foreign minister resident in Peking was still under negotiation, and had not been fully settled as a permanent diplomatic arrangement between the Peking government and the Treaty Powers. Dr. Parker was given the appointment of commissioner on account of his long residence in China and his ability to speak the Chinese language, but not on account of any special training as a diplomat, nor for legal knowledge. It was through Mr. M. N. Hitchcock, an American merchant of the firm of Messrs. King & Co., and a mutual friend of Dr. Parker and myself, that I became the Doctor's private secretary. I knew Dr. Parker while I was at

Mrs. Gutzlaff's School, and he doubtless knew I had recently graduated from Yale, which was his Alma Mater also. His headquarters were in Canton, but he spent his summers in Macao. I was with him only three months. My salary was $15 a month (not large enough to spoil me at any rate). He had very little for me to do, but I thought that by being identified with him, I might possibly come in contact with Chinese officials. However, this was far from being the case. Seeing that I could neither learn anything from him, nor enlarge my acquaintance with the Chinese officials, I gave up my position as his secretary and went over to Hong Kong to try to study law. Through my old friend, Andrew Shortrede, who generously extended to me the hospitality of his house, I succeeded in securing the position of the interpretership in the Hong Kong Supreme Court. The situation paid me $75 a month. Having this to fall back upon, I felt encouraged to go ahead in my effort to study law. Accordingly, I was advised to apprentice myself to an attorney or solicitor–at–law. In the English court of practice, it seems that there are two distinct classes of lawyers—attorneys or solicitors, and barristers. The first prepares in writing all evidences, facts, and proofs of a case, hands them to the barrister or counsel, who argues the case in court according to law.

I apprenticed myself to an attorney, who was recommended to me by my old patron and friend, Shortrede. I was not aware that by going into the British Colony in Hong Kong to become an attorney, I was stepping on the toes of the British legal fraternity, nor that by apprenticing myself to an attorney instead of to the new attorney–general of the Colony, who, without my knowledge, wanted me himself, I had committed another mistake, which eventually necessitated my leaving Hong Kong altogether.

First of all, all the attorneys banded themselves together against me, because, as they openly stated in all the local papers except the "China Mail". if I were allowed to practice my profession, they might as well pack up and go back to England, for as I had complete knowledge of both English and Chinese I would eventually monopolize all the Chinese legal business. So they made it too hot for me to continue in my studies.

In the next place, I was not aware that the attorney–general wanted me to apprentice myself to him, for he did all he could in his capacity as attorney–general of the Colony to use his influence to open the way for me to become an attorney, by draughting a special colonial ordinance to admit Chinese to practice in the Hong Kong Colony as soon as I could pass my examinations. This ordinance was sent to the British government to be sanctioned by Parliament before it became valid and a colonial law. It was sanctioned and thus became a colonial ordinance.

In the meanwhile, Anstey, the attorney–general, found out that I had already apprenticed myself to Parson, the attorney. From that time forth I had no peace. I was between two fires—the batteries operated by the attorneys opened on me with redoubled energy, and the new battery, operated by the attorney–general, opened its fire. He found fault with my interpreting, which he had never done previously. Mr. Parson saw how things stood. He himself was also under a hot fire from both sides. So in order to save himself, he told me plainly and candidly that he had to give me up and made the article of apprenticeship between us null and void. I, on my part, had to give up my position as interpreter in the

Supreme Court. Parson, himself, not long after I had abandoned my apprenticeship and my position as interpreter, for reasons satisfactory to himself, gave up his business in Hong Kong and returned to England. So master and pupil left their posts at pretty nearly the same time.

A retrospective view of my short experience in Hong Kong convinced me that it was after all the best thing that I did not succeed in becoming a lawyer in Hong Kong, as the theatre of action there would have been too restricted and circumscribed. I could not have come in touch with the leading minds of China, had I been bound up in that rocky and barren Colony. Doubtless I might have made a fortune if I had succeeded in my legal profession, but as circumstances forced me to leave the Colony, my mind was directed northward to Shanghai, and in August, 1856, I left Hong Kong in the tea clipper, "Florence", under Captain Dumaresque, of Boston. He was altogether a different type of man from the captain of the "Eureka" which brought me out in 1855. He was kind, intelligent and gentlemanly. When he found out who I was, he offered me a free passage from Hong Kong to Shanghai. He was, in fact, the sole owner of the vessel, which was named after his daughter, Florence. The passage was a short one—lasting only seven days—but before it was over, we became great friends.

Not long after my arrival in Shanghai, I found a situation in the Imperial Customs Translating Department, at a salary of Tls. 75 a month, equivalent to $100 Mexican. For want of a Chinese silver currency the Mexican dollar was adopted. This was one point better than the interpretership in the Hong Kong Supreme Court. The duties were not arduous and trying. In fact, they were too simple and easy to suit my taste and ambition. I had plenty of time to read. Before three months of trial in my new situation, I found that things were not as they should be, and if I wished to keep a clean and clear record and an untarnished character, I could not remain long in the service. Between the interpreters who had been in the service marry years and the Chinese shippers there existed a regular system of graft. After learning this, and not wishing to be implicated with the others in the division of the spoils in any way or shape, I made up my mind to resign. So one day I called upon the Chief Commissioner of Customs, ostensibly to find out what my future prospects were in connection in the Customs Service— whether or not there were any prospects of my being promoted to the position of a commissioner. I was told that no such prospects were held out to me or to any other Chinese interpreter. I, therefore, at once decided to throw up my position. So I sent in my resignation, which was at first not accepted. A few days after my first interview, Lay, the chief commissioner, strenuously tried to persuade me to change my mind, and offered as an inducement to raise my salary to Tls. 200 a month, evidently thinking that I was only bluffing in order to get higher wages. It did not occur to him that there was at least one Chinaman who valued a clean reputation and an honest character more than money; that being an educated man, I saw no reason why I should not be given the same chances to rise in the service of the Chinese government as an Englishman, nor why my individuality should not be recognized and respected in every walk of life. He little thought that I had aspirations even higher than his, and that I did not care to associate myself with a pack of Custom–house interpreters and inspectors, who were known to take bribes; that a man who expects others to respect him, must first respect himself. Such were my promptings. I did not state the real cause of my quitting the service, but at the end of four months' trial I left the service in order to try my fortune in new fields more congenial.

My friends at the time looked upon me as a crank in throwing up a position yielding me Tls. 200 a month for something uncertain and untried. This in their estimation was the height of folly. They little realized what I was driving at. I had a clean record and I meant to keep it clean. I was perfectly aware that in less than a year since my return to China, I had made three shifts. I myself began to think I was too mercurial to accomplish anything substantial, or that I was too dreamy to be practical or too proud to succeed in life. But in a strenuous life one needs to be a dreamer in order to accomplish possibilities. We are not called into being simply to drudge for an animal existence. I had had to work hard for my education, and I felt that I ought to make the most of what little I had, not so much to benefit myself individually as to make it a blessing common to my race. By these shifts and changes I was only trying to find my true bearing, and how I could make myself a blessing to China.

Chapter VIII　Experiences in Business

The next turn I took, after leaving the Imperial Customs, was clerk in an English house— tea and silk merchants. During the few months that I was with them, I gained quite an insight into mercantile business, and the methods of conducting it, which proved to be profitable knowledge and experience to me later on. Six months after I had entered upon my new sphere as a make-shift, the firm dissolved partnership, which once more threw me out of a position, and I was again cast upon the sea of uncertainty. But during my connection with the firm, two little incidents occurred which I must not fail to relate.

One Thursday evening, as I was returning home from a prayer meeting held in the Union Chapel in Shanghai, I saw ahead of me on Szechuen Road in front of the Episcopal church, a string of men; each had a Chinese lantern swinging in the air over his head, and they were singing and shouting as they zigzagged along the road, evidently having a jolly, good time, while Chinese on both sides of the road were seen dodging and scampering about in great fright in all directions, and acting as through they were chased by the Old Nick himself. I was at a distance of about one hundred yards from the scene. I took in the situation at once. My servant, who held a lantern ahead of me, to light the way, was so frightened that he began to come back towards me. I told him not to be afraid, but walk right straight ahead. Pretty soon we confronted three or four of the fellows, half tipsy. One of them snatched the lantern from my servant and another, staggering about, tried to give me a kick. I walked along coolly and unconcerned till I reached the last batch of two or three fellows. I found these quite sober and in their senses and they were lingering behind evidently to enjoy the fun and watch the crowd in their hilarious antics. I stopped and parleyed with them, and told them who I was. I asked them for the names of the fellows who snatched my boy's lantern and of the fellow who tried to kick me. They declined at first, but finally with the promise that I would not give them any trouble, they gave me the name of one of the fellows, his position on the vessel, and the name of the vessel he belonged to. It turned out that the man was the first mate of the ship "Eureka," the very vessel that brought me out to China, in 1855, and which happened to be consigned to the firm I was working for. The next morning, I wrote a note to the captain, asking him to hand the note to his first officer. The captain, on receiving the note, was quite excited, and handed it to the first mate, who immediately came ashore and apologized. I made it very pleasant for him and told him that Americans in China were held in high esteem by the people, and every American landing in China should be jealous of the high estimation in which they were held and not do anything to compromise it. My motive in writing the note was merely to get him on shore and give him this advice. He was evidently pleased with my friendly attitude and extended his hand for a shake to thank me for the advice. He invited me to go on board with him to take a glass of wine and be good friends. I thanked him for his offer, but declined it, and we parted in an amicable way.

My second incident, which happened a couple of months after the first, did not have such a peaceful ending.

After the partnership of the firm, in whose employ I was, dissolved, an auction sale of the furniture of the firm took place. In the room where the auction was proceeding, I happened to be standing in a mixed crowd of Chinese and foreigners. A stalwart six–footer of a Scotchman happened to be standing behind me. He was not altogether a stranger to me, for I had met him in the streets several times. He began to tie a bunch of cotton balls to my queue, simply for a lark. But I caught him at it and in a pleasant way held it up and asked him to untie it. He folded his arms and drew himself straight up with a look of the utmost disdain and scorn. I at once took in the situation, and as my countenance sobered, I reiterated my demand to have the appendage taken off. All of a sudden, he thrust his fist against my mouth, without drawing any blood, however. Although he stood head and shoulders above me in height, yet I was not at all abashed or intimidated by his burly and contemptuous appearance. My dander was up and oblivious to all thoughts of our comparative size and strength, I struck him back in the identical place where he punched me, but my blow was a stinger and it went with lightening rapidity to the spot without giving him time to think. It drew blood in great profusion from lip and nose. He caught me by the wrist with both his hands. As he held my right wrist in his powerful grasp, for he was an athlete and a sportsman, I was just on the point of raising my right foot for a kick, which was aimed at a vital point, when the head partner of the firm, who happened to be near, suddenly stepped in between and separated us. I then stood off to one side, facing my antagonist, who was moving off into the crowd. As I moved away, I was asked by a voice from the crowd:

"Do you want to fight?"

I said, "No, I was only defending myself. Your friend insulted me and added injury to insult. I took him for a gentlemen, but he has proved himself a blackguard."

With the stinging remark, which was heard all over the room, I retired from the scene into an adjoining room, leaving the crowd to comment on the incident. The British Consul, who happened to be present on the occasion, made a casual remark on the merits of the case and said, as I was told afterwards by a friend, that "The young man was a little too fiery; if he had not taken the law into his own hands, he could have brought suit for assault and battery in the consular court, but since he has already retaliated and his last remark before the crowd has inflicted a deeper cut to his antagonist than the blow itself, he has lost the advantage of a suit".

The Scotchman, after the incident, did not appear in public for a whole week. I was told he had shut himself up in his room to give his wound time to heal, but the reason he did not care to show himself was more on account of being whipped by a little Chinaman in a public manner; for the affair, unpleasant and unfortunate as it was, created quite a sensation in the settlement. It was the chief topic of conversation for a short time among foreigners, while among the Chinese I was look upon with great respect, for since the foreign settlement on the extra-territorial basis was established close to the city of Shanghai, no Chinese within its jurisdiction had ever been known to have the courage and pluck to defend his rights, point blank, when they had been violated or trampled upon by a foreigner. Their meek and mild disposition had allowed personal insults and affronts to pass unresented and unchallenged, which naturally had the tendency to encourage arrogance and insolence on the part of ignorant foreigners. The time will soon come, however, when the people of China will be so educated and enlightened as to know what their rights are, public and private, and to have the moral courage to assert and defend them whenever they are invaded. The triumph of Japan over Russia in the recent war has opened the eyes of the Chinese world. It will never tolerate injustice in any way or shape, much less will it put up with foreign aggression and aggrandizement any longer. They see now in what plight their national ignorance, conceit and conservatism, in which they had been fossilized, had placed them. They were on the verge of being partitioned by the European Powers and were saved from the catastrophe only by the timely intervention of the United States government. What the future will bring forth, since the Emperor Kwangsu and Dowager Empress Chi Hsi have both passed away, no one can predict.

The breaking up of the firm by which I was employed, once more, as stated before, and for the fourth time, threw me out of a regular business. But I was not at all disconcerted or discouraged, for I had no idea of following a mercantile life as a permanent calling. Within the past two years, my knowledge of the Chinese language had decidedly improved. I was not in hot haste to seek for a new position. I immediately took to translating as a means of bridging over the breaks of a desultory life. This independent avocation, though not a lucrative one, nevertheless led the way to a wider acquaintance with the educated and mercantile classes of the Chinese; to widen my acquaintance was my chief concern. My translating business brought me in contact with the comprador of one of the leading houses in Shanghai. The senior partner of this house died in 1857. He was well–known and thought much of by both the Chinese and the foreign mercantile body. To attest their high regard for his memory, the prominent Chinese merchants drew up an elaborate and eulogistic epitaph on the occasion of his death. The surviving members of the firm selected two translators to translate the epitaph. One was the interpreter in the British Consulate General, a brother to the author of "The Chinese and their Rebellions", and the other was (through the influence of the comprador) myself. To my great surprise, my translation was given the preference and accepted by the manager of the firm. The Chinese committee were quite elated that one of their countrymen knew enough English to bring out the inner sense of their epitaph. It was adopted and engraved on the monument. My name began to be known among the Chinese, not as a fighter this time, but as a Chinese student educated in America.

Soon after this performance, another event unexpectedly came up in which I was again called upon to act; that was the inundation of the Yellow River, which had converted the northern part of Kiangsu province into a sea, and made homeless and destitute thousands of people of that locality. A large body of refugees had wandered to and flocked near Shanghai. A Chinese deputation, consisting of the leading merchants and gentry, who knew or had heard of me, called and asked me to draw up a circular appealing to the foreign community for aid and contributions to relieve the widespread suffering among the refugees. Several copies were immediately put into circulation and in less than a week, no less than $20000 were subscribed and paid. The Chinese

Committee were greatly elated over their success and their joy was unbounded. To give a finish touch to this stroke of business, I wrote in the name of the committee a letter of acknowledgement and thanks to the foreign community for the prompt and generous contribution it had made. This was published in the Shanghai local papers— "The Shanghai Mail" and "Friend of China"—so that inside of three months after I had started my translating business, I had become widely known among the Chinese as the Chinese student educated in America. I was indebted to Tsang Kee Foo, the comprador, for being in this line of business, and for the fact that I was a well-educated Chinese—a man highly respected and trusted for his probity and intelligence. His long connection with the firm and his literary taste had gathered around him some of the finest Chinese scholars from all parts of China, while his business transactions brought him in touch with the leading Chinese capitalists and business men in Shanghai and elsewhere. It was through him that both the epitaph and the circular mentioned above were written; and it was Tsang Kee Foo who introduced me to the celebrated Chinese mathematician, Li Jen Shu, who years afterwards brought me to the notice of Viceroy Tsang Kwoh Fan—the distinguished general and statesman, who, as will be seen hereafter, took up and promoted the Chinese Educational Scheme. In the great web of human affairs, it is almost impossible to know who among our friends and acquaintances may prove to be the right clue to unravel the skein of our destiny. Tsang Kee Foo introduced me to Li Jen Shu, the latter introduced me to Tsang Kwoh Fan, who finally through the Chinese Educational Scheme grafted Western education to the Oriental culture, a union destined to weld together the different races of the world into one brotherhood.

My friend Tsang Kee Foo afterwards introduced me to the head or manager of Messrs. Dent & Co., who kindly offered me a position in his firm as comprador in Nagasaki, Japan, soon after that country was opened to foreign trade. I declined the situation, frankly and plainly stating my reason, which was that the compradorship, though lucrative, is associated with all that is menial, and that as a graduate of Yale, one of the leading colleges in America, I could not think of bringing discredit to my Alma Mater, for which I entertained the most profound respect and reverence, and was jealous of her proud fame. What would the college and my classmates think of me, if they should hear that I was a comprador—the head servant of servants in an English establishment? I said there were cases when a man from stress of circumstances may be compelled to play the part of a menial for a shift, but I was not yet reduced to that strait, though I was poor financially. I told him I would prefer to travel for the firm as its agent in the interior and correspond directly with the head of the firm. In that case, I would not sacrifice my manhood for the sake of making money in a position which is commonly held to be servile. I would much prefer to pack tea and buy silk as an agent—either on a salary or on commission. Such was my ground for declining. I, however, thanked him for the offer. This interview took place in the presence of my friend, Tsang Kee Foo, who without knowing the details of the conversation, knew enough of the English language to follow the general tenor of the talk. I then retired and left the manager and my friend to talk over the result. Tsang afterwards told me that Webb said, "Yung Wing is poor but proud. Poverty and pride usually go together, hand in hand." A few days afterwards Tsang informed me that Webb had decided to send me to the tea districts to see and learn the business of packing tea.

Chapter IX My First Trip to the Tea Districts

On the 11th of March, 1859, I found myself on board of a Woo–Sik–Kwei, a Chinese boat built in Woo–Sik, a city situated on the boarders of the Grand Canal, within a short distance of the famous city of Suchau—a rival of the city of Hangzhau, for wealth, population, silk manufacture and luxury. The word "Kwei" means "fast", Therefore, Woo–Sik–Kwei means fast boats of Woo–Sik. These passenger boats which piled between the principal cities and marts situated near the waters of the canal and lake system in southern Kianksu were usually built of various sizes and nicely fitted up for the comfort and convenience of the public. Those intended for officials, and the wealthy classes, were built on a larger scale and fitted up in a more pretentious style. They were all flatbottom boats. They sailed fairly well before the wind, but against it, they were either tracked by lines from the masts to the trackers on shore, or by sculling, at which the Chinese are adepts. They can give a boat a great speed by a pair of sculls resting on steel pivots that are fastened at the stern, one on each side, about the middle of the scull, with four men on each scull; the blades are made to play in the water astern, right and left, which pushes and sends the boat forward at a surprisingly rapid rate. But in recent years steam has made its way into China and steam launches have superseded these native craft which are fast disappearing from the smooth waters of Kiangsu province—very much as the fast sailing ships, known as Baltimore Clippers, that in the fifties and sixties were engaged in the East India and China trade, have been gradually swept from the ocean by steam.

At the end of three days, I was landed in the historic city of Hangchau, which is the capital of Chehkiang. It is situated on a plain of uneven ground, with hills in the southwest and west, and northeast. It covers an area of about three or four square miles. It is of a rectangular shape. Its length is from north to south; its breadth, from east to west. On the west, lies the Si–Hoo or West Lake, a beautiful sheet of limpid water with a gravelly or sandy bottom, stretching from the foot of the city wall to the foot of the mountains which appear in the distance in the rear, rising into the clouds like lofty bulwarks guarding the city on the north.

The Tsientang River, about two miles distant, flanks the city on the east. It takes its rise from the high mountain range of Hwui Chow in the southeast and follows a somewhat irregular course to the bay of the same name, and rushes down the rocky declivities like a foaming steed and empties itself into the bay about forty miles east of the city. This is one of the rivers that have periodical bores in which the tidal waters in their entrance to the bay create a noise like thunder, and the waves rise to the height of eight or ten feet.

Hangchau, aside from her historic fame as having been the seat of the government of the Sung Dynasty of the 12th and 13th centuries, has always maintained a wide reputation for fine buildings, public and private, such as temples, pagodas, mosques and bridges, which go to lend enchantment to the magnificent natural scenery with which she is singularly endowed. But latterly, age and the degeneration of the times have done their work of mischief. Her past glory is fast sinking into obscurity; she will never recover her former prestige, unless a new power arises to make her once more the capital of a regenerated government.

On the 15th of March, I left Hangchau to ascend the Tsientang River, at a station called Kang Kow, or mouth of the river, about two miles east of the city, where boats were waiting for us. Several hundreds of these boats of a peculiar and unique type were riding near the estuary of the river. These boats are called Urh Woo, named after the district where they were built. They vary from fifty to one hundred feet in length, from stem to stern, and are ten or fifteen feet broad, and draw not more than two or three feet of water when fully loaded. They are all flat-bottom boats, built of the most limber and flexible material that can be found, as they are expected to meet strong currents and run against rocks, both in their ascent and descent, on account of the irregularity and rocky bottom of the river. These boats, when completely equipped and covered with bamboo matting, look like huge cylinders, and are shaped like cigars. The interior from stem to stern is divided into separate compartments, or rooms, in which bunks are built to accommodate passengers. These compartments and bunks are removed when room is needed for cargoes. These boats ply between Hangchau and Sheong Shan and do all the interior transportation by water between these entrepôts in Chehkiang and Kiangsi Sheong Shan is the important station of Chehkiang, and Yuh-Shan is that of Kiangsi. The distance between the two entrepôts is about fiftylis, or about sixteen English miles, connected by one of the finest macadamized roads in China. The road is about thirty feet wide, paved with slabs of granite and flanked with greenish–colored cobbles. A fine stone arch which was erected as a landmark of the boundary line separating Chehkiang and Kiangsi provinces, spans the whole width of the road. On both sides of the key–stone of the arch are carved four fine Chinese characters, painted in bright blue, viz., Leang Hsing Tung Chu: 两省 通衢．

This is one of the most notable arch–ways through which the inter–provincial trade has been carried on for ages past. At the time when I crossed from Sheong Shan to Yuh–Shan, the river ports of Hankau, Kiukiang, Wuhu and Chinkiang were not opened to foreign trade and steamboats had not come in to play their part in the carrying trade of the interior of China. This magnificent thoroughfare was crowded with thousands of porters bearing merchandise of all kinds to and fro—exports and imports for distribution. It certainly presented an interesting sight to the traveler, as well as a profound topic of contemplation to a Chinese patriot.

The opening of the Yangtze River, which is navigable as far as Kaingchau, on the borders of Szechwan province, commanding the trade of at least six or seven provinces along its whole course of nearly three thousand miles to the ocean, presents a spectacle of unbounded possibilities for the amelioration of nearly a third of the human race, if only the grasping ambition of the West will let the territorial integrity and the independent sovereignty of China remain intact. Give the people of China a fair chance to work out the problems of their own salvation, as for instance the solution of the labor question, which has been so radically disorganized and broken up by steam, electricity and machinery. This has virtually taken the breath and bread away from nine-tenths of the people of China, and therefore this immovable mass of population should be given ample time to recover from its demoralization.

To go back to my starting point at Kang Kow, the entrance to the river, two miles east of Hangchau, we set sail, with a fair wind, at five o'clock in the morning of the 15th of March, and in the evening at ten o'clock we anchored at a place named the "Seven Dragons", after having made about one hundred miles during the day. The eastern shore in this part of the Tsientang River is evidently of red sandstone formation, for we could see part of the strata submerged in the water and excavations of the stone may be seen strewn about on the shore. In fact, red sandstone buildings may be seen scattered about here and there. But the mountain about the Seven Dragons is picturesque and romantic.

Early the next day, we again started, but the rain poured down in torrents. We kept on till we reached the town of Lan Chi and came to anchor in the evening, after having made about forty miles. This is the favorite entrepôt where the Hupeh and Hunan congou teas were brought all the way from the tea districts of these provinces, to be housed and transshipped to Shanghai via Hangchau. Lan Chi is an entrepôts of only one street, but its entire length is six miles. It is famous for its nice hams, which are known all over China. On account of the incessant rain, we stopped half a day at Lan Chi. In the afternoon the sky began to clear and at twelve o'clock in the night we again started and reached the walled city of Ku Chow, which was besieged by the Taiping rebels in March, 1858, just a year before; after four months' duration the siege was raised and no great damage was done. We put up in an inn for the night. Ku Chow is a departmental city of Chehkiang and is about thirty miles distant from Sheong Shan, already mentioned in connection with Yuh–Shan. We were delayed by the Custom House officials, as well as on account of the scarcity of porters and chair–bearers to take us over to Sheong Shan. We arrived at Yuh–Shan from Sheong Shan by chair in the evening. We put up in an inn for the night, having first engaged fishing boats to take us to the city of Kwangshun, thirty miles from Yuh–Shan, we were in Kiangsi territory, and our route now lay in a west by north direction, down stream towards the Po Yang Lake, whose southern margin we passed, and reached Nan Cheong, the capital of Kiangsi province. The city presented a fine outward appearance. We did not stop long enough to go through the city and see its actual condition since its evacuation by the rebels.

Our route from Nan Cheong was changed in a west by south direction, making the great entrepôts of Siang Tan our final goal. In this route, we passed quite a number of large cities that had nothing of special importance, either commercially or historically, to relate. We passed Cheong Sha, the capital of Hunan, in the night. We arrived at Siang Tan on the morning of the 15th of April. Siang Tan is one of the noted entrepôts in the interior of China and used to be the great distributing center of imports when foreign trade was confined to the single port of Canton. It was also the emporium where the tea and silk goods of China were centered and housed, to be carried down to Canton for exportation to foreign countries. The overland transport trade between Siang Tan and Canton was immense. It gave employment to at least one hundred thousand porters, carrying merchandise over the Nan Fung pass, between the two cities, and supported a large population along both sides of the thoroughfare. Steam, wars and treaties of very recent dates have not only broken up this system of labor and changed the complexion of the whole labor question throughout China, but will also alter the economical, industrial and political conditions of the Chinese Empire during the coming years of her history.

At Siang Tan, our whole party, composed of tea—men, was broken up and each batch began its journey to the district assigned it, to begin the work of purchasing raw tea and preparing it to be packed for shipment in Shanghai.

I stayed in Siang Tan about ten days and then made preparations for a trip up to the department of Kingchau in Hupeh province, to look into the yellow silk produced in a district called Ho—Yung.

We left Siang Tan on the 26th of April, and proceeded northward to our place of destination. Next morning at eight o'clock we reached Cheong Sha, the capital of Hunan province. As the day was wet and gloomy, we stopped and tried to make the best of it by going inside of the city to see whether there was anything worth seeing, but like all Chinese cities, it presented the same monotonous appearance of age and filth, the same unchangeable style of architecture and narrow streets. Early next morning, we resumed our boat journey, crossed the Tung Ting Lake and the great river Yangtze till we entered the mouth of the King Ho which carried us to Ho Yung. On this trip to hunt after the yellow silk—not the golden fleece—we were thirteen days from Siang Tan. The country on both banks of the King Ho seemed quiet and peaceful and people were engaged in agricultural pursuits. We saw many buffaloes and donkeys, and large patches of wheat, interspersed with beans. A novel sight presented itself which I have never met with elsewhere in China. A couple of country lassies were riding on a donkey, and were evidently in a happy mood, laughing and talking as they rode by. Arriving in Ho Yung, we had some difficulty in finding an inn, but finally succeeded in securing quarters in a silk hong. No sooner were we safely quartered, than a couple of native constables called to know who we were; our names and business were taken down. Our host, the proprietor of the hong, who knew the reason of our coming, explained things to the satisfaction of the men, who went away perfectly satisfied that we were honest traders and no rebel spies. We were left to transact our business unmolested. As soon as our object was known, numerous samples of yellow silk were brought for our inspection. We selected quite a number of samples, which altogether weighed about sixty–five pounds, and had them packed to be taken to Shanghai.

At the end of a fortnight, we concluded to take our journey back. Accordingly, on the 26th of May we bade Ho Yung farewell, and started for the tea district of Nih Kia Shi, in the department of Cheong Sha, via Hankau. We arrived at Hankau on the 5th of June, and put up in a native inn. The weather was hot and muggy, and our quarters were narrow and cut off from fresh air. Three days after our arrival, three deputies visited us to find out who we were. It did not take long to convince them that we were not rebel spies. We showed them the package of yellow silk, which bore marks of a war–tax which we had to pay on it, all along the route from Ho Yung to Hankau. We were left unmolested.

The port of Hankau had not been opened for foreign trade, though it was well understood that it was to be opened very soon. Before its capture by the Taiping rebels, or rather before the Taiping rebels had made their appearance on the stage of action, Hankau was the most important entrepôts in China. When the Taiping rebels captured Woochang in 1856, Hankau and Han Yang fell at the same time, and the port was destroyed by fire and was reduced to ashes. At the time of my visit, the whole place was rebuilt and trade began to revive. But the buildings were temporary shifts. Now the character of the place is completely changed and the foreign residences and warehouses along the water's edge have given it altogether a European aspect, so that the Hankau of today may be regarded as the Chicago or St. Louis of China, and in no distant day she is destined to surpass both in trade, population and wealth. I was in Hankau a few days before I crossed the Yangtze–Kiang to the black tea district of Nih Kia Shi.

We left Hankau on the 30th of June and went over to the tea packing houses in Nih Kia Shi and Yang Liu Tung on the 4th of July. I was in those two places over a month and gained a complete knowledge of the whole process of preparing the black tea for the foreign market. The process is very simple and can be easily learned. I do not know through what preparations the Indian and Assam teas have to go, where machinery is used, but they cannot be very elaborate. Undoubtedly, since the fifties, manual labor, the old standby in preparing tea for foreign consumption, has been much improved with a view of retaining a large percentage of the tea trade in China. The reason why a large percentage of the tea business has passed away from China to India is not because machinery is used in the one case and manual labor is retained in the other, but chiefly on account of the quality of the tea that is raised in the different soil of the two countries. The Indian or Assam tea is much stronger (in proportion to the same quantity) than the Chinese tea. The Indian tea is 2–1 to Chinese tea, in point of strength, whereas the Chinese tea is 2–1 to the Indian tea in point of delicacy and flavor. The Indian is rank and strong, but the Chinese tea is superior in the quality of its fine aroma. The higher class of tea-drinkers in America, Europe and Russia prefer China tea to Indian, whereas the laboring and common class in those countries take to Indian and Assam, from the fact that they are stronger and cheaper.

In the latter part of August I decided to return to Shanghai, not by way of Siang Tan, but via Hankau, down the Yangtze River to Kiu Kang and across the Poh Yang Lake. I arrived at Hankau again the second time on the 29th of August, having left there two months previous, in July. This time I came in a Hunan junk loaded with tea for Shanghai. At Ho Kow, the southern shore of the Poh Yang Lake, I had to follow the same route I took in March, and on the 21st of September I landed at Hangchau and from there I took a Woo–Sik–Kwei for Shanghai, where I arrived in the night of the 30th of September, the time consumed on this journey having been seven months—from March to October. It was my first journey into the interior of China, and it gave me a chance to gain an insight into the actual condition of the people, while a drastic rebellion was going on in their midst. The zone of the country through which I had passed had been visited by the rebels and the imperialists, but was, to all outward appearance, peaceful and quiet. To what extent the people had suffered both from rebel and imperialist devastations in those sections of the country, no one can tell. But there was one significant fact that struck me forcibly and that was the sparseness of population, which was at variance with my preconceived notions regarding the density of population in China which I had gathered from books and accounts of travelers. This was particularly noticeable through that section of Chehkiang, Kiangsi, Hunan and Hupeh, which I visited. The time of the year, when crops of all kinds needed to be planted, should have brought out the peasantry into the open fields with oxen, mules, donkeys, buffaloes and horses, as indispensable accessories to farm life. But comparatively few farmers were met with.

Shortly after my arrival from the interior, in October, an English friend of mine requested me to go to Shaun Hang to buy raw silk for him. Shaun Hang is a city located in a silk district about twenty miles southwest of Hangchau, and noted for its fine quality of silk. I was about two months in this business, when I was taken down with fever and ague and was compelled to give it up. Shaun Hang, like most Chinese cities, was filthy and unhealthy and the water that flowed through it was as black as ink. The city was built in the lowest depression of a valley, and the outlet of the river was so blocked that there was hardly any current to carry off the filth that had been accumulating for ages. Hence the city was literally located in cesspool—a breeding place for fever and ague, and epidemics of all kinds. But I soon recovered from the attack of the fever and ague and as soon as I could stand on my legs again, I immediately left the malarial atmosphere, and was, in a short time, breathing fresher and purer air.

Chapter X   My Visit to the Taipings

In the fall of 1859 a small party of two missionaries, accompanied by Tsang Laisun, planned a trip to visit the Taiping rebels in Nanking. I was asked to join them, and I decided to do so. My object in going was to find out for my own satisfaction the character of the Taipings; whether or not they were the men fitted to set up a new government in the place of the Manchu Dynasty. Accordingly, on the 6th of November, 1859, we left Shanghai in a Woo–Sik–Kwei boat, with a stiff northeast breeze in our favor, though we had to stem an ebb tide for an hour. The weather was fine and the whole party was in fine spirits. We happened to have an American flag on board, and on the spur of the moment, it was flung to the breeze, but on a sober second thought, we had it hauled down so as not to attract undue attention and have it become the means of thwarting the purpose of our journey. Instead of taking the Sung–Kiang route which was the highway to Suchau, we turned off into another one in order to avoid the possibility of being hauled up by the imperialists and sent back to Shanghai, as we were told that an imperial fleet of Chinese gun–boats was at anchor at Sung Kiang. We found the surrounding country within a radius of thirty miles of Shanghai to be very quiet and saw no signs of political disturbance. The farmers were

205

busily engaged in gathering in their rice crops.

It might be well to mention here that during my sojourn in the interior, the Taiping rebels had captured the city of Suchau, and there was some apprehension on the part of foreigners in the settlement that they might swoop down to take possession of the city of Shanghai, as well as the foreign settlement. That was the reason the Sung Kiang River was picketed by Chinese gunboats, and the foreign pickets were extended miles beyond the boundary line of the foreign concession.

We reached Suchau on the morning of the 9th of November without meeting with any difficulty or obstacles all the way, nor were we challenged either by the imperialists or rebels, which went to show how loosely and negligently even in time of war, things were conducted in China. On arriving at the Lau Gate of the city, we had to wait at the station where tickets were issued to those who went into the city and taken from those who left, for Suchau was then under martial law. As we wished to go into the city to see the commandant, in order to get letters of introduction from him to the chiefs of other cities along our route to Nanking, we had to send two of our party to headquarters to find out whether we were permitted to enter. At the station, close to the Lau Gate, we waited over an hour. Finally our party appeared accompanied by the same messenger who had been deputed by the head of the police to accompany them to the commandant's office. Permission was given us, and all four went in. The civil officer was absent, but we were introduced to the military commandant, Liu. He was a tall man, dressed in red. His affected hauteur at the start was too thin to disguise his want of a solid character. He became very inquisitive and asked the object of our journey to Nanking. He treated us very kindly, however, and gave us a letter of introduction to the commandant in Tan Yang, and furnished us with passports all the way through the cities of Woo Sik and Cheong Chow. In the audience hall of Commandant Liu, we were introduced to four foreigners—two Americans, one Englishman, and a French noble. One of the Americans said he was a doctor, the Englishman was supposed to be a military officer, and the Frenchman, as stated above, claimed to be a nobleman. Doubtless they were all adventurers. Each had his own ax to grind. One of the Americans had a rifle and cartridges for sale. He asked quite an exorbitant price for them and they were summarily rejected. The Frenchmen said he had lost a fortune and had come to China to make it up. Our missionary companions were much pleased after being entertained by Liu in hearing him recite the doxology, which he did glibly. Towards evening, when we returned to our boat, he sent us a number of chickens and a goat to boot. We were thus amply provisioned to prosecute our journey to Tan Yang. We left Suchau on the morning of the 11th of November. On our arrival at Woo Sik, our passports were examined and we were very courteously treated by the rebels. We were invited to dinner by the chief in command. After that he sent us fruits and nuts, and came on board himself to see us off. We held quite a long conversation with him, which ended in his repeating the doxology.

November 12th we left Woo Sik and started for Cheong Chow. From Suchau onward we were on the Grand Canal. The road on the bank of the canal was in good condition. Most of the people we saw and met were rebels, traveling between Tan Yang and Suchau, and but few boats were seen passing each other. All the country surrounding the canal between those cities seemed to have been abandoned by the peasantry and the cultivated fields were covered with rank grass and weeds, instead of flourishing crops. A traveler, not knowing the circumstances, would naturally lay the blame wholly upon the Taiping rebels, but the imperialists in their conflicts with the rebels, were as culpable as their enemies. The rebels whom we met on the public road were generally very civil and tried in every way to protect the people in order to gain their confidence. Incendiarism, pillage, robbery and ill-treatment of the people by the rebels were punished by death. We reached Cheong Chow in the night. We found nearly all the houses along the road between Woo Sik and Cheong Chow to be completely deserted and emptied of all their inmates. There were occasionally a few of the inhabitants to be seen standing on the bank with small baskets peddling eggs, oranges and cakes, vegetables and pork. They were principally old people, with countenances showing their suffering and despair. On November 13, at six o'clock in the morning, we resumed our journey to Tan Yang. As we drew near Tan Yang, the people seemed to have regained their confidence and the fields seemed to be cultivated. The conduct of the rebels towards them was considerate and commendable. During the morning we saw a force of one thousand men marching towards Tan Yang. We did not quite reach Tan Yang and came to anchor for the night in plain sight of it.

Early next morning, we went into the city to see the Commandant Liu, to present to him the letter we received in Suchau, but he was absent from the city. The man next to Liu, a civilian, came out to meet us. He was very affable and treated us kindly and with great civility. One of our party referred to the religions character of the Taipings.

Chin then gave us his views of Christianity, as taught by Hung Siu

Chune—the leader of the rebellion. He said:

"We worship God the Heavenly Father, with whom Jesus and the Holy Spirit constitute the true God; that Shang Ti is the True Spirit."

He then repeated the doxology. He said the rebels have two doxologies—the old and the new; they had discarded the new and adopted the old. He said, the Tien Wong—the Celestial Emperor—was taken up to Heaven and received orders from the Heavenly Father to come and exterminate all evil and rectify all wrong; to destroy idolatry and evil spirits, and finally to teach the people the knowledge of God. He did not know whether the Tien Wong was translated to Heavenly bodily or in spirit, or both. He said the Tien Wong himself explained that he could not hold the same footing with God himself; that the homage paid to God was an act of religious worship, but that rendered to the Tien Wong was merely an act of court etiquette, which ministers and officers always paid to their sovereigns and in every dynasty, and could not be construed as acts of worship. He also said that Tien Wong was a younger brother of Christ, but that it did not follow that he was born of the same mother. Tien Wong, he claimed, was a younger brother of Christ in the sense that he was especially appointed by God to instruct the people. Christ was also appointed by God to reform and redeem the world. With regard to the three cups of tea—he said that they were intended as a thank–offering, and were not propitiatory in their character.

"Whenever we drink a cup of tea, we offer thanksgiving to the Heavenly Father. The three cups of tea have no reference to the Trinity whatever. One cup answers the same purpose. The number three was purposely chosen, because it is the favorite number with the Chinese—

it is even mentioned in the Chinese classics."

As for redemption, he said, "No sacrificial offering can take away our sins; the power of redemption is in Christ; he redeems us and it is our duty to repent of our sins. Even the Tien Wong is very circumspect and is afraid to sin against God."

In the matter of the soldiery keeping aloof from the people in time of war, he said, "It has been an immemorial custom, adopted by almost every dynasty, that the people should go to the country, and the soldiers be quartered in the city. When a city is captured or taken, it is easy to subjugate the surrounding country."

The places we saw in ruins, both at Suchau and all the way up the canal, were partly destroyed by Cheong Yuh Leang's troops in their retreat, partly by local predatory parties for the sake of plunder, and partly by the Taipings themselves. When Chung Wong was in Suchau, he did all he could to suppress incendiarism by offering rewards of both money and rank to those who took an active part in suppressing it. He issued three orders:

1. That soldiers were not allowed to kill or slaughter the inhabitants.

2. They were prohibited from slaughtering cattle.

3. They were prohibited from setting fire to houses.

A violation of any of these orders was attended with capital punishment. When he came down to Woo Sik, he had a country elder decapitated for allowing local bandits to burn down the houses of the people. This was the information we gathered from our conversation with Chin. He also said that Yung Wing and Chung Wong were both talented men—not only in military but also in civil affairs.

He gave us a long account of the capture of different places by the rebels, and how they had been defeated before Nanking, when that city was laid siege to by the imperialists in the early part of 1860. He also showed us a letter by a chief at Hwui Chow regarding the utter defeat and rout of Tsang Kwoh Fan, who was hemmed in by an immense force of the rebels. Tsang was supposed to have been killed in the great battle. He said that Cheong Yuh Leang, the imperialist general, who laid siege to Nanking, after his defeat went to Hangchau for medical treatment for hemorrhage of the lungs; that all the country along the canal, north of the Yangtze, was in the hands of the rebels, and that Princes Chung and Ying were marching up the river to take possession of Hupeh, and that Shih Ta Kai, another chief, was assigned the conquest of Yun Nan, Kwai Chow and Sze Chune provinces. At that time Chin Kiang was being besieged by the rebels, and Chi Wong was in command of an army of observation in Kiang Nan. Such was the rambling statement given us by Chin regarding the disposition of the rebel forces under different chiefs or princes.

After dining with him in the evening, we repaired to our boat for the night. The next morning, November 15th, we again went into the city and called upon Liu, but, failing to see him, we again called upon Chin to arrange for the conveyance of our luggage and ourselves from Tan Yang to Nanking. The aide told us to send all our things in Chin's office and that our boat, if left in Tan Yang until our return, would be well cared for and protected during our absence. So next morning, the 16th of November, we started on foot and walked fifteen miles from Tan Yang to a village called Po Ying, about six miles from the city of Ku Yung, where we halted to pass the night. We had some difficulty in securing a resting place. The people were poor and had no confidence in strangers. We, however, after some coaxing, were supplied with straws spread out on the ground, and the next morning we gave the old woman a dollar. We had boiled rice gruel, cold chicken and crackers for our breakfast. When we reached Ku Yung about nine o'clock on the 17th of November, we found that every gate of the city was closed against us, as well as all others, because a rumor was afloat that the rebels before Chin Kiang were defeated, and that they were flocking towards Ku Yung for shelter. So we concluded to continue on our journey towards Nanking, though our missionary friends came near deciding to return to Tan Yang and wend our way back to Shanghai. We proceeded not far from Ku Yung, when we finally proceeded in getting chairs and mules to prosecute our journey.

On the 18th of November, after a trying and wearisome journey, we reached Nanking. I was the first one to reach the South Gate, waiting for the rest of the party to come up before entering. We were reported inside of the gate and messengers accompanied us to the headquarters of the Rev. Mr. Roberts, close by the headquarters of Hung Jin, styled Prince Kan.

After our preliminary introduction to the Rev. Mr. Roberts, I excused myself, and leaving the rest of the party to continue their conversation with him, retired to my quarters to clean up and get rested from the long and tedious journey. In fact, I had little or nothing to say while in Mr. Roberts' presence, nor did I attempt to make myself known to him. I had seen him often in Macao when in Mrs. Gutzlaff's school, twenty or more years before, and I had recognized him at once as soon as I set my eyes on him. He certainly appeared old to me, being dressed in his yellow satin robe of state and moving leisurely in his clumsy Chinese shoes. Exactly in what capacity he was acting in Nanking, I was at a loss to know; whether still as a religious adviser to Hung Siu Chune, or playing the part of secretary of state for the Taiping Dynasty, no one seemed able to tell.

The next day (the 19th of November) I was invited to call on Kan Wong. He was a nephew of Hung Siu Chune, the rebel chief who was styled Tien Wong or the Celestial Sovereign. Before Hung Jin came to Nanking, I had made his acquaintance, in 1856, at Hong Kong. He was then connected with the London Mission Association as a native preacher and was under Dr. James Legge, the distinguished translator of the Chinese classics. I saw considerable of him while in Hong Kong and even then he had expressed a wish that he might see me some day in Nanking. He was then called Hung Jin, but since he had joined his uncle in Nanking, he was raised to the position of prince. Kan means "Protecting," and Kan Wong signifies "Protecting Prince." He greeted me very cordially and evidently was glad to see me. After the usual exchange of conventionalities, he wanted to know what I thought of the Taipings; whether I thought well enough of their cause to identify myself with it. In reply, I said I had no intention of casting my lot with them, but came simply to see him and pay my respects. At the same time, I wanted to find out for my own satisfaction the actual condition of things in Nanking. I said the journey from Suchau to Nanking had suggested several things to me, which I thought might be of interest to him. They were as follows:

1. To organize an army on scientific principles.

2. To establish a military school for the training of competent military officers.

3. To establish a naval school for a navy.

4. To organize a civil government with able and experienced men to act as advisers in the different departments of administration.

5. To establish a banking system, and to determine on a standard of weight and measure.

6. To establish an educational system of graded schools for the people, making the Bible one of the text books.

7. To organize a system of industrial schools.

These were the topics that suggested themselves to me during the journey. If the Taiping government would be willing, I said, to adopt these measures and set to work to make suitable appropriations for them, I would be perfectly willing to offer my services to carry them out. It was in that capacity that I felt I could be of the most service to the Taiping cause. In any other, I would simply be an encumbrance and a hindrance to them.

Such was the outcome of my first interview. Two days later, I was again invited to call. In the second interview, we discussed the merits and the importance of the seven proposals stated in our first interview. Kan Wong, who had seen more of the outside world than the other princes or leaders, and even more than Hung Siu Chune himself, knew wherein lay the secret of the strength and power of the British government and other European powers, and fully appreciated the paramount importance and bearing of these proposals. But he was alone and had no one to back him in advocating them. The other princes, or leaders, were absent from the city, carrying on their campaign against the imperialists. He said he was well aware of the importance of these measures, but nothing could be done until they returned, as it required the consent of the majority to any measure before it could be carried out.

A few days after this a small parcel was presented to me as coming from Kan Wong. On opening it, I found to my great surprise a wooden seal about four inches long and an inch wide, having my name carved with the title of "E," 乂 which means "Righteousness," and designates the fourth official rank under that of a prince, which is first. My title was written out on a piece of yellow satin stamped with the official seal of the Kan Wong. I was placed in a quandary and was at a loss to know its purport—whether it was intended to detain me in Nanking for good or to commit me irretrievably to the Taiping cause, *nolens volens*. At all events, I had not been consulted in the matter and Kan Wong had evidently acted on his own responsibility and taken it for granted that by conferring on me such a high rank as the fourth in the official scale of the Taipings, I might be induced to accept and thus identify myself with the Taiping cause—of the final success of which I had strong doubts, judging from the conduct, character and policy of the leading men connected with it. I talked the matter over with my associates, and came to the decision that I must forthwith return the seal and decline the tempting bauble. I went in person to thank Kan Wong for this distinguished mark of his high consideration, and told him that at any time when the leaders of the Taipings decided to carry out either one or all of my suggestions, made in my first interview with him, I should be most happy to serve them, if my services were needed to help in the matter. I then asked him as a special favor for a passport that would guarantee me a safe conduct in traveling through the territory under the jurisdiction of the Taipings, whether on business or pleasure. The passport was issued to me the next day, on the 24th of December, and we were furnished with proper conveyances and provisions to take us back to the city of Tan Yang, where our boat lay under the protection of Chin, second in command of the city, waiting our return from Nanking. We started on our return trip for Shanghai on the 27th of December by the same route as we came, and arrived safely in Tan Yang in the early part of January, 1861. On my way back to Shanghai, I had ample time to form an estimate of the Taiping Rebellion—its origin, character and significance.

Chapter XI Reflections on the Taiping Rebellion

Rebellions and revolutions in China are not new and rare historic occurrences. There have been at least twenty–four dynasties and as many attendant rebellions or revolutions. But with the exception of the Feudatory period, revolutions in China (since the consolidation of the three Kingdoms into the one Empire under the Emperor Chin) meant only a change of hands in the government, without a change either of its form, or principles. Hence the history of China for at least two thousand years, like her civilization, bears the national impress of a monotonous dead level—jejune in character, wanting in versatility of genius, and almost devoid of historic inspiration.

The Taiping Rebellion differs from its predecessors in that in its embryo state it had taken onto itself the religious element, which became the vital force that carried it from the defiles and wilds of Kwangsi province in the southwest to the city of Nanking in the northeast, and made it for a period of fifteen years a constantly impending danger to the Manchu Dynasty, whose corruption, weakness and maladministration were the main causes that evoked the existence of this great rebellion.

The religious element that gave it life and character was a foreign product, introduced into China by the early Protestant missionaries, of whom Dr. Robert Morrison was the first English pioneer sent out by the London Mission, followed a decade later by the Rev. Icabod J. Roberts, an American missionary. These two missionaries may properly claim the credit, if there is any, of having contributed (each in his particular sphere) in imparting to Hung Siu Chune a knowledge of Christianity. Dr. Morrison, on his part, had translated the Bible into Chinese, and the Emperor Khang Hsi's dictionary into English; both these achievements gave the missionary work in China a basis to go upon in prosecuting the work of revising and of bringing the Bible to the Chinese standard of literary taste, so as to commend it to the literary classes, and in making further improvements in perfecting the Chinese–English dictionary, which was subsequently done by such men as Dr. Medhurts, Bishop Boone, Dr. Legge, E. C. Bridgeman, and S. Wells Williams.

Besides these works of translation, which undoubtedly called for further revision and improvement, Dr. Morrison also gave China a native convert—Leang Alifah—who became afterwards a noted preacher and the author of some religious tracts.

Hung Siu Chune, in his quest after religious knowledge and truths, got hold of a copy of Dr. Morrison's Bible and the tracts of Leang Afah. He read and studied them, but he stood in need of a teacher to explain to him many points in the Bible, which appeared to him mysterious and obscure. He finally made the acquaintance of the Rev. Mr. Icabod J. Roberts, an American missionary from Missouri, who happened to make his headquarters in Canton. Hung Siu Chune called upon him often, till their acquaintance ripened into a close and lasting friendship, which was kept up till Hung Siu Chune succeeded in taking Nanking, when Mr. Roberts was invited to reside there in the double capacity of a religious teacher and a state adviser. This was undoubtedly done in recognition of Mr. Roberts' services as Hung's teacher and friend while in Canton. No one knew what had become of Mr. Roberts when Nanking fell and reverted to the imperialists in 1864.

It was about this time, when he was sedulously seeking Mr. Roberts' religious instructions at Canton, that Hung failed to pass his first competitive examination as a candidate to compete for official appointment, and he decided to devote himself exclusively to the work of preaching the Gospel to his own people, the Hakkas of Kwang Tung and Kwangsi. But as a colporter and native preacher, Hung had not reached the climax of his religious experience before taking up his stand as the leader of his people in open rebellion against the Manchu Dynasty.

We must go back to the time when, as a candidate for the literary competitive examinations, he was disappointed. This threw him into a fever, and when he was tossing about in delirium, he was supposed to have been translated to Heaven, where he was commanded by the Almighty to fill and execute the divine mission of his life, which was to destroy idolatry, to rectify all wrong, to teach the people a knowledge of the true God, and to preach redemption through Christ. In view of such a mission, he at once assumed himself to be the son of God, coequal with Christ, whom he called his elder brother.

It was in such a state of mental hallucination that Hung Siu Chune appeared before his little congregation of Hakkas—migrating strangers—in the defiles and wilds of Kwangsi. Their novel and strange conduct as worshippers of Shang Ti—the Supreme Ruler— their daily religious exercises, their prayers, and their chanting of the doxology as taught and enjoyed by him, had attracted a widespread attention throughout all the surrounding region of Kwangsi. Every day fresh accessions of new comers flocked to their fold and swelled their ranks, till their numerical force grew so that the local mandarins were baffled and at their wits' end to know what to do with these believers of Christianity. Such, in brief, was the origin, growth and character of the Christian element working among the simple and rustic mountaineers of Kwangsi and Kwang Tung.

It is true that their knowledge of Christianity, as sifted through the medium of the early missionaries from the West, and the native converts and colporters, was at best crude and elementary, but still they were truths and great power, potential enough to turn simple men and religiously—inclined women into heroes and heroines who faced dangers and death with the utmost indifference, as was seen subsequently, when the government had decided to take the bull by the horns and resorted to persecution as the final means to break up this religious, fanatical community. In their conflicts with the imperial forces, they had neither guns nor ammunition, but fought with broomsticks, flails and pitchforks. With these rustic and farming implements they drove the imperialist hordes before them as chaff and stubble before a hurricane. Such was their pent—up religious enthusiasm and burning ardor.

Now this religious persecution was the side issue that had changed the resistance of Hung Siu Chune and his followers, in their religious capacity, into the character of a political rebellion. It is difficult to say whether or not, if persecution had not been resorted to, Hung Siu Chune and his followers would have remained peaceably in the heart of China and developed a religious community. We are inclined to think, however, that even if there had been no persecution, a rebellion would have taken place, from the very nature of the political situation.

Neither Christianity nor religious persecution was the immediate and logical cause of the rebellion of 1850. They might be taken as incidents or occasions that brought it about, but they were not the real cause of its existence. These may be found deeply seated in the vitals of the political constitution of the government. Foremost among them was the corruption of the administrative government. The whole official organization, from head to foot, was honeycombed and tainted by a system of bribery, which passed under the polite and generic term of "presents", similar in character to what is now known as "graft". Next comes the exploitation of the people by the officials, who found an inexhaustible field to build up their fortunes. Finally comes the inevitable and logical corollary to official bribery and exploitation, namely, that the whole administrative government was founded on a gigantic system of fraud and falsehood.

The rebellion rose in the arena of China with an enigmatic character like that of the Sphinx, somewhat puzzling at the start. The Christian world throughout the whole West, on learning of its Christian tendencies, such as the worship of the true and living God; Christ the Savior of the world; the Holy Spirit, the purifier of the soul; the destruction of temples and idols that was found wherever their victorious arms carried them; the uncompromising prohibition of the opium habit; the observance of a Sabbath; the offering of prayers before

221

and after meals; the invocation of divine aid before a battle—all these cardinal points of a Christian faith created a world–wide impression that China, though the instrumentality of the Taipings, was to be evangelized; that the Manchu Dynasty was to be swept out of existence, and a "Celestial Empire of Universal Peace", as it was named by Hung Siu Chune, was going to be established, and thus China, by this wonderful intervention of a wise Providence, would be brought within the pale of Christian nations. But Christendom was a little too credulous and impulsive in the belief. It did not stop to have the Christianity of the Taipings pass through the crucible of a searching analysis.

Their first victory over their persecutors undoubtedly gave Hung Siu Chune and his associates the first intimation of a possible overturning of the Manchu Dynasty and the establishment of a new one, which he named in his religious ecstasy "The Celestial Empire of Universal Peace". To the accomplishment of this great object, they bent the full force of their iconoclastic enthusiasm and religious zeal.

En route from Kwang Si, their starting point, to Nanking, victory had perched on their standard all the way. They had dispatched a division of their army to Peking, and, on its way to the northern capitol, it had met with a repulse and defeat at Tientsin from whence they had turned back to Nanking. In their victorious march through Hunan, Hupeh, Kiang Si and part of An Hwui, their depleted forces were replenished and reinforced by fresh and new accessions gathered from the people of those provinces. They were the riffraff and scum of their populations. This rabble element added no new strength to their fighting force, but proved to be an encumbrance and caused decided weakness. They knew no discipline, and had no restraining religious power to keep them from pillage, plunder and indiscriminate destruction. It was through such new accessions that the Taiping cause lost its prestige, and was defeated before Tientsin and forced to retreat to Nanking. After their defeat in the North, they began to decline in their religious character and their bravery. Their degeneracy was accelerated by the capture of Yung Chow, Suchau and Hangchau, cities noted in Chinese history for their great wealth as well as for their beautiful women. The capture of these centers and a materialistic civilization poured into their laps untold wealth and luxury which tended to hasten their downfall.

The Taiping Rebellion, after fifteen years of incessant and desultory fighting, collapsed and passed into oblivion, without leaving any traces of its career worthy of historical commemoration beyond the fact that it was the outburst of a religious fanaticism which held the Christian world in doubt and bewilderment, by reason of its Christian origin. It left no trace of its Christian element behind either in Nanking, where it sojourned for nearly ten years, or in Kwang Si, where it had its birth. In China, neither new political ideas nor political theories or principles were discovered which would have constituted the basal facts of a new form of government. So that neither in the religious nor yet in the political world was mankind in China or out of China benefited by that movement. The only good that resulted from the Taiping Rebellion was that God made use of it as a dynamic power to break up the stagnancy of a great nation and wake up its consciousness for a new national life, as subsequent events in 1894, 1895, 1898, 1900, 1901, and 1904–5 fully demonstrated.

Chapter XII Expedition to the Taiping Tea District

My Nanking visit was utterly barren of any substantial hope of promoting any scheme of educational or political reform for the general welfare of China or for the advancement of my personal interest. When I was thoroughly convinced that neither the reformation nor the regeneration of China was to come from the Taipings, I at once turned my thoughts to the idea of making a big fortune as my first duty, and as the first element in the successful carrying out of other plans for the future.

One day, while sauntering about in the tea garden inside the city of Shanghai, I came across a few tea-merchants regaling themselves with that beverage in a booth by themselves, evidently having a very social time. They beckoned to me to join their party. In the course of the conversation, we happened to touch on my late journey through the tea districts of Hunan, Hupeh and Kiang Si and also my trip to Nanking. Passing from one topic of conversation to another, we lighted upon the subject of the green tea district of Taiping in An Hwui province. It was stated that an immense quantity of green tea could be found there, all packed and boxed ready for shipment, and that the rebels were in possession of the goods, and that whoever had the hardihood and courage to risk his life to gain possession of it would become a millionaire. I listened to the account with deep and absorbing interest, taking in everything that was said on the subject. It was stated that there were over 1000000 chests of tea there. Finally the party broke up, and I wended my way to my quarters completely absorbed in deep thought. I reasoned with myself that this was a chance for me to make a fortune, but wondered who would be foolhardy enough to furnish the capital, thinking that no business man of practical experience would risk his money in such a wild goose adventure, surrounded as it was with more than ordinary dangers and difficulties, in a country where highway robbery, lawlessness and murder were of daily occurrence. But with the glamor of a big fortune confronting me, all privations, dangers and risks of life seemed small and faded into airy nothing.

My friend, Tsang Mew, who had been instrumental in having me sent traveling into the interior a year before, was a man of great business experience. He had a long head and a large circle of business acquaintances, besides being my warm friend, so I concluded to go to him and talk over the whole matter, as I knew he would not hesitate to give me his best advice. I laid the whole subject before him. He said he would consider the matter fully and in a few days let me know what he had decided to do about it. After a few days, he told me that he had had several consultations with the head of the firm, of which he was comprador, and between them the company had decided to take up my project.

The plan of operation as mapped out by me was as follows: I was to go to the district of Taiping by the shortest and safest route possible, to find out whether the quantity of tea did exist; whether it was safe to have treasure taken up there to pay the rebels for the tea; and whether it was possible to have the tea supply taken down by native boats to be transshipped by steamer to Shanghai. This might be called the preliminary expedition. Then, I was to determine which of the two routes would be the more feasible—there being two, one by the way of Wuhu, a treaty port, and another by way of Ta Tung, not a treaty port, a hundred miles above Wuhu. Wuhu and the whole country leading to Taiping, including the district itself, was under the jurisdiction of the rebels, whereas Ta Tung was still in possession of the imperialists. From Wuhu to Taiping by river the distance was about two hundred and fifty miles, whereas, by way of Ta Tung, the way, though shorter, was mostly overland, which made transportation more difficult and expensive, besides having to pay the imperialists heavy war-tax at Ta Tung, while duty and war-tax were entirely free at Wuhu.

In this expedition of inspection, I chose Wuhu as the basis of my operation. I started with four Chinese tea-men, natives of Taiping who had fled to Shanghai as refugees when the whole district was changed into a theatre of bloody conflicts between the imperialists and rebel forces for two years. On the way up the Wuhu River, we passed three cities mostly deserted by their inhabitants, but occupied by rebels. Paddy fields on both sides of the river were mostly left uncultivated and deserted, overrun with rank weeds and tall grass. As we ascended towards Taiping, the whole region presented a heart-rending and depressing scene of wild waste and devastation. Whole villages were depopulated and left in a dilapidated condition. Out of a population of 500000 only a few dozen people were seen wandering about in a listless, hopeless condition, very much emaciated and looking like walking skeletons.

After a week's journey we reached the village of San Kow, where we were met and welcomed by three tea—men who had been in Shanghai about four years previous. It seemed that they had succeeded in weathering the storm which had swept away the bulk of the population and left them among the surviving few. They were mighty glad to see us, and our appearance in the village seemed to be a God—send. Among the houses that were left intact, I selected the best of them to be my headquarters for the transaction of the tea business. The old tea—men were brought in to co—operate in the business and they showed us where the tea was stored. I was told that in San Kow there were at least five hundred thousand boxes, but in the whole district of Taiping there were at least a million and a half boxes, about sixty pounds of tea to a box.

At the end of another week, I returned to Wuhu and reported all particulars. I had found that the way up from Wuhu by river to Taiping was perfectly safe and I did not anticipate any danger to life or treasure. I had seen a large quantity of the green tea myself and found out that all that was needed was to ship as much treasure as it was safe to have housed in Wuhu, and from there to have it transferred in country tea—boats, well escorted by men in case of any emergency. I also sent samples of the different kinds of green tea to Shanghai to be inspected and listed. These proved to be satisfactory and the order came back to buy as much of the stock as could be bought.

I was appointed the head of all succeeding expeditions to escort treasure up the river to San Kow and cargoes of tea from there to Wuhu. In one of these expeditions, I had a staff of six Europeans and an equal number of Chinese tea-men. We had eight boxes of treasure containing altogether Tls. 40000. A tael, in the sixties, according to the exchange of that period, was equal to \$1.33, making the total amount of Mexican dollar to be a little over \$53000. We had a fleet of eight tea-boats, four large ones and four smaller ones. The treasure was divided into two equal parts and was placed in the two largest and staunchest boats. The men were also divided into two squads, three Europeans and three Chinese in one large boat and an equal number in the other. We were well provided with firearms, revolvers and cutlasses. Besides the six Europeans, we had about forty men including the boatmen, but neither the six tea-men nor the boatmen could be relied upon to show fight in case of emergency. The only reliable men I had to fall back upon, in case of emergency, were the Europeans; even in these I was not sure I could place implicit confidence, for they were principally runaway sailors of an adventurous character picked up in Shanghai by the company and sent up to Wuhu to escort the treasure up to the interior. Among them was an Englishman who professed to be a veterinary doctor. He was over six feet tall in his stocking feet, a man of fine personal appearance, but he did not prove himself to be of very stout heart, as may be seen presently. Thus prepared and equipped, we left for Wuhu in fine spirits. We proceeded on our journey a little beyond the city of King Yuen, which is about half the way to San Kow. We could have gone a little beyond King Yuen, but thinking it might be safer to be near the city, where the rebel chief had seen my passport, obtained in Nanking, and knew that I had influential people in

Nanking, we concluded to pass the night in a safe secluded little cove in the bend of the river just large enough for our little boats to moor close to each other, taking due precaution to place the two largest ones in the center, flanked by the other boats on the right and left of them; the smaller boats occupied the extreme ends of the line.

Before retiring, I had ordered all our firearms to be examined and loaded and properly distributed. Watchmen were stationed in each boat to keep watch all night, for which they were to be paid extra. The precautionary steps having thus been taken, we all retired for the night. An old tea-man and myself were the only ones who lay wide awake while the rest gave unmistakable signs of deep sleep. I felt somewhat nervous and could not sleep. The new moon had peeked in upon us occasionally with her cold smile, as heavy and dark clouds were scudding across her path. Soon she was shut in and disappeared, and all was shrouded in pitch darkness. The night was nearly half spent, when my ears caught the distant sound of whooping and yelling which seemed to increase in volume. I immediately started up to dress myself and quietly woke up the Europeans and Chinese in both boats. As the yelling and whooping drew nearer and nearer it seemed to come from a thousand throats, filling the midnight air with unearthly sounds. In another instant countless torch lights were seen dancing and whirling in the dismal darkness right on the opposite bank. Fortunately the river was between this marauding band and us, while pitch darkness concealed our boats from their sight. In view of such impending danger, we held a council of war. None of us were disposed to fight and endanger our lives in a conflict in which the odds were fearfully against us, there being about a thousand to one. But the English veterinary doctor was the foremost and most strenuous of the Europeans to advocate passive surrender. His countenance actually turned pale and he trembled all over, whether from fear or the chilly atmosphere of the night I could not tell. Having heard from each one what he had to say, I could do nothing but step forward and speak to them, which I did in this wise: "Well, boys, you have all decided not to fight in case we are attacked, but to surrender our treasure. The ground for taking such a step is that we are sure to be outnumbered by a rebel host. So that in such a dilemma discretion is the better part of valor, and Tls. 40000 are not worth sacrificing our lives for. But by surrendering our trust without making an effort of some kind to save it, we would be branded as unmitigated cowards, and we could never expect to be trusted with any responsible commission again. Now, I will tell you what I propose to do. If the rebel horde should come over and attempt to seize our treasure, I will spring forward with my yellow silk passport, and demand to see their chief, while you fellows with your guns and arms must stand by the treasure. Do not fire and start the fight. By parleying with them, it will for the moment check their determination to plunder, and they will have a chance to find out who we are, and where I obtained the passport; and even if they should carry off the treasure, I shall tell their chief that I will surely report the whole proceeding in Nanking and recover every cent of our loss."

These remarks seemed to revive the spirit and courage of the men, after which we all sat on the forward decks of our boats anxiously waiting for what the next moment would bring forth. While in this state of expectancy, our hearts palpitating in an audible fashion, our eyes were watching intently the opposite shore. All the shouting and yelling seemed to have died away, and nothing could be seen but torches moving about slowly and leisurely in regular detachments, each detachment stopping occasionally and then moving on again. This was kept up for over two hours, while they constantly receded from us. I asked an old boatman the meaning of such movements and was told that the marauding horde was embarking in boats along the whole line of the opposite shore and was moving down steam. It was three o'clock in the morning, and it began to rain. A few of the advance boats had passed us without discovering where we were. They were loaded with men and floated by us in silence. By four o'clock the last boats followed the rest and soon disappeared from sight. Evidently, from the stillness that characterized the long line of boats as they floated down steam, the buccaneering horde was completely used up by their looting expedition, and at once abandoned themselves to sound sleep when they got on board the boats. We thanked our stars for such a narrow escape from such an unlooked–for danger. We owed our safety to the darkness of the night, the rain and to the fact that we were on the opposite shore in a retired cove. By five o'clock all our anxieties and fears were laid aside and turned into joy and thankfulness. We resumed our journey with light hearts and reached San Kow two days later in peace and safety. In less than two weeks we sent down to Wuhu, escorted by Europeans and tea–men, the first installment, consisting of fifteen boatloads of tea to be transshipped by steamer to Shanghai. The next installment consisted of twelve boatloads. I escorted that down the river in person. The river, in some places, especially in the summer, was quite shallow and a way had to be dug to float the boats down. In one or two instances the boatmen were very reluctant to jump into the water to do the work of deepening the river, and on one occasion I had to jump in, with the water up to my waist, in order to set them an example. When they caught the idea and saw me in the water, every man followed my example and vied with each other in clearing a way for the boats, for they saw I meant business and there was no fooling about it either.

I was engaged in this Taiping tea business for about six months, and took away about sixty-five thousand boxes of tea, which was hardly a tenth part of the entire stock found in the district. Then I was taken down with the fever and ague of the worst type. As I could get no medical relief at Wuhu, I was obliged to return to Shanghai, where I was laid up sick for nearly two months. Those two months of sickness had knocked all ideas of making a big fortune out of my head. I gave up the Taiping tea enterprise, because it called for a greater sacrifice of health and wear upon my nervous system than I was able to stand. The King Yuen midnight incident, which came near proving a disastrous one for me, with the marauding horde of unscrupulous cutthroats, had been quite a shock on my nervous system at the time and may have been the primal cause of my two months' sickness; it served as a sufficient warning to me not to tax my nervous system by further encounters and disputes with the rebel chiefs, whose price on the tea we bought of them was being increased every day. A dispassionate and calm view of the enterprise convinced me that I would have to preserve my life, strength and energy for a higher and worthier object than any fortune I might make out of this Taiping tea, which, after all, was plundered property. I am sure that no fortune in the world could be brought in the balance to weigh against my life, which is of inestimable value to me.

Although I had made nothing out of the Taiping teas, yet the fearless spirit, the determination to succeed, and the pluck to be able to do what few would undertake in face of exceptional difficulties and hazards, that I had exhibited in the enterprise, were in themselves assets worth more to me than a fortune. I was well–known, both among foreign merchants and native business men, so that as soon as it was known that I had given up the Taiping tea enterprise on account of health, I was offered a tea agency in the port of Kew Keang for packing teas for another foreign firm. I accepted it as a temporary shift, but gave it up in less than six months and started a commission business on my own account. I continued this business for nearly three years and was doing as well as I had expected to do. It was at this time while in Kew Keang that I caught the first ray of hope of materializing the educational scheme I had been weaving during the last year of my college life.

Chapter XIII My Interviews with Tsang Kwoh Fan

In 1863, I was apparently prospering in my business, when, to my great surprise, an unexpected letter from the city of Ngan Khing, capital of An Whui province, was received. The writer was an old friend whose acquaintance I had made in Shanghai in 1857. He was a native of Ningpo, and was in charge of the first Chinese gunboat owned by the local Shanghai guild. He had apparently risen in official rank and had become one of Tsang Kwoh Fan's secretaries. His name was Chang Shi Kwei. In this letter, Chang said he was authorized by Viceroy Tsang Kwoh Fan to invite me to come down to Ngan Khing to call, as he (the Viceroy) had heard of me and wished very much to see me. On the receipt of the letter I was in a quandary and asked myself many questions: What could such a distinguished man want of me? Had he got wind of my late visit to Nanking and of my later enterprise to the district of Taiping for the green tea that was held there by the rebels? Tsang Kwoh Fan himself had been in the department of Hwui Chow fighting the rebels a year before and had been defeated, and he was reported to have been killed in battle. Could he have been told that I had been near the scene of his battle and had been in communication with the rebels, and did he want, under a polite invitation, to trap me and have my head off? But Chang, his secretary, was an old friend of many years' standing. I knew his character well; he wouldn't be likely to play the cat's paw to have me captured. Thus deliberating from one surmise to another, I concluded not to accept the invitation until I had learned more of the great man's purpose in sending for me.

In reply to the letter, I wrote and said I thanked His Excellency for his great condescension and considered it a great privilege and honor to be thus invited, but on account of the tea season having set in (which was in February), I was obliged to attend to the orders for packing tea that were fast coming in; but that as soon as they were off my hands, I would manage to go and pay my respects to His Excellency.

Two months after receiving the first letter, a second one came urging me to come to Ngan Khing as early as possible. This second letter enclosed a letter written by Li Sien Lan, the distinguished Chinese mathematician, whose acquaintance I had also made while in Shanghai. He was the man who assisted a Mr. Wiley, a missionary of the London Board of Missions, in the translation of several mathematical works into Chinese, among which was the Integral and Differential Calculus over which I well remember to have "flunked and fizzled" in my sophomore year in college; and, in this connection, I might as well frankly own that in my make-up mathematics was left out. Mr. Li Sien Lan was also an astronomer. In his letter, he said he had told Viceroy Tsang Kwoh Fan who I was and that I had had a foreign education; how I had raised a handsome subscription to help the famine refugees in 1857; that I had a strong desire to help China to become prosperous, powerful and strong. He said the viceroy had some important business for me to do, and that Chu and Wha, who were interested in machinery of all kinds, were also in Ngan Khing, having been invited there by the Viceroy. Mr. Li's letter completely dispelled all doubts and misgivings on my part as to the viceroy's design in wishing to see me, and gave me an insight as to his purpose for sending me.

As an answer to these letters, I wrote saying that in a couple of months I should be more at liberty to take the journey. But my second reply did not seem to satisfy the strong desire on the part of Tsang Kwoh Fan to see me. So in July, 1863, I received a third letter from Chang and a second one from Li. In these letters the object of the viceroy was clearly and frankly stated. He wanted me to give up my mercantile business altogether and identify myself under him in the service of the state government, and asked whether or not I could come down to Ngan Khing at once. In view of this unexpected offer, which demanded prompt and explicit decision, I was not slow to see what possibility there was of carrying out my educational scheme, having such a powerful man as Tsang Kwoh Fan to back it. I immediately replied that upon learning the wishes of His Excellency, I had taken the whole situation into consideration, and had concluded to go to his headquarters at Ngan Khing, just as soon as I had wound up my business, which would take me a complete month, and that I would start by August at the latest. Thus ended the correspondence which was really the initiatory step of my official career.

Tsang Kwoh Fan was a most remarkable character in Chinese history. He was regarded by his contemporaries as a great scholar and a learned man. Soon after the Taiping Rebellion broke out and began to assume vast proportions, carrying before it province after province,

Tsang began to drill an army of his own compatriots of Hunan who had always had the reputation of being brave and hardy fighters. In his work of raising a disciplined army, he secured the co–operation of other Hunan men, who afterwards took a prominent part in building up a flotilla of river gunboats. This played a great and efficient part as an auxiliary force on the Yangtze River, and contributed in no small measure to check the rapid and ready concentration of the rebel forces, which had spread over a vast area on both banks of the great Yangtze River. In the space of a few years the lost provinces were gradually recovered, till the rebellion was narrowed down within the single province of Kiang Su, of which Nanking, the capital of the rebellion, was the only stronghold left. This finally succumbed to the forces of Tsang Kwoh Fan in 1864.

To crush and end a rebellion of such dimensions as that of the Taipings was no small task. Tsang Kwoh Fan was made the generalissimo of the imperialists. To enable him to cope successfully with the Taipings, Tsang was invested with almost regal power. The revenue of seven or eight provinces was laid at his feet for disposal, also official ranks and territorial appointments were at his command. So Tsang Kwoh Fan was literally and practically the supreme power of China at the time. But true to his innate greatness, he was never known to abuse the almost unlimited power that was placed in his hands, nor did he take advantage of the vast resources that were at his disposal to enrich himself or his family, relatives or friends. Unlike Li Hung Chang, his protégé and successor, who bequeathed Tls. 40000000 to his descendants after his death, Tsang died comparatively poor, and kept the escutcheon of his official career untarnished and left a name and character honored and revered for probity, patriotism and purity. He had great talents, but he was modest. He had a liberal mind, but he was conservative. He was a perfect gentleman and a nobleman of the highest type. It was such a man that I had the great fortune to come in contact with in the fall of 1863.

After winding up my business in New Keang, I took passage in a native boat and landed at Ngan Khing in September. There, in the military headquarters of Viceroy Tsang Kwoh Fan, I was met by my friends, Chang Si Kwei, Li Sien Lan, Wha Yuh Ting and Chu Siuh Chune, all old friends from Shanghai. They were glad to see me, and told me that the viceroy for the past six months, after hearing them tell that as a boy I had gone to America to get a Western education, had manifested the utmost curiosity and interest to see me, which accounted for the three letters which Chang and Li had written urging me to come. Now, since I had arrived, their efforts to get me there had not been fruitless, and they certainly claimed some credit for praising me up to the viceroy. I asked them if they knew what His Excellency wanted me for, aside from the curiosity of seeing a native of China made into a veritable Occidental. They all smiled significantly and told me that I would find out after one or two interviews. From this, I judged that they knew the object for which I was wanted by the Viceroy, and perhaps, they were at the bottom of the whole secret.

The next day I was to make my début, and called. My card was sent in, and without a moment's delay or waiting in the ante-room I was ushered into the presence of the great man of China. After the usual ceremonies of greeting, I was pointed to a seat right in front of him. For a few minutes he sat in silence, smiling all the while as though

he were much pleased to see me, but at the same time his keen eyes
scanned me over from head to foot to see if he could discover anything
strange in my outward appearance. Finally, he took a steady look into
my eyes which seemed to attract his special attention. I must confess
I felt quite uneasy all the while, though I was not abashed. Then came
his first question.

"How long were you abroad?"

"I was absent from China eight years in pursuit of a Western
education."

"Would you like to be a soldier in charge of a company?"

"I should be pleased to head one if I had been fitted for it. I have
never studied military science."

"I should judge from your looks, you would make a fine soldier,
for I can see from your eyes that you are brave and can command."

"I thank Your Excellency for the compliment. I may have
the courage of a soldier, but I certainly lack military training and
experience, and on that account I may not be able to meet Your
Excellency's expectations."

When the question of being a soldier was suggested, I thought
he really meant to have me enrolled as an officer in his army against
the rebels; but in this I was mistaken, as my Shanghai friends told me
afterwards. He simply put it forward to find out whether my mind was at
all martially inclined. But when he found by my response that the bent
of my thought was something else, he dropped the military subject and
asked me my age and whether or not I was married. The last question
closed my first introductory interview, which had lasted only about half
an hour. He began to sip his tea and I did likewise, which according

to Chinese official etiquette means that the interview is ended and the guest is at liberty to take his departure.

I returned to my room, and my Shanghai friends soon flocked around me to know what had passed between the Viceroy and myself. I told them everything, and they were highly delighted.

Tsang Kwoh Fan, as he appeared, in 1863, was over sixty years of age, in the very prime of life. He was five feet, eight or nine inches tall, strongly built and well-knitted together and in fine proportion. He had a broad chest and square shoulders surmounted by a large symmetrical head. He had a broad and high forehead; his eyes were set on a straight line under triangular-shaped eyelids, free from that obliquity so characteristic of the Mongolian type of countenance usually accompanied by high cheek bones, which is another feature peculiar to the Chinese physiognomy. His face was straight and somewhat hairy. He allowed his side whiskers their full growth; they hung down with his full beard which swept across a broad chest and added dignity to a commanding appearance. His eyes though not large were keen and penetrating. They were of a clear hazel color. His mouth was large but well compressed with thin lips which showed a strong will and a high purpose. Such was Tsang Kwoh Fan's external appearance, when I first met him at Ngan Khing. Regarding his character, he was undoubtedly one of the most remarkable men of his age and time. As a military general, he might be called a self-made man; by dint of his indomitable persistence and perseverance, he rose from his high scholarship as a Hanlin (Chinese LL. D.) to be a generalissimo of all the imperial forces that were levied against the Taiping rebels, and in less than a decade after he headed his Hunan raw recruits, he succeeded in reducing the wide devastations of the rebellion that covered a territorial area of three of the richest provinces of China to a single one of Kiang Nan, till finally, by the constriction of his forces, he succeeded in crusling the life out of the rebellion by the fall and capture of Nanking. The Taiping Rebellion was of fifteen years' duration, from 1850 to 1865. It was no small task to bring it to its extinction. Its rise and progress had cost the Empire untold treasures, while 25000000 human lives were immolated in that political hecatomb. The close of the great rebellion gave the people a breathing respite. The Dowager Empress had special reasons to be grateful to the genius of Tsang Kwoh Fan, who was instrumental in restoring peace and order to the Manchu Dynasty. She was not slow, however, to recognize Tsang Kwoh Fan's merits and moral worth and created him a duke. But Tsang's greatness was not to be measured by any degree of conventional nobility; it did not consist in his victories over the rebels, much less in his re-capture of Nanking. It rose from his great virtues: his pure, unselfish patriotism, his deep and far-sighted statesmanship, and the purity of his official career. He is known in history as "the man of rectitude". This was his posthumous title conferred on him by imperial decree.

To resume the thread of my story, I was nearly two weeks in the viceroy's headquarters, occupying a suite of rooms in the same building assigned to my Shanghai friends—Li, Chang, Wha and Chu. There were living in his military headquarters at least two hundred officials, gathered there from all parts of the Empire, for various objects and purposes. Besides his secretaries, who numbered no less than a hundred, there were expectant officials, learned scholars, lawyers, mathematicians, astronomers and machinists; in short, the picked and noted men of China were all drawn there by the magnetic force of his character and great name. He always had a great admiration for men if distinguished learning and talents, and loved to associate and mingle with them. During the two weeks of my sojourn there, I had ample opportunity to call upon my Shanghai friends, and in that way incidentally found out what the object of the Viceroy was in urging me to be enrolled in the government services. It seemed that my friends had had frequent interviews with the Viceroy in regard to having a foreign machine shop established in China, but it had not been determined what kind of a machine shop should be established. One evening they gave me a dinner, at ahich time the subject of the machine shop was brought up and it became the chief topic. After each man had expressed his views on the subject excepting myself, they wanted to know what my views were, intimating that in all likelihood in my next interview with the Viceroy he would bring up the subject. I said that as I was not an expert in the matter, my opinions or suggestions might not be worth much, but nevertheless from my personal observation in the United States and from a common–sense point of view, I would say that a machine shop in the present state of China should be of a general and fundamental character and not one for specific purposes. In other words, I told them they ought to have a machine shop that would be able to create or reproduce other machine shops of the same character as itself; each and all of these should be able to turn out specific machinery for the manufacture of specific things. In plain words, they would have to have general and fundamental machinery in order to turn out specific machinery. A machine shop consisting of lathes of different kinds of sizes, planers and drills would be able to turn out machinery for making guns, engines, agricultural implements, clocks, etc. In a large country like China, I told them, they would need many primary or fundamental machine shops, but that after they had one (and a first-class one at that) they could make it the mother shop for reproducing others—perhaps better and more improved. If they had a number of them, it would enable them to have the shops co-operate with each other in case of need. It would be cheaper to have them reproduced and multiplied in China, I said, where labor and material were cheaper, than in Europe and America. Such was my crude idea of the subject. After I had finished, they were apparently much pleased and interested, and expressed the hope that I would state the same views to the Viceroy if he should ask me about the subject.

Several days after the dinner and conversation, the Viceroy did send for me. In this interview he asked me what in my opinion was the best thing to do for China at that time. The question came with such a force of meaning, that if I had not been for warned by my friends a few evenings before, or if their hearts had not been set on the introduction of a machine shop, and they had not practically won the Viceroy over to their pet scheme, I might have been strongly tempted to launch forth upon my educational scheme as a reply to the question as to what was the best thing to do for China. But in such an event, being a stranger to the Viceroy, having been brought to his notice simply through the influence of my friends, I would have run a greater risk of jeopardizing my pet scheme of education than if I were left to act independently. My obligations to them were great, and I therefore decided that my constancy and fidelity to their friendship should be correspondingly great. So, instead of finding myself embarrassed in answering such a large and important question, I had a preconceived answer to give, which seemed to dove-tail into his views already crystallized into definite form, and which was ready to be carried out at once. So my educational scheme was put in the background, and the machine shop was allowed to take precedence. I repeated in substance what I had said to my friends previously in regard to establishing a mother machine shop, capable of reproducing other machine shops of like character, etc. I especially mentioned the manufacture of rifles, which, I said, required for the manufacture of their component parts separate machinery, but that the machine shop I would recommend was not one adapted for making the rifles, but adapted to turn out specific machinery for the making of rifles, cannons, cartridges or anything else.

"Well," said he, "this is a subject quite beyond my knowledge. It would be well for you to discuss the matter with Wha and Chu, who are more familiar with it than I am and we will decide what is best to be done."

This ended my interview with the Viceroy. After I left him, I met my friends, who were anxious to know the result of the interview. I told them of the outcome. They were highly elated over it. In our last conference it was decided that the matter of the character of the machine shop was to be left entirely to my discretion and judgment, after consulting a professional mechanical engineer. At the end of another two weeks, Wha was authorized to tell me that the Viceroy, after having seen all the four men, had decided to empower me to go abroad and make purchases of such machinery as in the opinion of a professional engineer would be the best and the right machinery for China to adopt. It was also left entirely to me to decided where the machinery should be purchased—either in England, France or the United States of America.

The location of the machine shop was to be at a place called Kow Chang Meu, about four miles northwest of the city of Shanghai. The Kow Chang Meu machine shop was afterwards known as the Kiang Nan Arsenal, an establishment that covers several acres of ground and embraces under its roof all the leading branches of mechanical work. Millions have been invested in it since I brought the first machinery from Fitchburg, Mass., in order to make it one of the greatest arsenals east of the Cape of Good Hope. It may properly be regarded as a lasting monument to commemorate Tsang Kwoh Fan's broadmindedness as well as far-sightedness in establishing Western machinery in China.

Chapter XIV My Mission to America to Buy Machinery

A week after my last interview with the Viceroy and after I had been told that I was to be entrusted with the execution of the order, my commission was made out and issued to me. In addition to the commission, the fifth official rank was conferred on me. It was a nominal civil rank, with the privilege of wearing the blue feather, as was customary only in war time and limited to those connected with the military service, but discarded in the civil service, where the peacock's feather is conferred only by imperial sanction. Two official dispatches were also made out, directing me where to receive the Tls. 68000, the entire amount for the purchase of the machinery. One-half of the amount was to be paid by the Taotai of Shanghai, and other half by the Treasurer of Canton. After all the preliminary preparations had been completed, I bade farewell to the Viceroy and my Shanghai friends and started on my journey.

On my arrival in Shanghai in October, 1863, I had the good fortune to meet Mr. John Haskins, an American mechanical engineer, who came out to China with machinery for Messrs. Russel & Co. He

had finished his business with that firm and was expecting soon to
return to the States with his family—a wife and a little daughter. He
was just the man I wanted. It did not take us long to get acquainted
and as the time was short, we soon came to an understanding. We
took the overland route from Hong Kong to London, via the Isthmus of
Suez. Haskins and his family took passage on the French Messagerie
Imperial line, while I engaged mine on board of one of the Peninsular
& Oriental steamers. In my route to London, I touched at Singapore,
crossed the Indian Ocean, and landed at Ceylon, where I changed
steamers for Bengal up the Red Sea and landed at Cairo, where I had
to cross the Isthmus by rail. The Suez Canal was not finished; the work
of excavating was still going on. Arriving at Alexandria, I took passage
from there to Marseilles, the southern port of France, while Haskins
and his family took a steamer direct for Southampton. From Marseilles
I went to Paris by rail. I was there about ten days, long enough to give
me a general idea of the city, its public buildings, churches, gardens,
and of Parisian gaiety. I crossed the English channel from Calais to
Dover and went thence by rail to London—the first time in my life to
touch English soil, and my first visit to the famous metropolis. While
in London, I visited Whitworth's machine shop, and had the pleasure
of renewing my acquaintance with Thomas Christy, whom I knew in
China in the '50's. I was about a month in England, and then crossed
the Atlantic in one of the Cunard steamers and landed in New York in
the early spring of 1864, just ten years after my graduation from Yale
and in ample time to be present at the decennial meeting of my class
in July. Haskins and his family had preceded me in another steamer
for New York, in order that he might get to work on the drawings and

247

specifications of the shop and machinery and get them completed as soon as possible. In 1864, the last year of the great Civil War, nearly all the machine shops in the country, especially in New England, were preoccupied and busy in executing government orders, and it was very difficult to have my machinery taken up. Finally Haskins succeeded in getting the Putnam Machine Co., Fitchburg, Mass., to fill the order.

While Haskins was given sole charge of superintending the execution of the order, which required at least six months before the machinery could be completed for shipment to China, I took advantage of the interim to run down to New Haven and attend the decennial meeting of my class. It was to me a joyous event and I congratulated myself that I had the good luck to be present at our first re-union. Of course, the event that brought me back to the country was altogether unpretentious and had attracted little or no public attention at the time, because the whole country was completely engrossed in the last year of the great Civil War, yet I personally regarded my commission as an inevitable and preliminary step that would ultimately lead to the realization of my educational scheme, which had never for a moment escaped my mind. But at the meeting of my class, this subject of my life plan was not brought up. We had a most enjoyable time and parted with nearly the same fraternal feeling that characterized our parting at graduation. After the decennial meeting, I returned to Fitchburg and told Haskins that I was going down to Washington to offer my services to the government as a volunteer for the short period of six months, and that in case anything happened to me during the six months so that I could not come back to attend to the shipping of the machinery to Shanghai, he should attend to it. I left him all the papers—the cost and description of the machinery, the bills of lading, insurance, and freight, and directed him to send everything to the Viceroy's agent in Shanghai. This precautionary step having been taken, I slipped down to Washington.

Brigadier–General Barnes of Springfield, Mass., happened to be the general in charge of the Volunteer Department. His headquarters were at Willard's Hotel. I called on him and made known to him my object, that I felt as a naturalized citizen of the United States, it was my bounden duty to offer my services as a volurteer courier to carry despatches between Washington and the nearest Federal camp for at least six months, simply to show my loyalty and patriotism to my adopted country, and that I would furnish my own equipments. He said that he remembered me well, having met me in the Yale Library in New Haven, in 1853, on a visit to his son, William Barnes, who was in the college at the time I was, and who afterwards became a prominent lawyer in San Francisco. General Barnes asked what business I was engaged in. I told him that since my graduation in 1854 I had been in China and had recently returned with an order to purchase machinery for a machine shop ordered by Viceroy and Generalissimo Tsang Kwoh Fan. I told him the machinery was being made to order in Fitchburg, Mass., under the supervision of an American mechanical engineer, and as it would take at least six months before the same could be completed, I was anxious to offer my services to the government in the meantime as an evidence of my loyalty and patriotism to my adopted country. He was quite interested and pleased with what I said.

"Well, my young friend," said he, "I thank you very much for your offer, but since you are charged with a responsible trust to execute for the Chinese government, you had better return to Fitchburg to attend to it. We have plenty of men to serve, both as couriers and as fighting men to go to the front." Against this preemptory decision, I could urge nothing further, but I felt that I had at least fulfilled my duty to my adopted country.

Chapter XV   My Second
Return to China

The machinery was not finished till the early spring of 1865. It was shipped direct from New York to Shanghai, China; while it was doubling the Cape of Good Hope on its way to the East, I took passage in another direction, back to China. I wanted to encircle the globe once in my life, and this was my opportunity. I could say after that, that I had circumnavigated the globe. So I planned to go back by way of San Francisco. In order to do that, I had to take into consideration the fact that the Union Pacific from Chicago to San Francisco via Omaha was not completed, nor was any steamship line subsidized by the United States government to cross the Pacific from San Francisco to any seaport, either in Japan or China at the time. On that account I was obliged to take a circuitous route, by taking a coast steamer from New York to Panama, cross the Isthmus, and from there take passage in another coast steamer up the Mexican coast to San Francisco, Cal.

At San Francisco, I was detained two weeks where I had to wait for a vessel to bridge me over the broad Pacific, either to Yokohama or Shanghai. At that time, as there was no other vessel advertised to sail for the East, I was compelled to take passage on board the "Ida de Rogers", a Nantucket bark. There were six passengers, including myself. We had to pay $500 each for passage from San Francisco to Yokohama. The crew consisted of the captain, who had with him his wife, and a little boy six years old, a mate, three sailors and a cook, a Chinese boy. The "Ida de Rogers" was owned by Captain Norton who hailed from Nantucket. She was about one hundred and fifty feet long— an old tub at that. She carried no cargo and little or no ballast, except bilge-water, which may have come from Nantucket, for aught I know. The skipper, true to the point of the country where they produce crops of seamen of microscopic ideas, was found to be not at all deficient in his close calculations of how to shave closely in every bargain and, in fact, in everything in life. In this instance, we had ample opportunity to find out under whom we were sailing. Before we were fairly out of the "Golden Gate", we were treated every day with salted mackerel, which I took to be the daily and fashionable dish of Nantucket. The cook we had made matters worse, as he did not seem to know his business and was no doubt picked up in San Francisco just to fill the vacancy. The mackerel was cooked and brought on the table without being freshened, and the Indian meal cakes that were served with it, were but half baked, so that day after day we practically all left the table disgusted and half starved. Not only was the food bad and unhealthy, but the skipper's family was a very low type. The skipper himself was a most profane man, and although I never heard the wife swear, yet she seemed to enjoy her husband's oaths. Their little boy who was not more than six years old, seemed to have surpassed the father in profanity. It may be said that the young scamp had mastered his shorter and longer catechism of profanity completely, for he was not wanting in expressions of the most disgusting and repulsive kind, as taught him by his sire, yet his parents sat listening to him with evident satisfaction, glancing around at the passengers to catch their approval. One of the passengers, an Englishman, who stood near listening and smoking his pipe, only remarked ironically, "You have a smart boy there." At this the skipper nodded, while the mother seemed to gloat over her young hopeful. Such a scene was of daily occurrence, and one that we could not escape, since we were cooped up in such narrow quarters on account of the smallness of the vessel. There was not even a five–foot deck where one could stretch his legs. We were most of the time shut up in the dining room, as it was the coolest spot we could find. Before our voyage was half over, we had occasion to land at one of the most northerly islands of the Hawaiian group for fresh water and provisions. While the vessel was being victualed, all the passengers landed and went out to the country to take a stroll, which was great relief. We were gone nearly all day. We all re–embarked early in the evening. It seemed that the captain had filled the forward hold with chickens and young turkeys. We congratulated ourselves that the skipper after all had swung round to show a generous streak, which had only needed an opportunity to show itself, and that for the rest of the voyage he was no doubt going to feed us on fresh chickens and turkeys to make up for the salted mackerel, which might have given us the scurvy had we continued on the same diet. For the first day or so, after we resumed our voyage, we had chicken and fish for our breakfast and dinners, but that was the last we saw of the fresh provisions. We saw no turkey on the table. On making inquiry, the cook told us that both the chickens and the turkeys were bought, not for our table, but for speculation, to be sold on arrival in Yokohama. Unfortunately for the skipper, the chickens and turkeys for want of proper food and fresh air, had died a few days before our arrival at the port.

Immediately upon reaching Yokohama, I took passage in a P. & O. steamer for Shanghai.

On my arrival there, I found the machinery had all arrived a month before; it had all been delivered in good condition and perfect working order. I had been absent from China a little over a year. During that time Viceroy Tsang Kwoh Fan, with the co-operation of his brother, Tsang Kwoh Chuen, succeeded in the capture of Nanking, which put an end to the great Taiping Rebellion of 1850.

On my arrival in Shanghai, I found that the Viceroy had gone up to Chu Chow, the most northerly department of Kiangsu province, close to the border line of Shan Tung, and situated on the canal. He made that his headquarters in superintending the subjugation of the Nienfi or Anwhui rebels, against whom Li Hung Chang had appointed as his lieutenant in the field. I was requested to go up to Chu Chow to make a report in person regarding the purchase of the machinery.

On my journey to Chu Chow, I was accompanied by my old friend Wha Yuh Ting part of the way. We went by the Grand Canal from Sinu-Mew at the Yangtze up as far as Yang Chow, the great entrepôt for the Government Salt Monopoly. There we took mule carts overland to Chu Chow. We were three days on our journey. Chu Chow is a departmental city and here, as stated before, Viceroy Tsang made his quarters. I was there three days. The Viceroy complimented me highly for what I had done. He made my late commission to the States to purchase machinery the subject of a special memorial to the government. Such a special memorial on any political event invariably gives it political prominence and weight, and in order to lift me at once from a position of no importance to a territorial civil appointment of the bona fide fifth rank, was a step seldom asked for or conceded. He made out my case to be an exceptional one, and the following is the language he used in his memorial:

"Yung Wing is a foreign educated Chinese. He has mastered the English language. In his journey over thousands of miles of ocean to the extreme ends of the earth to fulfill the commission I entrusted to him, he was utterly oblivious to difficulties and dangers that lay in his way. In this respect even the missions of the Ancients present no parallel equal to his. Therefore, I would recommend that he be promoted to the expectancy of one of the Kiangsu subprefects, and he is entitled to fill the first vacancy presenting itself, in recognition of his valuable services."

His secretary, who drew up the memorial at his dictation, gave me a copy of the memorial before I left Chu Chow for Shanghai, and congratulated me on the great honor the Viceroy had conferred on me. I thanked the Viceroy before bidding him good–bye, and expressed the hope that my actions in the future would justify his high opinion of me.

In less than two months after leaving him, an official document from the Viceroy reached me in Shanghai, and in October, 1865, I was a full–fledged mandarin of the fifth rank. While waiting as an expectant subprefect, I was retained by the provincial authorities as a government interpreter and translator. My salary was $250 per month. No other expectant official of the province—not even an expectant Taotai (an official of the fourth rank)—could command such a salary.

Ting Yih Chang was at the time Taotai of Shanghai. He and I

became great friends. He rose rapidly in official rank and became successively salt commissioner, provincial treasurer and Taotai or governor of Kiang Nan. Through him, I also rose in official rank and was decorated with the peacock's feather. While Ting Yih Chang was salt commissioner, I accompanied him to Yang Chow and was engaged in translating Colton's geography into Chinese, for about six months. I then returned to Shanghai to resume my position as government interpreter and translator. I had plenty of time on my hands. I took to translating "Parsons on Contracts", which I thought might be useful to the Chinese. In this work I was fortunate in securing the services of a Chinese scholar to help me. I found him well versed in mathematics and in all Chinese official business, besides being a fine Chinese scholar and writer. He finally persuaded me not to continue the translation, as there was some doubt as to whether such a work, even when finished, would be in demand, because the Chinese courts are seldom troubled with litigations on contracts, and in all cases of violation of contracts, the Chinese code is used.

In 1867, Viceroy Tsang Kwoh Fan, with Li Hung Chang's co-operation, succeeded in ending the Nienfi rebellion, and came to Nanking to fill his viceroyalty of the two Kiangs.

Before taking up his position as viceroy of the Kiangs permanently, he took a tour of inspection through his jurisdiction and one of the important places he visited was Shanghai and the Kiang Nan Arsenal—an establishment of his own creation. He went through the arsenal with undisguised interest. I pointed out to him the machinery which I bought for him in America. He stood and watched its automatic movement, with unabated delight, for this was the first time he had seen machinery, and how it worked. It was during this visit that I succeeded in persuading him to have a mechanical school annexed to the arsenal, in which Chinese youths might be taught the theory as well as the practice of mechanical engineering, and thus enable China in time to dispense with the employment of foreign mechanical engineers and machinists, and to be perfectly independent. This at once appealed to the practical turn of the Chinese mind, and the school was finally added to the arsenal. They are doubtless turning out at the present time both mechanical engineers and machinists of all descriptions.

Chapter XVI Proposal of My Educational Scheme

Having scored in a small way this educational victory, by inducing the Viceroy to establish a mechanical training school as a corollary to the arsenal, I felt quite worked up and encouraged concerning my educational scheme which had been lying dormant in my mind for the past fifteen years, awaiting an opportunity to be brought forward.

Besides Viceroy Tsang Kwoh Fan, whom I counted upon to back me in furthering the scheme, Ting Yih Chang, an old friend of mine, had become an important factor to be reckoned with in Chinese politics. He was a man of progressive tendencies and was alive to all practical measures of reform. He had been appointed governor of Kiangsu province, and after his accession to his new office, I had many interviews with him regarding my educational scheme, in which he was intensely interested. He told me that he was in correspondence with Wen Seang, the prime minister of China, who was a Manchu, and that if I were to put my scheme in writing, he would forward it to Peking, and ask Wen Seang to use his influence to memorialize the government for its adoption. Such an unexpected piece of information came like a clap of thunder and fairly lifted me off my feet. I immediately left Suchau for Shanghai. With the help of my Nanking friend, who had helped me in the work of translating "Parsons on Contracts", I drew up four proposals to be presented to Governor Ting, to be forwarded by him to Minister Wen Seang, at Peking. They were as follows:

First proposal

The first proposal contemplated the organization of a Steamship Company on a joint stock basis. No foreigner was to be allowed to be a stockholder in the company. It was to be a purely Chinese company, managed and worked by Chinese exclusively.

To insure its stability and success, an annual government subsidy was to be made in the shape of a certain percentage of the tribute rice carried to Peking from Shanghai and Chinkiang, and elsewhere, where tribute rice is paid over to the government in lieu of taxes in money. This tribute rice heretofore had been taken to Peking by flat-bottom boats, via the Grand Canal. Thousands of these boats were built expressly for this rice transportation, which supported a large population all along the whole route of the Grand Canal.

On account of the great evils arising from this mode of transportation, such as the great length of time it took to take the rice to Peking, the great percentage of loss from theft, and from fermentation, which made the rice unfit for food, part of the tribute rice was carried by sea in Ningpo junks as far as Tientsin, and from thence transshipped again in flat-bottom boats to Peking. But even the Ningpo junk system was attended with great loss of time and much damage, almost as great as by flat-bottomed scows. My proposition was to use steam to do the work, supplanting both the flat-bottomed scows and the Ningpo junk system, so that the millions who were dependent on rice for subsistence might find it possible to get good and sound rice. This is one of the great benefits and blessings which the China Merchant Steamship Co. has conferred upon China.

Second proposal

The second proposition was for the government to send picked Chinese youths abroad to be thoroughly educated for the public service. The scheme contemplated the education of one hundred and twenty students as an experiment. These one hundred and twenty students were to be divided into four installments of thirty students each, one installment to be sent out each year. They were to have fifteen years to finish their education. Their average age was to be from twelve to fourteen years. If the first and second installments proved to be a success, the scheme was to be continued indefinitely. Chinese teachers were to be provided to keep up their knowledge of Chinese while in the United States. Over the whole enterprise two commissioners were to be appointed, and the government was to appropriate a certain percentage of the Shanghai customs to maintain the mission.

Third proposal

The third proposition was to induce the government to open the mineral resources of the country and thus in an indirect way lead to the necessity of introducing railroads to transport the mineral products from the interior to the ports.

I did not expect this proposition to be adopted and carried out, because China at that time had no mining engineers who could be depended upon to develop the mines, nor were the people free from their Fung Shui superstition.[①] I had no faith whatever in the success of the proposition, but simply put it in writing to show how ambitious I was to have the government wake up to the possibilities of the development of its vast resources.

Fourth proposal

The encroachment of foreign powers upon the independent sovereignty of China has always been watched by me with the most intense interest. No one who is at all acquainted with Roman Catholicism can fail to be impressed with the unwarranted pretensions and assumptions of the Romish church in China. She claims civil jurisdiction over her proselytes, and takes civil and criminal cases out of Chinese courts. In order to put a stop to such insidious and crafty workings to gain temporal power in China, I put forth this proposition: to prohibit missionaries of any religious sect or denomination from exercising any kind of jurisdiction over their converts, in either civil or criminal cases. These four propositions were carefully drawn up, and were presented to Governor Ting for transmission to Peking.

Of the four proposals, the first, third, and fourth were put in to chaperone the second, in which my whole heart was enlisted, and which above all others was the one I wanted to be taken up; but not to give it too prominent a place, at the suggestion of my Chinese

---

① The doctrine held by the Chinese in relation to the spirits or genii that rule over winds and waters, especially running streams and subterranean waters. This doctrine is universal and inveterate among the Chinese, and in a great measure prompts their hostility to railroads and telegraphs, since they believe that such structures anger the spirits of the air and waters and consequently cause floods and typhoons.——*Standard Dictionary*

teacher, it was assigned a second place in the order of the arrangement. Governor Ting recognized this, and accordingly wrote to Prime Minister Wen Seang and forwarded the proposals to Peking. Two months later, a letter from Ting, at Suchau, his headquarters, gave me to understand that news from Peking had reached him that Wen Seang's mother had died, and he was obliged, according to Chinese laws and customs, to retire from office and go into mourning for a period of twenty-seven months, equivalent to three years, and to abstain altogether from public affairs of all kinds. The news threw a cold blanket over my educational scheme for the time being. No sooner had one misfortune happened than another took its place, worse than the first—Wen Seang himself, three months afterwards, was overtaken by death during his retirement. This announcement appeared in the Peking "Gazette", which I saw, besides being officially informed of it by Governor Ting. No one who had a pet scheme to promote or a hobby to ride could feel more blue than I did, when the cup of joy held so near to his lips was dashed from him. I was not entirely disheartened by such circumstances, but had an abiding faith that my educational scheme would in the end come out all right. There was an interval of at least three years of suspense and waiting between 1868 and 1870. I kept pegging at Governor Ting, urging him to keep the subject constantly before Viceroy Tsang's mind. But like the fate of all measures of reform, it had to abide its time and opportunity.

The time and the opportunity for my educational scheme to materialize finally came. Contrary to all human expectations, the opportunity appeared in the guise of the Tientsin Massacre. No more did Samson, when he slew the Timnath lion, expect to extract honey from its carcass than did I expect to extract from the slaughter of the French nuns and Sisters of Charity the educational scheme that was destined to make a new China of the old, and to work out an Oriental civilization on an Occidental basis.

The Tientsin Massacre took place early in 1870. It arose from the gross ignorance and superstition of the Tientsin populace regarding the work of the nuns and Sisters of Charity, part of whose religious duty it was to rescue foundlings and castaway orphans, who were gathered into hospitals, cared for and educated for the services of the Roman Catholic church. This beneficent work was misunderstood and misconstrued by the ignorant masses, who really believed in the rumors and stories that the infants and children thus gathered in were taken into the hospitals and churches to have their eyes gouged out for medical and religious purposes. Such diabolical reports soon spread like wild–fire till popular excitement was worked up to its highest pitch of frenzy, and the infuriated mob, regardless of death and fearless of law, plunged headlong into the Tientsin Massacre. In that massacre, a Protestant church was burned and destroyed, as was also a Roman Catholic church and hospital; several nuns or Sisters of Charity were killed.

At the time of this occurrence, Chung Hou was viceroy of the Metropolitan province. He had been ambassador to Russia previously, but in this unfortunate affair, according to Chinese law, he was held responsible, was degraded from office and banished. The whole imbroglio was finally settled and patched up by the payment of an indemnity to the relatives and friends of the victims of the massacre and the rebuilding of the Roman Catholic and Protestant churches, another Catholic hospital, besides a suitable official apology made by the government for the incident. Had the French government not been handicapped by the impending German War which threatened her at the time, France would certainly have made the Tientsin Massacre a casus belli, and another slice of the Chinese Empire would have been annexed to the French possessions in Asia. As it was, Tonquin, a tributary state of China, was afterwards unscrupulously wrenched from her.

In the settlement of the massacre, the Imperial commissioners appointed were: Viceroy Tsang Kwoh Fan, Mow Chung His, Liu *** and Ting Yih Chang, Governor of Kiang Su. Li Hung Chang was still in the field finishing up the Nienfi rebellion, otherwise he, too, would have been appointed to take part in the proceedings of the settlement. I was telegraphed for by my friend, Ting Yih Chang, to be present to act as interpreter on the occasion, but the telegram did not reach me in time for me to accompany him to Tientsin; but I reached Tientsin in time to witness the last proceedings. The High Commissioners, after the settlement with the French, for some reason or other, did not disband, but remained in Tientsin for several days. They evidently had other matters of State connected with Chung Hou's degradation and banishment to consider.

Chapter XVII   The Chinese Educational Mission

Taking advantage of their presence, I seized the opportunity to press my educational scheme upon the attention of Ting Yih Chang and urged him to present the subject to the Board of Commissioners of which Tsang Kwoh Fan was president. I knew Ting sympathized with me in the scheme, and I knew, too, that Tsang Kwoh Fan had been well informed of it three years before through Governor Ting. Governor Ting took up the matter in dead earnest and held many private interviews with Tsang Kwoh Fan as well as with the other members of the Commission. One evening, returning to his headquarters very late, he came to my room and awakened me and told me that Viceroy Tsang and the other Commissioners had unanimously decided to sign their names conjointly in a memorial to the government to adopt my four propositions. This piece of news was too much to allow me to sleep any more that night; while lying on my bed, as wakeful as an owl, I felt as though I were treading on clouds and walking in air. Two days after this stirring piece of news, the memorial was jointly signed with Viceroy Tsang Kwoh Fan's name heading the list, and was on its way to Peking by pony express. Meanwhile, before the Board of Commissioners disbanded and Viceroy Tsang took his departure for Nanking, it was decided that Chin Lan Pin, a member of the Hanlin College, who had served twenty years as a clerk in the Board of Punishment, should be recommended by Ting to co-operate with me in charge of the Chinese Educational Commission. The ground upon which Chin Lan Pin was recommended as a co-commissioner was that he was a Han Lin and a regularly educated Chinese, and the enterprise would not be so likely to meet with the opposition it might have if I were to attempt to carry it out alone, because the scheme in principle and significance was against the Chinese theory of national education, and it would not have taken much to create a reaction to defeat the plan on account of the intense conservatism of the government. The wisdom and the shrewd policy of such a move appealed to me at once, and I accepted the suggestion with pleasure and alacrity. So Chin Lan Pin was written to and came to Tientsin. The next day, after a farewell dinner had been accorded to the Board of Commissioners before it broke up, Governor Ting introduced me to Chin Lan Pin, whom I had never met before and who was to be my associate in the educational scheme. He evidently was pleased to quit Peking, where he had been cooped up in the Board of Punishment for twenty years as a clerk. He had never filled a government position in any other capacity in his life, nor did he show any practical experience in the world of business and hard facts. In his habits he was very retiring, but very scholarly. In disposition he was kindly and pleasant, but very timid and afraid of responsibilities of even a feather's weight.

In the winter of 1870, Tsang Kwoh Fan, after having settled the Tientsin imbroglio, returned to Nanking, his headquarters as the viceroy of the two Kiangs. There he received the imperial rescript sanctioning his joint memorial on the four proposals submitted through Ting Yih Chang for adoption by the government. He notified me on the subject. It was a glorious piece of news, and the Chinese educational project thus became a veritable historical fact, marking a new era in the annals of China. Tsang invited me to repair to Nanking, and during that visit the most important points connected with the mission were settled, viz.: the establishment of a preparatory school; the number of students to be selected to be sent abroad; where the money was to come from to support the students while there; the number of years they were to be allowed to remain there for their education.

The educational commission was to consist of two commissioners, Chin Lan Pin and myself. Chin Lan Pin's duty was to see that the students should keep up their knowledge of Chinese while in America; my duty was to look after their foreign education and to find suitable homes for them. Chin Lan Pin and myself were to look after their expenses conjointly. Two Chinese teachers were provided to keep up their studies in Chinese, and an interpreter was provided for the Commission. Yeh Shu Tung and Yung Yune Foo were the Chinese teachers and Tsang Lai Sun was the interpreter. Such was the composition of Chinese Educational Commission.

As to the character and selection of the students: the whole number to be sent abroad for education was one hundred and twenty; they were to be divided into four installments of thirty members each, one installment to be sent each year for four successive years at about the same time. The candidates to be selected were not to be younger than twelve or older than fifteen years of age. They were to show respectable parentage or responsible and respectable guardians. They were required to pass a medical examination, and an examination in their Chinese studies according to regulation—reading and writing in Chinese—also to pass an English examination if a candidate had been in an English school. All successful candidates were required to repair every day to the preparatory school, where teachers were provided to continue with their Chinese studies, and to begin the study of English or to continue with their English studies, for at least one year before they were to embark for the United States.

Parents and guardians were required to sign a paper which stated that without recourse, they were perfectly willing to let their sons or protégés go abroad to be educated for a period of fifteen years, from the time they began their studies in the United States until they had finished, and that during the fifteen years, the government was not to be responsible for death or for any accident that might happen to any student.

The government guaranteed to pay all their expenses while they were being educated. It was to provide every installment with a Chinese teacher to accompany it to the United States, and to give each installment of students a suitable outfit. Such were the requirements and the organization of the student corps.

Immediately upon my return to Shanghai from Nanking after my long interview with the Viceroy, my first step was to have a preparatory school established in Shanghai for the accommodation of at least thirty students, which was the full complement for the first installment. Liu Kai Sing, who was with the Viceroy for a number of years as his first secretary in the Department of Memorials, was appointed superintendent of the preparatory school in Shanghai. In him, I found an able coadjutor as well as a staunch friend who took a deep interest in the educational scheme. He it was who prepared all the four installments of students to come to this country.

Thus the China end of the scheme was set afloat in the summer of 1871. To make up the full complement of the first installment of students, I had to take a trip down to Hong Kong to visit the English government schools to select from them a few bright candidates who had had some instruction both in English and Chinese studies. As the people in the northern part of China did not know that such an educational scheme had been projected by the government, there being no Chinese newspapers published at the time to spread the news among the people, we had, at first, few applications for entrance into the preparatory school. All the applications came from the Canton people, especially from the district of Heang Shan. This accounts for the fact that nine–tenths of the one hundred and twenty government students were from the south.

In the winter of 1871, a few months after the preparatory school had begun operations, China suffered an irreparable loss by the death of Viceroy Tsang Kwoh Fan, who died in Nanking at the ripe age of seventy–one years. Had his life been spared even a year longer, he would have seen the first installment of thirty students started for the United States—the first fruit of his own planting. But founders of all great and good works are not permitted by the nature and order of things to live beyond their ordained limitations to witness the successful developments of their own labor in this world; but the consequences of human action and human character, when once their die is cast, will reach to eternity. Sufficient for Tsang Kwoh Fan that he had completed his share in the educational line well. He did a great and glorious work for China and posterity, and those who were privileged to reap the benefit of his labor will find ample reason to bless him as China's great benefactor. Tsang, as a statesman, a patriot, and as a man, towered above his contemporaries even as Mount Everest rises above the surrounding heights of the Himalaya range, forever resting in undisturbed calmness and crowned with the purity of everlasting snow. Before he breathed his last, I was told that it was his wish that his successor and protégé, Li Hung Chang, be requested to take up his mantle and carry on the work of the Chinese Educational Commission.

Li Hung Chang was of an altogether different make-up from his distinguished predecessor and patron. He was of an excitable and nervous temperament, capricious and impulsive, susceptible to flattery and praise, or, as the Chinese laconically put it, he was fond of wearing tall hats. His outward manners were brusque, but he was inwardly kind-hearted. As a statesman he was far inferior to Tsang; as a patriot and politician, his character could not stand a moment before the searchlight of cold and impartial history. It was under such a man that the Chinese Educational Commission was launched forth.

In the latter part of the summer of 1872 the first installment of Chinese students, thirty in number, were ready to start on the passage across the Pacific to the United States. In order that they might have homes to go to on their arrival, it devolved upon me to precede them by one month, leaving Chin Lan Pin, the two Chinese teachers and their interpreter to come on a mail later. After reaching New York by the Baltimore and Ohio, via Washington, I went as far as New Haven on my way to Springfield, Mass., where I intended to meet the students and other members of the commission on their way to the East by the Boston and Albany Railroad. At New Haven, the first person I called upon to announce my mission was Prof. James Hadley. He was indeed glad to see me, and was delighted to know that I had come back with such a mission in my hands. After making my wants known to him, he immediately recommended me to call upon Mr. B. G. Northrop, which I did, Mr. Northrop was then Commissioner of Education for Connecticut. I told him my business and asked his advice. He strongly recommended me to distribute and locate the students in New England families, either by twos or fours to each family, where they could be cared for and at the same time instructed, till they were able to join classes in graded schools. This advice I followed at once. I went on to Springfield, Mass., which city I considered was the most central point from which to distribute the students in New England; for this reason I chose Springfield for my headquarters. This enabled me to be very near my friends, Dr. A. S. McClean and his worthy wife, both of whom had been my steadfast friends since 1854.

But through the advice of Dr. B. G. Northrop and other friends, I made my permanent headquarters in the city of Hartford, Conn., and for nearly two years our headquarters were located on Sumner Street. I did not abandon Springfield, but made it the center of distribution and location of the students as long as they continued to come over, which was for three successive years, ending in 1875.

In 1874, Li Hung Chang, at the recommendation of the commission, authorized me to put up a handsome, substantial building on Collins Street as the permanent headquarters of the Chinese Educational

271

Commission in the United States. In January, 1875, we moved into our new headquarters, which was a large, double three-story house spacious enough to accommodate the Commissioners, teachers and seventy-five students at one time. It was provided with a schoolroom where Chinese was exclusively taught; a dining room, a double kitchen, dormitories and bath rooms. The motive which led me to build permanent headquarters of our own was to have the educational mission as deeply rooted in the United States as possible, so as not to give the Chinese government any chance of retrograding in this movement. Such was my proposal, but that was not God's disposal as subsequent events plainly proved.

Chapter XVIII Investigation of the Coolie Traffic in Peru

In the spring of 1873, I returned to China on a flying visit for the sole purpose of introducing the Gatling gun—a comparatively new weapon of warfare of a most destructive character. I had some difficulty in persuading the Gatling Company to give me the sole agency of the gun in China, because they did not know who I was, and were unacquainted with my practical business experience. In fact, they did not know how successfully I had carried on the Taiping Green Tea Expedition in 1860–1, in the face of dangers and privations which few men dared to face. However, I prevailed on the president of the company, Dr. Gatling himself, the inventor of the gun, to entrust me with the agency. Exactly a month after my arrival in Tientsin, I cabled the company an order for a battery of fifty guns, which amounted altogether to something over $100000, a pretty big order for a man who it was thought could not do anything. This order was followed by subsequent orders. I was anxious that China should have the latest modern guns as well as the latest modern educated men. The Gatling Company was satisfied with my work and had a different opinion of me afterwards.

While I was in Tientsin, attending to the gun business, the Viceroy told me that the Peruvian commissioner was there waiting to make a treaty with China regarding the further importation of coolie labor into Peru. He wanted me to call on the commissioner and talk with him on the subject, which I did. In his conversation, he pictured to me in rosy colors how well the Chinese were treated in Peru; how they were prospering and doing well there, and said that the Chinese government ought to conclude a treaty with Peru to encourage the poorer class of Chinese to emigrate to that country, which offered a fine chance for them to better themselves. I told him that I knew something about the coolie traffic as it was carried on in Macao; how the country people were inveigled and kidnapped, put into barracoons and kept there by force till they were shipped on board, where they were made to sign labor contracts either for Cuba or Peru. On landing at their destination, they were then sold to the highest bidder, and made to sign another contract with their new masters, who took special care to have the contract renewed at the end of every term, practically making slaves of them for life. Then I told him something about the horrors of the middle passage between Macao and Cuba or Peru; how whole cargoes of them revolted in mid-ocean, and either committed wholesale suicide by jumping into the ocean, or else overpowered the captain and the crew, killed them and threw them overboard, and then took their chances in the drifting of the vessel.

Such were some of the facts and horrors of the coolie traffic I pictured to the Peruvian Commissioner. I told him plainly that he must not expect me to help him in this diabolical business. On the contrary, I told him I would dissuade the Viceroy from entering into a treaty with Peru to carry on such inhuman traffic. How the Peruvian's countenance changed when he heard me deliver my mind on the subject! Disappointment, displeasure and anger were visible in his countenance. I bade him good morning, for I was myself somewhat excited as I narrated what I had seen in Macao and what I had read in the papers about the coolie traffic. Indeed, one of the first scenes I had seen on my arrival in Macao in 1855 was a string of poor Chinese coolies tied to each other by their cues and led into one of the barracoons like abject slaves. Once, while in Canton, I had succeeded in having two or three kidnappers arrested, and had them put into wooden collars weighing forty pounds, which the culprits had to carry night and day for a couple of months as a punishment for their kidnapping.

Returning to the Viceroy, I told him I had made the call, and narrated my interview. The Viceroy, to make my visit short, then said, "You have come back just in time to save me from cabling you. I wish you to return to Hartford as quickly as possible and make preparations to proceed to Peru at once, to look into the condition of the Chinese coolies there."

On my return to Hartford, I found that Chin Lan Pin had also been instructed by the government to look after the condition of the Chinese coolies in Cuba. These collateral or side missions were ordered at Li Hung Chang's suggestion. I started on my mission before Chin Lan Pin did. My friend, the Rev. J. H. Twichell, and Dr. E. W. Kellogg, who afterwards became my brother–in–law, accompanied me on my trip. I finished my work inside of three months, and had my report completed before Chin started on his journey to Cuba. On his return, both of our reports were forwarded to Viceroy Li, who was in charge of all foreign diplomatic affairs.

My report was accompanied with two dozen photographs of Chinese coolies, showing how their backs had been lacerated and torn, scarred and disfigured by the lash, I had these photographs taken in the night, unknown to anyone except the victims themselves, who were, at my request, collected and assembled together for the purpose. I knew that these photographs would tell a tale of cruelty and inhumanity perpetrated by the owners of haciendas, which would be beyond cavil and dispute.

The Peruvian Commissioner, who was sent out to China to negotiate a treaty with Viceroy Li Hung Chang to continue the coolie traffic to Peru, was still in Tientsin waiting for the arrival of my report. A friend of mine wrote me that he had the hardihood to deny the statements in my report, and said that they could not be supported by facts. I had written to the Viceroy beforehand that he should hold the photographs in reserve, and keep them in the background till the Peruvian had exhausted all his arguments, and then produce them. My correspondent wrote me that the Viceroy followed my suggestion, and the photographs proved to be so incontrovertible and palpable that the Peruvian was taken by surprise and was dumbfounded. He retired completely crestfallen. Since our reports on the actual conditions of Chinese coolies in Cuba and Peru were made, no more coolies have been allowed to leave China for those countries. The traffic had received its death blow.

Chapter XIX   End of the Educational Mission

In the fall of 1875 the last installment of students arrived. They came in charge of a new commissioner, Ou Ngoh Liang, two new Chinese teachers and a new interpreter, Kwang Kee Cheu. These new men were appointed by Viceroy Li Hung Chang. I knew them in China, especially the new commissioner and the interpreter.

These changes were made at the request of Chin Lan Pin, who expected soon to return to China on a leave of absence. He was going to take with him the old Chinese teacher, Yeh Shu Tung, who had rendered him great and signal service in his trip to Cuba on the coolie question the year before. Tsang Lai Sun, the old interpreter, was also requested to resign and returned to China. These changes I had anticipated some time before and they did not surprise me.

Three months after Chin Lan Pin's arrival in Peking, word came from China that he and I were appointed joint Chinese ministers to Washington, and that Yeh Shu Tung, the old Chinese teacher, was appointed secretary to the Chinese Legation. This was great news to me to be sure, but I did not feel ecstatic over it; on the contrary, the more I reflected on it, the more I felt depressed. But my friends who congratulated me on the honor and promotion did not take in the whole situation as it loomed up before my mind in all its bearings. As far as I was concerned, I had every reason to feel grateful and honored, but how about my life work—the Chinese educational mission that I had in hand—and which needed in its present stage great watchfulness and care? If, as I reflected, I were to be removed to Washington, who was there left behind to look after the welfare of the students with the same interest that I had manifested? It would be like separating the father from his children. This would not do, so I sat down and wrote to the Viceroy a letter, the tenor of which ran somewhat as follows: I thanked him for the appointment which I considered to be a great honor for any man to receive from the government; and said that while I appreciated fully its significance, the obligations and responsibilities inseparably connected with the position filled me with anxious solicitude that my abilities and qualifications might not be equal to their satisfactory fulfillment. In view of such a state of mind, I much preferred, if I were allowed to have my preference in the matter, to remain in my present position as a commissioner of the Chinese mission in Hartford and to continue in it till the Chinese students should have finished their education and were ready to return to China to serve the State in their various capacities. In that event I should have discharged a duty to "Tsang the Upright", and at the same time fulfilled a great duty to China. As Chin Lan Pin had been appointed minister at the same time, he would doubtless be able alone to meet the expectations of the government in his diplomatic capacity.

The letter was written and engrossed by Yung Yune Foo, one of the old Chinese teachers who came over with the first installment of students at the same time Yeh Shu Tung came. In less than four months an answer was received which partially acceded to my request by making me an assistant or associate minister, at the same time allowing me to retain my position as Commissioner of Education, and in that capacity, to exercise a general supervision over the education of the students.

Ou Ngoh Liang, the new commissioner, was a much younger man than Chin. He was a fair Chinese scholar, but not a member of the Hanlin College. He was doubtless recommended by Chin Lan Pin. He brought his family with him, which consisted of his second wife and two children. He was a man of a quiet disposition and showed no inclination to meddle with settled conditions or to create trouble, but took rather a philosophical view of things; he had the good sense to let well enough alone. He was connected with the mission but a short time and resigned in 1876.

In 1876 Chin Lan Pin came as minister plenipotentiary and brought with him among his numerous retinue Woo Tsze Tung, a man whom I knew in Shanghai even in the '50's. He was a member of the Hanlin College, but for some reason or other, he was never assigned to any government department, nor was he ever known to hold any kind of government office. He showed a decided taste for chemistry, but never seemed to have made any progress in it, and was regarded by all his friends as a crank.

After Ou's resignation, Chin Lan Pin before proceeding to Washington to take up his official position as Chinese minister, strongly recommended Woo Tsze Tung to succeed Ou as commissioner, to which Viceroy Li Hung Chang acceded without thinking of the consequences to follow. From this time forth the educational mission found an enemy who was determined to undermine the work of Tsang Kwoh Fan and Ting Yih Cheong, to both of whom Woo Tsze Tung was more or less hostile. Woo was a member of the reactionary party, which looked upon the Chinese Educational Commission as a move subversive of the principles and theories of Chinese culture. This was told me by one of Chin's suite who held the appointment of chargé d'affaires for Peru. The making of Woo Tsze Tung a commissioner plainly revealed the fact that Chin Lan Pin himself was at heart an uncompromising Confucian and practically represented the reactionary party with all its rigid and uncompromising conservatism that gnashes its teeth against all and every attempt put forth to reform the government or to improve the general condition of things in China. This accounts for the fact that in the early stages of the mission, I had many and bitter altercations with him on many things which had to be settled for good, once and for all. Such as the school and personal expenses of the students; their vacation expenses; their change of costume; their attendance at family worship; their attendance at Sunday School and church services; their outdoor exercises and athletic games. These and other questions of a social nature came up for settlement. I had to stand as a kind of buffer between Chin and the students, and defended them in all their reasonable claims. It was in this manner that I must have incurred Chin's displeasure if not his utter dislike. He had never been out of China in his life until he came to this country. The only standard by which he measured things and men (especially students) was purely Chinese. The gradual but marked transformation of the students in their behavior and conduct as they grew in knowledge and stature under New England influence, culture and environment produced a contrast to their behavior and conduct when they first set foot in New England that might well be strange and repugnant to the ideas and senses of a man like Chin Lan Pin, who all his life had been accustomed to see the springs of life, energy and independence, candor, ingenuity and open–heartedness all covered up and concealed, and in a great measure smothered and never allowed their full play. Now in New England the heavy weight of repression and suppression was lifted from the minds of these young students; they exulted in their freedom and leaped for joy. No wonder they took to athletic sports with alacrity and delight!

Doubtless Chin Lan Pin when he left Hartford for good to go to Washington carried away with him a very poor idea of the work to which he was singled out and called upon to perform. He must have felt that his own immaculate Chinese training had been contaminated by coming in contact with Occidental schooling, which he looked upon with evident repugnance. At the same time the very work which he seemed to look upon with disgust had certainly served him the best turn in his life. It served to lift him out of his obscurity as a head clerk in the office of the Board of Punishment for twenty years to become a commissioner of the Chinese Educational Commission, and from that post to be a minister plenipotentiary in Washington. It was the stepping stone by which he climbed to political prominence. He should not have kicked away the ladder under him after he had reached his dizzy elevation. He did all he could to break up the educational scheme by recommending Woo Tsze Tung to be the Commissioner of Education, than whom he could not have had a more pliant and subservient tool for his purpose, as may be seen hereinafter.

Woo Tsze Tung was installed commissioner in the fall of 1876. No sooner was he in office than he began to find fault with everything that had been done. Instead of laying those complaints before me, he clandestinely started a stream of misrepresentation to Peking about the students; how they had been mismanaged; how they had been indulged and petted by Commissioner Yung; how they had been allowed to enjoy more privileges than was good for them; how they imitated American students in athletics; that they played more than they studied; that they formed themselves into secret societies, both religious and political; that they ignored their teachers and would not listen to the advice of the new commissioner; that if they were allowed to continue to have their own way, they would soon lose their love of their own country, and on their return to China, they would be good for nothing or worse than nothing; that most of them went to church, attended Sunday Schools and had become Christians; that the sooner this educational enterprise was broken up and all the students recalled, the better it would be for China, etc.

Such malicious misrepresentations and other falsehoods which we knew nothing of, were kept up in a continuous stream from year to year by Woo Tsze Tung to his friends in Peking and to Viceroy Li Hung Chang. The Viceroy called my attention to Woo's accusations. I wrote back in reply that they were malicious fabrications of a man who was known to have been a crank all his life; that it was a grand mistake to put such a man in a responsible position who had done nothing for himself or for others in his life; that he was only attempting to destroy the work of Tsang Kwoh Fan who, by projecting and fathering the educational mission, had the highest interest of China at heart; whereas Woo should have been relegated to a cell in an insane asylum or to an institution for imbeciles. I said further that Chin Lan Pin, who had recommended Woo to His Excellency as commissioner of Chinese Education, was a timid man by nature and trembled at the sight of the smallest responsibilities. He and I had not agreed in our line of policy in our diplomatic correspondence with the State Department nor had we agreed as commissioners in regard to the treatment of the Chinese students. To illustrate his extreme dislike of responsibilities: He was requested by the Governor to go to Cuba to find out the condition of the coolies in that island in 1873. He waited three months before he started on his journey. He sent Yeh Shu Tung and one of the teachers of the Mission accompanied by a young American lawyer and an interpreter to Cuba, which party did the burden of the work and thus paved the way for Chin Lan Pin and made the work easy for him. All he had to do was to take a trip down to Cuba and return, fulfilling his mission in a perfunctory way. The heat of the day and the burden of the labor were all borne by Yeh Shu Tung, but Chin Lan Pin gathered in the laurel and was made a minister plenipotentiary, while Yeh was given the appointment of a secretary of the legation. I mention these things not from any invidious motive towards Chin, but simply to show that often in the official and political world one man gets more praise and glory than he really deserves, while another is not rewarded according to his intrinsic worth. His Excellency was well aware that I had no axe to grind in making the foregoing statement. I further added that I much preferred not to accept the appointment of a minister to Washington, but rather to remain as commissioner of education, for the sole purpose of carrying it through to its final success. And, one time in the heat of our altercation over a letter addressed to the State Department, I told Chin Lan Pin in plain language that I did not care a rap either for the appointment of an assistant minister, or for that matter, of a full minister, and that I was ready and would gladly resign at any moment, leaving him free and independent to do as he pleased.

This letter in answer to the Viceroy's note calling my attention to Woo's accusations gave the Viceroy an insight into Woo's antecedents, as well as into the impalpable character of Chin Lan Pin. Li was, of course, in the dark as to what the Viceroy had written to Chin Lan Pin, but things both in the legation and the Mission apparently moved on smoothly for a while, till some of the students were advanced enough in their studies for me to make application to the State Department for admittance to the Military Academy at West Point and the Naval Academy in Annapolis. The answer to my application was: "There is no room provided for Chinese students." It was curt and disdainful. It breathed the spirit of Kearnyism and Sandlotism with which the whole Pacific atmosphere was impregnated, and which had hypnotized all the departments of the government, especially Congress, in which Blaine figured most conspicuously as the champion against the Chinese on the floor of the Senate. He had the presidential bee buzzing in his bonnet at the time, and did his best to cater for the electoral votes of the Pacific coast. The race prejudice against the Chinese was so rampant and rank that not only my application for the students to gain entrance to Annapolis and West Point was treated with cold indifference and scornful hauteur, but the Burlingame Treaty of 1868 was, without the least provocation, and contrary to all diplomatic precedents and common decency, trampled under foot unceremoniously and wantonly, and set aside as though no such treaty had ever existed, in order to make way for those acts of congressional discrimination against Chinese immigration which were pressed for immediate enactment.

When I wrote to the Viceroy that I had met with a rebuff in my attempt to have some of the students admitted to West Point and Annapolis, his reply at once convinced me that the fate of the Mission was sealed. He too fell back on the Burlingame Treaty of 1868 to convince me that the United States government had violated the treaty by shutting out our students from West Point and Annapolis.

Having given a sketch of the progress of the Chinese Educational Mission from 1870 to 1877–8, my letter applying for their admittance into the Military and Naval Academies might be regarded as my last official act as a commissioner. My duties from 1878 onwards were chiefly confined to legation work.

When the news that my application for the students to enter the Military and Naval Academies of the government had proved a failure, and the displeasure and disappointment of the Viceroy at the rebuff were known, Commissioner Woo once more renewed his efforts to break up the Mission. This time he had the secret cooperation of Chin Lan Pin. Misrepresentations and falsehoods manufactured out of the whole cloth went forth to Peking in renewed budgets in every mail, till a censor from the ranks of the reactionary party came forward and took advantage of the strong anti–Chinese prejudices in America to memorialize the government to break up the Mission and have all the students recalled.

The government before acceding to the memorial put the question to Viceroy Li Hung Chang first, who, instead of standing up for the students, yielded to the opposition of the reactionary party and gave his assent to have the students recalled. Chin Lan Pin, who from his personal experience was supposed to know what ought to be done, was the next man asked to give his opinion. He decided that the students had been in the United States long enough, and that it was time for them to return to China. Woo Tsze Tung, the Commissioner, when asked for his opinion, came out point blank and said that they should be recalled without delay and should be strictly watched after their return. I was ruled out of the consultation altogether as being one utterly incompetent to give an impartial and reliable opinion on the subject. Thus the fate of the educational mission was sealed, and all students, about one hundred in all, returned to China in 1881.

The breaking up of the Chinese Educational Commission and the recall of the young students in 1881, was not brought about without a strenuous effort on the part of some thoughtful men who had watched steadfastly over the development of human progress in the East and the West, who came forward in their quiet and modest ways to enter a protest against the revocation of the Mission. Chief among them were my lifelong friend, the Rev. J. H. Twichell, and Rev. John W. Lane, through whose persistent efforts Presidents Porter and Seelye, Samuel Clemens, T. F. Frelinghuysen, John Russell Young and others were enlisted and brought forward to stay the work of retrogression of the part of the Chinese. The protest was couched in the most dignified, frank and manly language of President Porter of Yale and read as follows:

To The Tsung Li Yamun

or

Office for Foreign Affairs.

"The undersigned, who have been instructors, guardians and friends of the students who were sent to this country under the care of the Chinese Educational Commission, beg leave to represent:

"That they exceedingly regret that these young men have been withdrawn from the country, and that the Educational Commission has been dissolved.

"So far as we have had opportunity to observe, and can learn from the representations of others, the young men have generally made a faithful use of their opportunities, and have made good progress in the studies assigned to them, and in the knowledge of the language, ideas, arts and institutions of the people of this country.

"With scarcely a single exception, their morals have been good; their manners have been singularly polite and decorous, and their behavior has been such as to make friends for themselves and their country in the families, the schools, the cities and villages in which they have resided.

"In these ways they have proved themselves eminently worthy of the confidence which has been reposed in them to represent their families and the great Chinese Empire in a land of strangers. Though children and youths, they have seemed always to understand that the honor of their race and their nation was committed to their keeping. As the result of their good conduct, many of the prejudices of ignorant and wicked men towards the Chinese have been removed, and more favorable sentiments have taken their place.

"We deeply regret that the young men have been taken away just at the time when they were about to reap the most important advantages from their previous studies, and to gather in the rich harvest which their painful and laborious industry had been preparing for them to reap. The studies which most of them have pursued hitherto have been disciplinary and preparatory. The studies of which they have been deprived by their removal, would have been the bright flower and the ripened fruit of the roots and stems which have been slowly reared under patient watering and tillage. We have given to them the same knowledge and culture that we give to our own children and citizens.

"As instructors and guardians of these young men, we should have welcomed to our schools and colleges the Commissioners of Education or their representatives and have explained to them our system and methods of instruction. In some cases, they have been invited to visit us, but have failed to respond to their invitations in person or by their deputies.

"We would remind your honorable body that these students were originally received to our homes and our colleges by request of the Chinese government through the Secretary of State with the express desire that they might learn our language, our manners, our sciences and our arts. To remove them permanently and suddenly without formal notice or inquiry on the ground that as yet they had learned nothing useful to China when their education in Western institutions, arts and sciences is as yet incomplete, seems to us as unworthy of the great Empire for which we wish eminent prosperity and peace, as it is discourteous to the nation that extended to these young men its friendly hospitality.

"We cannot accept as true the representation that they have derived evil and not good from our institutions, our principles and our manners. If they have neglected or forgotten their native language, we never assumed the duty of instructing them in it, and cannot be held responsible for this neglect. The Chinese government thought it wise that some of its own youth should be trained after our methods. We have not finished the work which we were expected to perform. May we not reasonably be displeased that the results of our work should be judged unfavorably before it could possibly be finished?

"In view of these considerations, and especially in view of the injury and loss which have fallen upon the young men whom we have learned to respect and love, and the reproach which has implicitly been brought upon ourselves and the great nation to which we belong— we would respectfully urge that the reasons for this sudden decision should be reconsidered, and the representations which have been made concerning the intellectual and moral character of our education should be properly substantiated. We would suggest that to this end, a committee may be appointed of eminent Chinese citizens whose duty it shall be to examine into the truth of the statements unfavorable to the young men or their teachers, which have led to the unexpected abandonment of the Educational Commission and to the withdrawal of the young men from the United States before their education could be finished."

Chapter XX   Journey to Peking and Death of My Wife

The treatment which the students received at the hands of Chinese officials in the first years after their return to China as compared with the treatment they received in America while at school could not fail to make an impression upon their innermost convictions of the superiority of Occidental civilization over that of China—an impression which will always appeal to them as cogent and valid ground for radical reforms in China, however altered their conditions may be in their subsequent careers. Quite a number of the survivors of the one hundred students, I am happy to say, have risen to high official ranks and positions of great trust and responsibility. The eyes of the government have been opened to see the grand mistake it made in breaking up the Mission and having the students recalled. Within only a few years it had the candor and magnanimity to confess that it wished it had more of just such men as had been turned out by the Chinese Educational Mission in Hartford, Conn. This confession, though coming too late, may be taken as a sure sign that China is really awakening and is making the best use of what few partially educated men are available. And these few Occidentally educated men have, in their turn, encouraged and stimulated both the government and the people. Since the memorable events of the China and Japan war, and the war between Japan and Russia, several hundreds of Chinese students have come over to the United States to be educated. Thus the Chinese educational scheme which Tsang Kwoh Fan initiated in 1870 at Tientsin and established in Hartford, Conn., in 1872, though rolled back for a period of twenty-five years, has been practically revived.

Soon after the students' recall and return to China in 1881, I also took my departure and arrived in Tientsin in the fall of that year on my way to Peking to report myself to the government after my term of office as assistant minister had expired. This was the customary step for all diplomatic officers of the government to take at the close of their terms. Chin Lan Pin preceded me by nearly a year, having returned in 1880.

While paying my visit to Li Hung Chang in Tientsin, before going up to Peking, he brought up the subject of the recall of the students. To my great astonishment he asked me why I had allowed the students to return to China. Not knowing exactly the significance of the inquiry, I said that Chin Lan Pin, who was minister, had received an imperial decree to break up the Mission; that His Excellency was in favor of the decree, so was Chin Lan Pin and so was Woo Tsze Tung. If I had stood out alone against carrying out the imperial mandate, would not I have been regarded as a rebel, guilty of treason, and lose my head for it? But he said that at heart he was in favor of their being kept in the States to continue their studies, and that I ought to have detained them. In reply I asked how I could have been supposed to read his heart at a distance of 45000 lis, especially when it was well known that His Excellency had said that they might just as well be recalled. If His Excellency had written to me beforehand not to break up the Mission under any circumstances, I would then have known what to do; as it was, I could not have done otherwise than to see the decree carried out. "Well," said he, in a somewhat angry and excited tone, "I know the author of this great mischief." Woo Tsze Tung happened to be in Tientsin at the time. He had just been to Peking and sent me word begging me to call and see him. Out of courtesy, I did call. He told me he had not been well received in Peking, and that Viceroy Li was bitter towards him when he had called and had refused to see him a second time. He looked careworn and cast down. He was never heard of after our last interview.

On my arrival in Peking, one of my first duties was to make my round of official calls on the leading dignitaries of the government—the Princes Kung and Ching and the presidents of the six boards. It took me nearly a month to finish these official calls. Peking may be said to be a city of great distances, and the high officials live quite far apart from each other. The only conveyances that were used to go about from place to place were the mule carts. These were heavy, clumsy vehicles with an axle-tree running right across under the body of a box, which was the carriage, and without springs to break the jolting, with two heavy wheels, one at each end of the axle. They were slow coaches, and with the Peking roads all cut up and seldom repaired, you can imagine what traveling in those days meant. The dust and smell of the roads were something fearful. The dust was nothing but pulverized manure almost as black as ink. It was ground so fine by the millions of mule carts that this black stuff would fill one's eyes and ears and penetrate deep into the pores of one's skin, making it impossible to cleanse oneself with one washing. The neck, head and hands had to have suitable coverings to keep off the dust. The water is brackish, making it difficult to take off the dirt, thereby adding to the discomforts of living in Peking.

I was in Peking about three months. While there, I found time to prepare a plan for the effectual suppression of the Indian opium trade in China and the extinction of the poppy cultivation in China and India. This plan was submitted to the Chinese government to be carried out, but I was told by Whang Wen Shiu, the president of the Tsung Li Yamun (Foreign Affairs), that for want of suitable men, the plan could not be entertained, and it was shelved for nearly a quarter of a century until recently when the subject became an international question.

I left Peking in 1882. After four months' residence in Shanghai, I returned to the United States on account of the health of my family.

I reached home in the spring of 1883, and found my wife in a very low condition. She had lost the use of her voice and greeted me in a hoarse low whisper. I was thankful that I found her still living though much emaciated. In less than a month after my return, she began to pick up and felt more like herself. Doubtless, her declining health and suffering were brought on partly on account of my absence and her inexpressible anxiety over the safety of my life. A missionary fresh from China happened to call on her a few days before my departure for China and told her that my going back to China was a hazardous step, as they would probably cut my head off on account of the Chinese Educational Mission. This piece of gratuitous information tended more to aggravate a mind already weighed down by poor health, and to have this gloomy foreboding added to her anxiety was more than she could bear. I was absent in China from my family this time nearly a year and a half, and I made up my mind that I would never leave it again under any conditions whatever. My return in 1883 seemed to act on my wife's health and spirit like magic, as she gradually recovered strength enough to go up to Norfolk for the summer. The air up in Norfolk was comparatively pure and more wholesome than in the Connecticut valley, and proved highly salubrious to her condition. At the close of the summer, she came back a different person from what she was when she went away, and I was much encouraged by her improved health. I followed up these changes of climate and air with the view of restoring her to her normal condition, taking her down to Atlanta, Georgia, one winter and to the Adirondacks another year. It seemed that these changes brought only temporary relief without any permanent recovery. In the winter of 1885, she began to show signs of a loss of appetite and expressed a desire for a change. Somerville, New Jersey, was recommended to her as a sanitarium. That was the last resort she went to for her health, for there she caught a cold which resulted in her death. She lingered there for nearly two months till she was brought home, and died of Bright's disease on the 28th of June, 1886. She was buried in Cedar Hill Cemetery in the home lot I secured for that purpose. Her death made a great void in my after-life, which was irreparable, but she did not leave me hopelessly deserted and alone; she left me two sons who are constant reminders of her beautiful life and character. They have proved to be my greatest comfort and solace in my declining years. They are most faithful, thoughtful and affectionate sons, and I am proud of their manly and earnest Christian characters. My gratitude to God for blessing me with two such sons will forever rise to heaven, an endless incense.

The two blows that fell upon me one after the other within the short span of five years from 1880 to 1886 were enough to crush my spirit. The one had scattered my life work to the four winds; the other had deprived me of a happy home which had lasted only ten years. The only gleam of light that broke through the dark clouds which hung over my head came from my two motherless sons whose tender years appealed to the very depths of my soul for care and sympathy. They were respectively seven and nine years old when deprived of their mother. I was both father and mother to them from 1886 till 1895. My whole soul was wrapped up in their education and well−being. My mother−in−law, Mrs. Mary B. Kellogg, assisted me in my work and stood by me in my most trying hours, keeping house for me for nearly two years.

Chapter XXI   My Recall to China

In 1894–5 war broke out between China and Japan on account of Korea. My sympathies were enlisted on the side of China, not because I am a Chinese, but because China had the right on her side, and Japan was simply trumping up a pretext to go to war with China, in order to show her military and naval prowess. Before the close of the war, it was impossible for me to be indifferent to the situation—I could not repress my love for China. I wrote to my former legation interpreter and secretary, two letters setting forth a plan by which China might prosecute the war for an indefinite time.

My first plan was to go over to London to negotiate a loan of $15000000, with which sum to purchase three or four ready built ironclads, to raise a foreign force of 5000 men to attack Japan in the rear from the Pacific coast—thus creating a diversion to draw the Japanese forces from Korea and give the Chinese government a breathing spell to recruit a fresh army and a new navy to cope with Japan. While this plan was being carried out, the government was to empower a commission to mortgage the Island of Formosa to some Western power for the sum of $400000000 for the purpose of organizing a national army and navy to carry on the war. These plans were embodied in two letters to Tsai Sik Yung, at that time secretary to Chang Tsze Tung, viceroy of Hunan and Hupeh. They were translated into Chinese for the Viceroy. That was in the winter of 1894. To my great surprise, Viceroy Chang approved of my first plan. I was authorized by cable to go over to London to negotiate the loan of $15000000. The Chinese minister in London, a Li Hung Chang man, was advised of my mission, which in itself was a sufficient credential for me to present myself to the minister. In less than a month after my arrival in London, I succeeded in negotiating the loan; but in order to furnish collaterals for it, I had to get the Chinese minister in London to cable the government for the hypothecation of the customs' revenue. I was told that Sir Robert Hart, inspector–general of customs, and Viceroy Li Hung Chang refused to have the customs' revenue hypothecated, on the ground that this revenue was hardly enough to cover as collateral the loan to meet the heavy indemnity demanded by Japan. The fact was: Viceroy Li Hung Chang and Chang Chi Tung were at loggerheads and opposed to each other in the conduct of the war. The latter was opposed to peace being negotiated by Li Hung Chang; but the former had the Dowager Empress on his side and was strenuous in his efforts for peace.

Hence Sir Robert Hart had to side with the Court party, and ignored Chang Chi Tung's request for the loan of $15000000; on that account the loan fell through, and came near involving me in a suit with the London Banking Syndicate.

I returned to New York and cabled for further instructions from Chang Chi Tung as to what my next step would be. In reply he cabled for me to come to China at once.

After thirteen years of absence from China, I thought that my connections with the Chinese government had been severed for good when I left there in 1883. But it did not appear to be so; another call to return awaited me, this time from a man whom I had never seen, of whose character, disposition and views I was altogether ignorant, except from what I knew from hearsay. But he seemed to know all about me, and in his memorial to the government inviting me to return, he could not have spoken of me in higher terms than he did. So I girded myself to go back once more to see what there was in store for me. By this recall, I became Chang Chi Tung's man as opposed to Li Hung Chang.

Before leaving for China this time, I took special pains to see my two sons well provided for in their education. Dr. E. W. Kellogg, my oldest brother-in-law, was appointed their guardian. Morrison Brown Yung, the older son, had just succeeded in entering Yale, Sheffield Scientific, and was able to look out for himself. Bartlett G. Yung, the younger one, was still in the Hartford High School preparing for college. I was anxious to secure a good home for him before leaving the country, as I did not wish to leave him to shift for himself at his critical age. The subject was mentioned to my friends, Mr. and Mrs. Twichell. They at once came forward and proposed to take Bartlett into their family as one of its members, till he was ready to enter college. This is only a single instance illustrative of the large-hearted and broad spirit which has endeared them to their people both in the Asylum Hill church and outside of it. I was deeply affected by this act of self-denial and magnanimity in my behalf as well as in the behalf of my son Bartlett, whom I felt perfectly assured was in first-class hands, adopted as a member of one of the best families in New England. Knowing that my sons would be well cared for, and leaving the development of their characters to an all–wise and ever–ruling Providence, as well as to their innate qualities, I embarked for China, this time without any definite and specific object in view beyond looking out for what opening there might be for me to serve her.

On my arrival in Shanghai, in the early part of the summer of 1895, I had to go to the expense of furnishing myself with a complete outfit of all my official dresses, which cost me quite a sum. Viceroy Chang Chi Tung, a short time previous to my arrival, had been transferred from the viceroyalty of the two Hoos to the viceroyalty of the two Kiangs temporarily. Instead of going up to Wu Chang, the capital of Hupeh, I went up to Nanking, where he was quartered.

In Viceroy Chang Chi Tung, I did not find that magnetic attraction which at once drew me towards Tsang Kwoh Fan when I first met him at Ngan Khing in 1863. There was a cold, supercilious air enveloping him, which at once put me on my guard. After stating in a summary way how the loan of $15000000 fell through, he did not state why the Peking government had declined to endorse his action in authorizing the loan, though I knew at the time that Sir Robert Hart, the inspector–general of the Chinese customs, put forward as an excuse that the custom dues were hardly enough to serve as collateral for the big loan that was about to be negotiated to satisfy the war indemnity demanded by the Japanese government. This was the diplomatic way of coating over a bitter pill for Chang Chi Tung to swallow, when the Peking government, through the influence of Li Hung Chang, was induced to ignore the loan. Chang and Li were not at the time on cordial terms, each having a divergent policy to follow in regard to the conduct of the war.

Dropping the subject of the loan as a dead issue, our next topic of conversation was the political state of the country in view of the humiliating defeat China had suffered through the incompetence and corruption of Li Hung Chang, whose defeat both on land and sea had stripped him of all official rank and title and came near costing him his life. I said that China, in order to recover her prestige and become a strong and powerful nation, would have to adopt a new policy. She would have to go to work and engage at least four foreigners to act as advisers in the Department for Foreign Affairs, in the Military and Naval Departments and in the Treasury Department. They might be engaged for a period of ten years, at the end of which time they might be re-engaged for another term. They would have to be men of practical experience, of unquestioned ability and character. While these men were thus engaged to give their best advice in their respective departments, it should be taken up and acted upon, and young and able Chinese students should be selected to work under them. In that way, the government would have been rebuilt upon Western methods, and on principles and ideas that look to the reformation of the administrative government of China.

Such was the sum and substance of my talk in the first and only interview with which Chang Chi Tung favored me. During the whole of it, he did not express his opinion at all on any of the topics touched upon. He was as reticent and absorbent as a dry sponge. The interview differed from that accorded me by Tsang Kwoh Fan in 1863, in that Tsang had already made up his mind what he wanted to do for China, and I was pointed out to him to execute it. But in the case of Chang Chi Tung, he had no plan formed for China at the time, and what I presented to him in the interview was entirely new and somewhat radical; but the close of the Japan War justified me in bringing forward such views, as it was on account of that war that I had been recalled. If he had been as broad a statesman as his predecessor, Tsang Kwoh Fan, he could have said something to encourage me to entertain even a glimpse of hope that he was going to do something to reform the political condition of the government of the country at the close of the war. Nothing, however, was said, or even hinted at. In fact, I had no other interview with him after the first one. Before he left Nanking for Wu Chang, he gave me the appointment of Secretary of Foreign Affairs for Kiang Nan.

On the arrival of Liu Kwan Yih, the permanent viceroy of the two Kiang provinces, Chang Chi Tung did not ask me to go up to Wu Chang with him. This I took to be a pretty broad hint that he did not need my services any longer, that I was not the man to suit his purposes; and as I had no axe to grind, I did not make any attempt to run after my grind–stone. On the contrary, after three months' stay in Nanking under Viceroy Liu Kwan Yih, out of regard for official etiquette, I resigned the secretaryship, which was practically a sinecure—paying about $150 a month. Such was my brief official experience with Viceroys Chang Chi Tung and Liu Kwan Yih.

I severed my official connection with the provincial government of Kiang Nan in 1896, and took up my headquarters in Shanghai— imtrammeled and free to do as I pleased and go where I liked. It was then that I conceived the plan of inducing the central government to establish in Peking a government national bank. For this object I set to work translating into Chinese the National Banking Act and other

301

laws relating to national banks from the Revised Statutes of the United States with Amendments and additional Acts of 1875. In prosecuting this work, I had the aid of a Chinese writer, likewise the co-operation of the late Wong Kai Keh, one of the Chinese students who was afterwards the assistant Chinese commissioner in the St. Louis Exposition, who gave me valuable help. With the translation, I went up to Peking with my Chinese writer, and, at the invitation of my old friend, Chang Yen Hwan, who had been Chinese Minister in Washington from 1884 to 1888, I took up my quarters in his residence and remained there several months. Chang Yen Hwan at that time held two offices: one as a senior member of the Tsung Li Yamun (Office for Foreign Affairs); the other, as the first secretary in the Treasury Department of which Ung Tung Hwo, tutor to the late Emperor Kwang Su, was the president. Chang Yen Hwan was greatly interested in the National Banking scheme. He examined the translation critically and suggested that I should leave out those articles that were inapplicable to the conditions of China, and retain only such as were important and practicable. After the translation and selection were completed, he showed it to Ung Tung Hwo, president of the Treasury. They were both highly pleased with it, and had all the Treasury officials look it over carefully and pass their judgment upon it. In a few weeks' time, the leading officials of the Treasury Department called upon me to congratulate me upon my work, and said it ought to be made a subject of a memorial to the government to have the banking scheme adopted and carried out. Chang Yen Hwan came forward to champion it, hacked by Ung Tung Hwo, the president.

To have a basis upon which to start the National Bank of China, it was necessary to have the government advance the sum of Tls.

10000000; of this sum, upwards of Tls. 2000000 were to be spent on machinery for printing government bonds and bank–notes of different denominations and machinery for a mint; Tls. 2000000 for the purchase of land and buildings; and Tls. 6000000 were to be held in reserve in the Treasury for the purchase of gold, silver and copper for minting coins of different denominations for general circulation. This Tls. 10000000 was to be taken as the initiatory sum to start the National Bank with, and was to be increased every year in proportion to the increase of the commerce of the Empire.

We had made such progress in our project as to warrant our appointing a committee to go around to select a site for the Bank, while I was appointed to come to the United States to consult with the Treasury Department on the plan and scope of the enterprise and to learn the best course to take in carrying out the plan of the National Bank. The Treasury Department, through its president, Ung Tung Hwo, was on the point of memorializing for an imperial decree to sanction setting aside the sum of Tls. 10000000 for the purpose indicated, when, to the astonishment of Chang Yen Hwan and other promoters of the enterprise, Ung Tung Hwo, the president, received a telegraphic message from Shing Sun Whei, head of the Chinese Telegraphic Co., and manager of the Shanghai, China Steamship Navigation Co., asking Ung to suspend his action for a couple of weeks, till his arrival in Peking, Ung and Shing being intimate friends, besides being compatriots, Ung acceded to Shing's request. Shing Taotai, as he was called, was well–known to be a multimillionaire, and no great enterprise or concession of any kind could pass through without his finger in the pie. So in this banking scheme, he was bound to have his say. He had emissaries all over Peking who kept him well posted about everything going on in the capital as well as outside of it. He had access to the most powerful and influential princes in Peking, his system of graft reaching even the Dowager Empress through her favorite eunuch, the notorious Li Ling Ying. So Shing was a well-known character in Chinese politics. It was through his system of graft that the banking enterprise was defeated. It was reported that he came up to Peking with Tls. 300000 as presents to two or three princes and other high and influential dignitaries, and got away with the Tls. 10000000 of appropriation by setting up a bank to manipulate his own projects.

The defeat of the National Banking project owed its origin to the thoroughly corrupt condition of the administrative system of China. From the Dowager Empress down to the lowest and most petty underling in the Empire, the whole political fabric was honey-combed with what Americans characterize as graft—a species of political barnacles, if I may be allowed to call it that, which, when once allowed to fasten their hold upon the bottom of the ship of State were sure to work havoc and ruination; in other words, with money one could get anything done in China. Everything was for barter; the highest bid got the prize. The two wars—the one with Japan in 1894–5 and the other, the Japan and Russian War in 1904–5—have in some measure purified the Eastern atmosphere, and the Chinese have finally awakened to their senses and have come to some sane consciousness of their actual condition.

After the defeat of the national banking project at the hands of Shing Taotai, I went right to work to secure a railroad concession from the government. The railroad I had in mind was one between the two ports of Tientsin and Chinkiang; one in the north, the other in the south near the mouth of the Yangtze River, The distance between these ports in a bee line is about five hundred miles; by a circuitous route going around the province of Shan Tung and crossing the Yellow River into the province of Hunan through Anwhui, the distance would be about seven hundred miles. The German government objected to having this railroad cross Shan Tung province, as they claimed they had the monopoly of building railroads throughout the province, and would not allow another party to build a railroad across Shan Tung. This was a preposterous and absurd pretension and could not be supported either by the international laws or the sovereign laws of China. At that time, China was too feeble and weak to take up the question and assert her own sovereign rights in the matter, nor had she the men in the Foreign Office to show up the absurdity of the pretension. So, to avoid any international complications, the concession was issued to me with the distinct understanding that the road was to be built by the circuitous route above described. The road was to be built with Chinese, not with foreign capital. I was given six months' time to secure capital. At the end of six months, if I failed to show capital, I was to surrender the concession. I knew very well that it would be impossible to get Chinese capitalists to build any railroad at that time. I tried hard to get around the sticking point by getting foreign syndicates to take over the concession, but all my attempts proved abortive, and I was compelled to give up my railroad scheme also. This ended my last effort to help China.

I did not dream that in the midst of my work, Khang Yu Wei and his disciple, Leang Kai Chiu, whom I met often in Peking during the previous year, were engaged in the great work of reform which was soon to culminate in the momentous *coup d'état* of 1898.

Chapter XXII   The Coup D'etat of 1898

The *coup d'état* of September, 1898, was an event memorable in the annals of the Manchu Dynasty. In it, the late Emperor Kwang Su was arbitrarily deposed; treasonably made a prisoner of state; and had his prerogatives and rights as Emperor of the Chinese Empire wrested from him and usurped by the late Dowager Empress Chi Hsi.

Kwang Su, though crowned Emperor when he was five years of age, had all along held the sceptre only nominally. It was Chi Hsi who held the helm of the government all the time.

As soon as Kwang Su had attained his majority, and began to exercise his authority as emperor, the lynx eye of Chi Hsi was never lifted away from him. His acts and movements were watched with the closest scrutiny, and were looked upon in any light but the right one, because her own stand in the government had never been the legitimate and straight one since 1864, when her first regency over her own son, Tung Chi, woke in her an ambition to dominate and rule, which grew to be a passion too morbid and strong to be curbed.

In the assertion of his true manhood, and the exercise of his sovereign power, his determination to reform the government made him at once the cynosure of Peking, inside and outside of the Palace. In the eyes of the Dowager Empress Chi Hsi, whose retina was darkened by deeds perpetrated in the interest of usurpation and blinded by jealousy, Kwang Su appeared in no other light than as a dement, or to use a milder expression, an imbecile, fit only to be tagged round by an apron string, cared for and watched. But to the disinterested spectator and unprejudiced judge, Kwang Su was no imbecile, much less a dement. Impartial history and posterity will pronounce him not only a patriot emperor, but also a patriot reformer—as mentally sound and sane as any emperor who ever sat on the throne of China. He may be looked upon as a most remarkable historical character of the Manchu Dynasty from the fact that he was singled out by an all-wise Providence to be the pioneer of the great reform movement in China at the threshold of the twentieth century.

Just at this juncture of the political condition of China, the tide of reform had reached Peking. Emperor Kwang Su, under some mysterious influence, to the astonishment of the world, stood forth as the exponent of this reform movement. I determined to remain in the city to watch its progress. My headquarters became the rendezvous of the leading reformers of 1898. It was in the fall of that memorable year that the *coup d'état* took place, in which the young Emperor Kwang Su was deposed by the Dowager Empress, and some of the leading reformers arrested and summarily decapitated.

Being implicated by harboring the reformers, and in deep sympathy with them, I had to flee for my own life and succeeded in escaping from Peking. I took up quarters in the foreign settlement of Shanghai. While there, I organized the "Deliberative Association of China", of which I was chosen the first president. The object of the association was to discuss the leading question of the day, especially those of reform.

In 1899, I was advised for my own personal safety, to change my residence. I went to Hong Kong and placed myself under the protection of the British government.

I was in Hong Kong from 1900 till 1902, when I returned to the United States to see my younger son, Bartlett G. Yung, graduate from Yale University.

In the spring of 1901, I visited the Island of Formosa, and in that visit I called upon Viscount Gentaro Kodama, governor of the island, who, in the Russo—Japan War of 1904–5 was the chief of staff to Marshal Oyama in Manchuria. In the interview our conversation had to be carried on through his interpreter, as he, Kodama, could not speak English nor could I speak Japanese.

He said he was glad to see me, as he had heard a great deal of me, but never had the pleasure of meeting me. Now that he had the opportunity, he said he might as well tell me that he had most unpleasant if not painful information to give me. Being somewhat surprised at such an announcement, I asked what the information was. He said he had received from the viceroy of Fuhkein and Chehkiang an official despatch requesting him to have me arrested, if found in Formosa, and sent over to the mainland to be delivered over to the Chinese authorities. Kodama while giving this information showed neither perturbation of thought nor feeling, but his whole countenance was wreathed with a calm and even playful smile.

I was not disturbed by this unexpected news, nor was I at all excited. I met it calmly and squarely, and said in reply that I was entirely in his power, that he could deliver me over to my enemies whenever he wished; I was ready to die for China at any time, provided that the death was an honorable one.

"Well, Mr. Yung," said he, "I am not going to play the part of a constable for China, so you may rest at ease on this point. I shall not deliver you over to China. But I have another matter to call to your attention." I asked what it was. He immediately held up a Chinese newspaper before me, and asked who was the author of the proposition. Without the least hesitation. I told him I was the author of it. At the same time, to give emphasis to this open declaration, I put my opened right palm on my chest two or three times, which attracted the attention of everyone in the room, and caused a slight excitement among the Japanese officials present.

I then said, "With Your Excellency's permission, I must beg to make one correction in the amount stated; instead of $800000000, the sum stated in my proposition was only $400000000." At this frank and open declaration and the corrected sum, Kodama was evidently pleased and visibly showed his pleasure by smiling at me.

The Chinese newspaper Kodama showed me contained a proposition I drew up for Viceroy Chang Chi Tung to memorialize the Peking government for adoption in 1894–5, about six months before the signing of the Treaty of Shemonashiki by Viceroy Li Hung Chang. The proposal was to have the Island of Formosa mortgaged to a European Treaty power for a period of ninety–nine years for the sum of $400000000 in gold. With this sum China was to carry on the war with Japan by raising a new army and a new navy. This proposition was never carried through, but was made public in the Chinese newspapers, and a copy of it found its way to Kodama's office, where, strange to say, I was confronted with it, and I had the moral courage not only to avow its authorship but also a correction of the amount the island was to be mortgaged for.

To bring the interview to a climax, I said, should like circumstances ever arise, nothing would deter me from repeating the same proposition in order to fight Japan.

This interview with the Japanese governor of Formosa was one of the most memorable ones in my life. I thought at first that at the request of the Chinese viceroy I was going to he surrendered, and that my fate was sealed; but no sooner had the twinkling smile of Kodama lighted his countenance than my assurance of life and safety came back with redoubled strength, and I was emboldened to talk war on Japan with perfect impunity. The bold and open stand I took on that occasion won the admiration of the governor who then invited me to accompany him to Japan where he expected to go soon to be promoted. He said he would introduce me to the Japanese emperor and other leading men of the nation. I thanked him heartily for his kindness and invitation and said I would accept such a generous invitation and consider it a great honor to accompany him on his contemplated journey, but my health would not allow me to take advantage of it. I had the asthma badly at the time.

Then, before parting, he said that my life was in danger, and that while I was in Formosa under his jurisdiction he would see that I was well protected and said that he would furnish me with a bodyguard to prevent all possibilities of assassination. So the next day he sent me four Japanese guards to watch over me at night in my quarters; and in the daytime whenever I went out, two guards would go in advance of me and two behind my jinricksha to see that I was safe. This protection was continued for the few days I spent in Formosa till I embarked for Hong Kong. I went in person to thank the governor and to express my great obligation and gratitude to him for the deep interest he had manifested towards me.